Summit
Books

WE DID OK, KID

a memoir

ANTHONY HOPKINS

SUMMIT BOOKS
*New York   Amsterdam/Antwerp   London   Toronto
Sydney/Melbourne   New Delhi*

S

Summit Books
An Imprint of Simon & Schuster, LLC
1230 Avenue of the Americas
New York, NY 10020

For more than 100 years, Simon & Schuster has championed authors and the stories they create. By respecting the copyright of an author's intellectual property, you enable Simon & Schuster and the author to continue publishing exceptional books for years to come. We thank you for supporting the author's copyright by purchasing an authorized edition of this book.

No amount of this book may be reproduced or stored in any format, nor may it be uploaded to any website, database, language-learning model, or other repository, retrieval, or artificial intelligence system without express permission. All rights reserved. Inquiries may be directed to Simon & Schuster, 1230 Avenue of the Americas, New York, NY 10020 or permissions@simonandschuster.com.

Copyright © 2025 by Anthony Hopkins

All interior and insert images are courtesy of the author unless otherwise noted. Page 245, "*The Silence of the Lambs*, Best Actor, 1992": Copyright © Academy of Motion Picture Arts and Sciences

All rights reserved, including the right to reproduce this book or portions thereof in any form whatsoever. For information, address Simon & Schuster Subsidiary Rights Department, 1230 Avenue of the Americas, New York, NY 10020.

First Summit Books hardcover edition November 2025

SUMMIT BOOKS and colophon are registered trademarks of Simon & Schuster, LLC

Simon & Schuster strongly believes in freedom of expression and stands against censorship in all its forms. For more information, visit BooksBelong.com.

For information about special discounts for bulk purchases, please contact Simon & Schuster Special Sales at 1-866-506-1949 or business@simonandschuster.com.

The Simon & Schuster Speakers Bureau can bring authors to your live event. For more information or to book an event, contact the Simon & Schuster Speakers Bureau at 1-866-248-3049 or visit our website at www.simonspeakers.com.

Interior design by Carly Loman

Manufactured in the United States of America

10 9 8 7 6 5 4 3 2 1

Library of Congress Cataloging-in-Publication Data is available.

ISBN 978-1-6680-7550-0
ISBN 978-1-6680-7552-4 (ebook)

To Stella with love

Not to laugh, not to lament, not to curse, but to understand.

—BARUCH SPINOZA, *Tractatus Politicus*

introduction

WE DID OK, KID

One gray Sunday morning in 1941, in the sand dunes of Aberavon Beach, a friend of my father's, Cliff Mathers, handed me a cough lozenge. In those days, the war years, we saw few, if any, sweets or candies. Those were the years of rationing. Fumbling, I dropped the sweet in the sand, and I started to blubber. My father and Cliff laughed. I was given a second sweet. My father stooped down to reassure me. No more tears. Cliff snapped the photo. One of my earliest memories. I was three.

INTRODUCTION

Now, at the age of eighty-seven, I occasionally glance at that photo and am prompted to say to that confused little boy: "We did OK, kid."

Like most children, I was anxious and confused. But that's part of growing up—being too young to comprehend any meaning in existence. That strange feeling of being lost, not able to cope, has stayed with me through the many years of my life. I am surprised—or is the word *bemused*? *Bewildered*? Yes, *bewildered*—that I'm still here. No explanation.

The indelible birthmark stamped into my core is the feeling of never being quite "with it."

But I was made of tough stuff. My father was like that—no nonsense, no fuzziness. His guidance to me was: "Just get on with it. Stand up straight and don't complain." It was a good tip. Another: "Life is rough. So what? Never give in." A bit harsh, but it got me through. That was my father, the old man. Richard Arthur Hopkins.

Dead and gone now. I don't know if he exists in another dimension—an afterlife or any of that kind of wishful thinking. But he is deep inside me, like bits of broken china.

It is an isolated life. It has always been that way. But no sweat, no big deal. Quite a trip, in fact, 'cause I am not a victim. I have put those fractured pieces to use—loneliness, alienation, anxiety, whatever those shards were. And now I'm glad for them. Those irritants and goads have kept me moving; they got me here.

one

ELEPHANT HEAD

It was on another damp, gray Sunday—this one in September 1949—that I became, at the age of eleven, my own man. That was the afternoon my mother and father delivered me to a nineteenth-century redbrick boarding school on a hill above the town of Pontypool in Monmouthshire.

West Mon was a Gothic building with towering spires and, over the entryway, two bas-relief rams holding up a scroll that read SERVE AND OBEY. The building had a foreboding, haunted-house quality not improved by the bone-chilling Monmouthshire rain, rumbling thunder, and whipping wind. I hated it on sight.

I was left there because my mother was eager to give me a decent education. My father was so-so about the idea because it would take a lump of hard-earned cash to give me such an opportunity.

I was on my father's side, because I couldn't care less about school. Why waste the money? I had never been the sharpest knife in the cutlery drawer, and there seemed little hope for improvement. Already I had been written off by those utterly pallid-faced teachers in my previous elementary school in Port Talbot—branded "Dennis the Dunce" by one particularly unpleasant teacher.

To the kids on our street, I was "Elephant Head." My head *was* large and looked somewhat inappropriate stuck on top of a puny body. My parents thought I was afflicted by water on the brain, but Dr. Bray, a child specialist, assured them that I was normal.

"He just needs fattening up," the good doctor told them.

Being delivered by my parents to that West Mon school was not a catastrophic event. It just happened to be one of those inconvenient speed bumps on the highway of life, nothing more, but for some reason or other, that event planted in my brain a seed of indifference. I vowed, *I'll take my chances and never get close to my mother and father again—or anyone else, for that matter.* I no longer cared. I decided to live my life on my terms, to open my eyes to the future. Forget the past. *Childhood over. Copy that. Over and out.* The ghost had entered the machine.

After a brief meeting with the headmaster, Mr. Harrison,

and his ebullient, zaftig wife, followed by a quick look around the claustrophobic dormitory of sixteen beds crammed into a square room with hospital-green walls, my parents and I returned to the parking space at the steps of the school's main entrance. My mother and father got into their car to drive home. As they pulled out, the sun glinted off the windshield. Through the glare, I saw my mother wave to me. My father kept his eyes on the road, so I kept my arms at my sides and didn't wave back.

As their car—a well-polished Ford Model C Ten—disappeared down the driveway, I noted the number of their plate: BTX 698. For the rest of that wet fall afternoon, I kept muttering the number over and over: "BTX 698. BTX 698. BTX 698."

The school's motto was: "Believe, achieve, succeed, serve, and obey." The school song was even more depressing: "We march along with joyful song, with a song of victory." We had to sing this ridiculous thing at every morning assembly before the grim teaching staff.

One of the housemasters in that brick prison was a cold-hearted military type; he had been involved in the North Africa campaign against General Rommel. I called him "Lob" because his face was lobster red. He told me that my merits and prospects were "nothing but rags and tatters." I liked the funny, dramatic sound of *rags and tatters*.

"Hush, hush, hush," I said. "I am what I am what I am. I am the Rags and Bones and Tatters Man."

Also, I was good at playing the clown. I often goofed around as the scarecrow in *The Wizard of Oz*, Bela Lugosi as Dracula, or Boris Karloff as Frankenstein's monster. I was eerily good at copying any voices or sounds I heard. I could neigh like a horse or bark like a dog. I also did Bugs Bunny: "What's up, Doc?" Elmer Fudd. Daffy Duck. Porky Pig. "That's all, folks!"

When I did my rags-and-tatters routine, some of the boys laughed, and Lob responded by writing on the blackboard: *"For what are men better than sheep or goats that nourish a blind life within the brain?"* —*Alfred Lord Tennyson.*

We were told to write it out twenty times. I treated the encounter with a sinister humor. As I copied over the words, I bleated like goats and sheep. Lob charged down the aisle toward me. Slaps. More bleating. More slaps.

The more slaps I got, the more I leaned into my survival trick, a gaze of pure, dumb insolence. This look displayed my passive indifference to everything hostile around me. Show no reaction. Stare them down. Pretend they don't exist. I enjoyed this newly discovered power. Show no pain! Bury what pain there is, push it under the carpet, keep moving. It drove adults crazy, and that suited me fine.

Even though it was depressing having to live in that ghastly place, it was there that I experienced my first brush with William Shakespeare.

It was a Saturday night. We boys had been herded together in the school's assembly hall, not to sing the school song—thank God—but to watch a film, a real film with sound. The school had hired a film projector and a projector operator, Mr. Gordon Phillips. This was something new and exciting.

We sat there on our wooden seats and waited. Finally, Mr. Harrison, the headmaster, swept into the hall, gown billowing out to indicate the significance of this momentous event. He was joined by his big, booming, battleship wife, old Ma Harrison. Our teachers followed. Max Horton, Lob

Garnett, and others. Mr. Harrison warned us to be quiet—no talking, no fidgeting, no laughing. Any boy breaking these rules would be removed—and then, so we imagined, swiftly executed in the gymnasium.

"Now, *Hamlet* is a very important film," announced Mr. Harrison. "Mr. Laurence Olivier, the world's greatest Shakespearean actor, has directed this film, and furthermore, he is passionately committed to broadcasting the powerful words and wisdom of the Bard of Warwickshire, Mr. William Shakespeare."

Oh, God help us all! Not Shakespeare. Please spare us this tedious triviality.

Mr. Harrison rambled on for another five minutes about Shakespeare and Mr. Olivier. Finally, he paid tribute to our projectionist, Mr. Gordon Phillips from Griffithstown.

What a depressing hour this is going to be! I thought. We all turned to acknowledge Mr. Phillips from Griffithstown. Mr. Harrison told us to say: "Thank you, Mr. Phillips from Griffithstown." I felt I was in hell.

Mr. Phillips from Griffithstown, standing between two film projectors, poised and ready for action, was a rotund, shiny-faced young man. His hair had been plastered down with Brylcreem, and he was wearing a blue bow tie for the event. This really was hell.

On the stage, a large cinema screen had been set up.

The lights in the hall were dimmed. On the screen was the familiar trademark introduction of the J. Arthur Rank Organisation: The giant gong being struck, the words *A J. Arthur Rank Enterprise*, the dark screen. And then, suddenly, the massive opening chords of William Walton's music.

It was . . . *stunning*. The battlements scene. The ghost of

Hamlet's father. Inside the castle of Elsinore. Olivier. His opening soliloquy began:

O, that this too, too solid flesh would melt
Thaw and resolve itself into a dew!

I was transfixed to the very last line of the soliloquy.

But break, my heart; for I must hold my tongue.

I had never experienced an impact like that. It was explosive. I could not yet understand the structure of *Hamlet* and its nuance—its archaic words, new and unfamiliar language, the rhythm and phrasing.

But I felt that Olivier as Hamlet was speaking to me, referring to some long-vanished, ancient part of myself. It was an unearthly experience. The grief of Hamlet over his father's death and his mother's betrayal of her dead husband. I cried, overpowered by the epic depiction of damaged fathers and mothers and of how we're all haunted by the ghosts of memory. I was too young to grasp a modern sense of the words. But a force had broken into the center of whatever I was.

two

NINETY-THREE MILLION MILES AWAY

My abilities at that first boarding school amounted to zero, and so my poor parents had to rethink my education prospects. They were desperate and needed someone to help me pole-vault to the pinnacles of scholasticism, someone who could, they whispered, "put in a word or two, so to speak."

It was like being part of a complex Shakespearean comedy, all winks and asides. I suppose I should have felt honored, being the center of such plots, but I felt like a dope, selling myself. I wanted no part of it.

Finally, we were guided to a mysterious figure, a person who had pull. Uncle Eddie—whom I was told lived in the Rest Bay area of Porthcawl and had "no side to him at all," meaning he was a straight shooter—was to become my savior.

It so happened that this great man everyone called Uncle Eddie was related to my father's side of the family. They were "rotten with money," my father said. These were the aged aunts and uncles living in St. Mary's Street, the Rest Bay *crachach*. *Crachach* was the pejorative term used to describe the Welsh elite who controlled the education sectors in Wales.

Neither of my two grandfathers had that same loftiness. Grandpa Hopkins—or Grandpa H., as I called him—was a tough old bird. And he loved to show me just how tough he was.

Every morning, he would take a cold bath, and then work all day.

"I'm as hard as nails," he would say. He extended his right arm and clenched fist, then spread the fingers. "Look at that—not a tremor. That's real strength. You've got to be tough in this world. It's called survival of the fittest."

He was born in Neath, South Wales, in 1878, and according to legend—his own legend, perhaps—he ran away from his drunken father and stowed away on a railway truck to London. He found lodgings in Bermondsey, South East London. He had little money but managed to get a job cleaning and scraping floors in a German bakery near Piccadilly.

He soon learned that the bakery was a place of gloom and backbreaking labor, but eventually, he became a real craftsman, a baker, and a master confectioner. Later, he won trophies at bakery exhibitions in Earl's Court in London. I still have his silver cups, many of them inscribed. On one: ARTHUR RICHARD HOPKINS 1924, FIRST PRIZE FOR CURRANT BUNS.

Parts of his story were, perhaps, embellished, but I did get a feeling of authenticity, and I admired the old man. But he didn't seem to have much regard for me except when I played the piano for him. "Anthony has a rather large head," he said to my mother once. "What a pity there is nothing much in it."

Anyway, that was Grandpa Hopkins. He told me a story once about a young man called Gerald with whom he'd worked in that London bakery. Gerald had married a young woman, and they were trying to feed their baby girl, but there wasn't enough food. Gerald was gravely ill. My grandfather thought it was consumption—tuberculosis—as a dry hacking cough was one of his symptoms. One morning, Gerald didn't show up for work, and the shop foreman announced to everyone that the young man had died of pneumonia the night before. The other men in the bakery said nothing. Work proceeded as normal.

My grandfather Hopkins became an industrial agitator. He told my father he had once met Vladimir Lenin. It could have been a tall story, a portion of his own legend. But it also could have been true, because Lenin had exiled himself to London. Leon Trotsky also lived in London, where at the time there was a fervid and passionate political stirring of Marxism.

Eventually, Grandpa Hopkins and my grandmother, Emmy, returned to Wales with their three young children, Miriam, Richard, and Lorna, and they struggled to survive.

Wales has often been described as the "land of song." Dylan Thomas created a mythological version in *Under Milk Wood*. But the truth is that there is nothing quaint or romantic or folksy about the Wales my family knew.

In 1921, when my father was fourteen, he was suddenly pulled out of school to work in the family bakery business without pay, and he stayed there until 1936.

On the other side of the proverbial garden wall was my maternal grandfather. His name was Frederick Thomas Yeats. He'd been born in Pewsey in Wiltshire. He would say to me, whenever I got upset: "It's all spilled milk, water under the bridge. Let it be."

My grandfather found work on the railway lines and in the shunting yards of Swindon, then moved to South Wales, where the new steelworks foundry was being built. There he met Sophia Phillips, an apprentice seamstress in a Carmarthen dress shop. They married and settled in Port Talbot. Two girls were born. The first was my mother, Muriel, born in 1913.

They lost the second, Jenny, my grandfather's favorite, to diphtheria when she was nine. My mother was twelve. One day at breakfast they heard a bump on the landing above. Her father got up and went into the hall, and there was Jenny slumped against the banister. He rushed up the stairs and lifted her in his arms. She was dead.

My mother told me that on the day of Jenny's funeral, as the coffin was being carried out to the hearse, she heard her father weeping and sobbing helplessly, hopelessly, in the little passage at the back of their house.

But the next day, he showed up as usual for his job as a crane driver at the steelworks. When he was asked if he wanted to take a few days off, he said no.

"I can't bring her back, can I?" he said. "Why relive all that? She's gone. Once you're dead, you're dead. The past is dead—nothing there." And he never spoke of his beloved daughter again.

Back to Uncle Eddie—Eddie James—who was worshipped by his family and spoken of in hallowed whispers: "He often goes up to London. You know, business and things. He often has breakfast on the train with our minister of health, Nye Bevan."

Uncle Eddie was also an editor on the *Western Mail* newspaper in Cardiff. He knew "high-ups" on the Welsh board of education. What good this would do for me, I had no idea.

One stiflingly warm Sunday afternoon, we were invited by Aunt Patty to meet Uncle Eddie for tea at her house on Esplanade Avenue. As my father drove us out to Aunt Patty's, my mother, sitting in the passenger seat, turned to look at me. I was slouched in the back. She told me to sit up straight. "I hope you don't sit like that at Aunt Patty's! Sit up straight and behave yourself and stop fidgeting. And say please and thank you when Aunt Patty gives you a piece of cake. Don't slouch. And don't mumble when Uncle Eddie asks you a question."

I stared out the car window as we drove along the seafront, and my mind drifted back to the last family visit. It was another death-knell Sunday afternoon. We were all gathered, the entire Hopkins brood. At least it seemed that way. My father's two sisters, Mimi and Lorna; Uncle Billy; Uncle Jack; and Bobby, my first cousin—all of us stuffed like sardines into the musty front room of Uncle Davey Charles and Aunt Nettie's house on St. Mary's Street.

For the hundred and tenth time, my mother had told me to sit up straight and say please and thank you whenever Auntie Nettie chanced to offer me a stale Welsh cake on a daintily flowered porcelain plate.

Suddenly an exhilarating thought had struck me: *Why don't you just stand up now—yes, right now—and just go completely berserk and insane like those lunatics from Bedlam? Yes, why not? Go crazy right now and smash that silly flowered porcelain plate over your dear aunt Nettie's head.* Perhaps that was the first seed of vengeance planted in my backward brain. The seed of mayhem and danger.

As I sat in the car recalling that visit, I noticed my father looking at me in the rearview mirror. I saw his face and noted, not for the first time, how much he looked like the American singer Bing Crosby. I stared back at him. Dumb insolence. That drove him nuts.

"I don't know what'll become of him. He bloody worries me," he said to my mother.

"Oh, Dick, for goodness' sake, don't go on and on about it. And stop swearing. I hope you don't swear like that in Auntie Patty's house."

"Oh, to hell with bloody Auntie Patty. Auntie Patty this and Auntie Patty that. Bloody Bible-punching hypocrites, that's what they are. The whole bloody lot of them."

"Then why are we going there? Why do we always go see your father and your sisters?"

"Why? Because they're bloody rich, that's why! We're all hoping for some pickings. Bloody rubbish. That's what it is."

Doom and Gloom, the terrible Welsh twins, were in the car with us that heavy summer afternoon.

Finally, we pulled up to Auntie Patty's house on the seafront.

My father pressed the doorbell. Distant chimes. The front door was opened by a chubby young woman dressed in black with a white serving cap on her head. Dick pulled a face at my mother as if to say, *Oh, pardon me for breathing, please, all very grand. All very bay window.*

We were taken into the front room and invited to sit, make ourselves comfortable; Aunt Patty would be with us soon. I sat next to my mother on the sofa. I didn't know why I had to sit up straight, but I did try. My father stood and peered through the net-curtained window at weekenders from the whole of Wales, the children whooping and shouting as their worn-out parents drifted down the pavements of the Esplanade and the seafront alongside the lonely people from the valleys. Everyone, it seemed, was out and about that miserable afternoon.

My father was his usual agitated self, tweaking the curtain

aside, tapping the windowpane with his fingernail. "Strange, isn't it?"

"What's strange?" my mother asked wearily.

"All those people out there. What are they doing?"

"They're enjoying themselves, Dick. That's what people do. Normal people do things like that. Why don't you sit down? Stop tapping the window. You're like a bag of nerves."

"I don't want to sit down. I'm perfectly happy standing here. What time is it?"

"I don't know. Three something or other."

I heard a soft chime from a distant clock. Aunt Patty came into the room. She was a Victorian matriarch, small and compact but upright and strong with a sonorous contralto voice.

She went to my father, offered her hand. "Richard. How are you?"

"Hello, Aunt Patty. I'm well, thank you."

"Good. Good. Good. Very good." Aunt Patty turned to my mother. "It's Marjorie, isn't it?"

"Muriel," my mother replied.

"Muriel. Yes, of course. Muriel." Then she glanced at me. "And this is the boy?"

"Yes. Anthony."

"Anthony. Yes, of course. Anthony."

My mother signaled to me. "Say 'Hello, Aunt Patty.'"

I obeyed the command. "Hello, Aunt Patty."

The grand old lady looked me up and down, then touched my face. "So you're the problem boy, right?"

"Yes, I think so," I replied.

My mother became flustered. "Not a problem, Aunt Patty. He's a little slow, that's all."

"Being slow is a problem, don't you think?" responded Aunt Patty.

There was a silence. Aunt Patty gave me the once-over. She touched my tie. An improvement must be made somehow.

"Our Eddie told us that Anthony needed help to get into a public school. What happened with the West Mon school?" asked Aunt Patty.

"He was very unhappy there," my mother answered.

"Oh, well, happiness isn't everything, you know," replied Aunt Patty. "He must go to some school or other. What kind of school are you looking for, Richard?"

"We're hoping to get him into Cowbridge Grammar School."

Aunt Patty brushed some invisible crumbs from her blouse.

"Cowbridge accepts only the sons of professionals, such as doctors and solicitors, if you take my meaning. The sons of tradespeople? Well, West Mon is the best for tradespeople's boys. You want Eddie to pull a few strings. Correct?"

My mother answered, "If it's at all possible."

My father muttered something about leaving.

An awkward pause. Children's voices from the street. A car horn.

"Yes, well," said Aunt Patty. "Would you like some tea?" She went to the door and called out, "Bessie, prepare the tea for our visitors." She came back. "Eddie will be here in a moment," she said. "Every afternoon Eddie must take his nap. You know how it is."

My father couldn't miss an opportunity for sarcasm: "Every afternoon? Why? Does he get *tired*?"

His face was the picture of mock innocence. My mother glared at him. She knew what he was capable of.

"Well, you know how it is, Richard. He does have his work cut out for him. Editorship of the *Western Mail*, the Welsh board of education. Tomorrow, for instance, he's going up to London. Catching the seven o'clock from Cardiff. He has a meeting with Mr. Bevan and—"

"Oh, really? He knows Nye Bevan? He moves in high places, does he?"

His quiet sarcasm went flying over Aunt Patty's head.

"Yes, you could say that, Richard. You could say that. He never stops."

She turned to the doorway. "Here's Eddie."

Into the room came Eddie James—Eddie the Great. An imposing man, blessed with a noble head of silver hair, and wearing heavy, black-framed glasses. Uncle Eddie crossed the room to my father and gave him a bone-cracking, old-friend handshake.

"Richard! I know your father well." He spoke in a cultivated Welsh voice with rolling baritone vowels, like an opera singer. "Dear Arthur Richard, how is the old scoundrel? Still active in the Labour Party, I take it?"

My father was overwhelmed by Uncle Eddie's vibrant enthusiasm.

"Well, you know how it is, Uncle Eddie, he's getting old now. Retired from the business a few years ago."

"We are all getting old, Richard. Going down the hill, as they say." Uncle Eddie turned to nod to my mother. "Mrs. Hopkins."

"Muriel," corrected Aunt Patty.

"Muriel. Of course."

Uncle Eddie, from his towering affability, looked at me as if studying a specimen from another planet.

"And you, young man, you are the slow coach? Right?"

My mother whispered, on cue: "Stand up straight, take your hands out of your pockets, and say 'Nice to meet you, Uncle Eddie.'"

I obeyed.

"Yes. So your mother and your father are worried about you, correct?"

"I think so," I answered quietly.

"Speak up. Don't mumble."

Uncle Eddie flopped down into an armchair.

"What are you good at?"

Standing before this magisterial, silver-headed superman, I was at a loss.

My father suddenly offered me a helping hand.

"Tell Uncle Eddie about your interest in astronomy."

Uncle Eddie looked at me as if reevaluating the wretched boy in front of him. "Astronomy, eh? My pet subject," he said. "Tell me what you know."

"I know the names of the nine planets," I mumbled.

"Speak up. I can't hear you," he said.

"I know the names of the nine planets," I repeated.

"Go on, then."

I rattled them off: "Mercury, Venus, Earth, Mars, Jupiter, Saturn, Uranus, Neptune, and Pluto. Mercury is closest to the sun."

"Very good, well done."

My mother murmured her approval.

Uncle Eddie challenged me. "What else?"

"The sun is eight and a half light-minutes from Earth, ninety-three million miles away, and the nearest galaxy is Andromeda and that is two and a half million light-years from

Earth, and Galileo got in trouble by saying the sun was the center of the solar system, and Colonel Fawcett vanished in the Amazon jungle, and the *Titanic* hit an iceberg in 1912, and the Empire State Building in New York is the tallest building in the world—one thousand two hundred and fifty feet tall."

"That is impressive," said Uncle Eddie. "Where did you learn all these facts?"

"From Arthur Mee's *The Children's Encyclopedia*. My father bought them for me when I was six."

That was one of the greatest gifts of my life. I'd been to the dentist that day and it had hurt. When we got home in the afternoon, we saw on the doorstep a big box. It was so heavy that Mr. John from next door had to help my mother take it into the house and up the stairs. They opened it up on the table. A ten-volume encyclopedia. Ten perfect blue books in a row, just for me.

Even though it was a beautiful, sunny summer day, I was put to bed to recover from the dental appointment. Starting that day, I read all ten volumes. First I devoured the pages on Beethoven and Mozart, then the sections on the Milky Way, and then articles with headings like "Nature," "The Earth," "All Countries," and "Golden Deeds." I read the books again and again until the covers were falling off, memorizing without effort the lengths of the world's major rivers and the capital and flag of every country.

I'd stunned the room with my recitation, but I kept going until my father came up behind me, put his hand on my head, and told me that I mustn't tire out Uncle Eddie. "That's enough for now."

I stopped talking, but Uncle Eddie told my father: "It's all right, Richard. Let the boy talk. He seems to have a lot to say."

Eddie looked at me, not sternly, but in a kind of friendly way.

"How is your reading, Anthony? What is your favorite book? Do you have a favorite book?"

"*The Wind in the Willows*, by Kenneth Grahame, *Prester John*, by John Buchan, and *Oliver Twist* and *Great Expectations*, by Charles Dickens."

"*Great Expectations*? Good heavens. Charles Dickens, eh? And who is your favorite character? Pip?"

"No, the convict, Abel Magwitch. Also in *Oliver Twist*, I like Fagin and Bill Sikes."

"Oh my goodness. Mr. Magwitch, eh? The bad man. Well, well, I must say. And Fagin. He was a rum character, wasn't he? And Bill Sikes. Shakespeare? Do you like him?"

"Yes, *Hamlet*: 'To be or not to be: that is the question. / Whether 'tis nobler in the mind to suffer / the slings and arrows of outrageous fortune.' Also, *Julius Caesar*. I like Mark Antony's 'O mighty Caesar' speech and his 'Friends, Romans, countrymen.'"

Uncle Eddie laughed. "Good Lord, enough, enough."

Triumph. There was a tiny ripple of laughter in the room. I think even Aunt Patty laughed.

Uncle Eddie's verdict: "Well, Richard and Marj—I'm sorry, Muriel—I think Anthony is a bit of a dreamer. That's all. A dreamer. He'll probably shock all of us one fine day. Who knows? He writes? How is his spelling?"

"Very good," my mother replied. "I think he reads those encyclopedias every day, and he is good at drawing and playing the piano. *Moonlight Sonata*." They'd bought me a piano to encourage my interest, and it worked. I loved playing the piano and drawing.

Uncle Eddie nodded.

Suddenly he rose from his magisterial armchair. "Well, I think *application* is what he needs. Extra teaching. I am off to London in the morning, quite early, in fact, but I will telephone the headmaster of Cowbridge, Mr. Idwal Rees, a splendid chap—Cambridge, you know. Yes. I'll telephone him either tonight or tomorrow. Tomorrow will be best. I will telephone him from London. See what we can do. But the boy does need extra tuition in arithmetic and algebra."

On the drive back to Port Talbot, my mother told me she was proud of me. My father glanced at me in the rearview mirror.

"Yes. Well, let's hope your uncle Eddie can pull a few strings."

Indeed, Uncle Eddie did work his magic. He and Arthur Mee's *Children's Encyclopedia* got me into Cowbridge at age thirteen, the summer term of 1951. I had arrived. Or so I thought.

three

THE CROW

The Cowbridge headmaster at the time, J. Idwal Rees, was renowned as a great classics scholar, having graduated from St. John's College, Cambridge. He taught Greek and played international rugby for Wales. He was a strict disciplinarian and always smartly dressed in a black suit with a black gown. He used to glide along the corridors of the school and across the grounds. I called him the Crow. Even Uncle Eddie James's pulling of the strings to get me into the school did nothing to make me feel welcome.

One Saturday morning, the Crow, within earshot of the other boys in the dormitory, told me what he thought of me. "You're totally inept," he said. "Does anything go on in that thick skull of yours?"

Interesting word! thought I.

A short slap across my head. "Well, does it? Does anything go on in that inept brain of yours? Answer me."

"No. Not much," I replied.

Another slap across the head. "No—what?"

"Sir."

"Say it."

"No, sir."

"Exactly. And look at your hands. Shovel hands."

He wasn't wrong. I used to drop things and break things. I was strong but prone to awkwardness, always the one to fumble a dish in the dining hall or wrench loose a handle in the corridor. "You break everything you touch. You're a brainless cart horse. Elephant Head—isn't that what they call you?"

"Yes."

"Yes—what?"

"Sir."

The slap across my head wasn't painful. It was a marker, a notch on the rifle butt. The brainless cart horse remark was interesting. Who knew? Perhaps a cart horse would be a preferable form of existence to a dead-end schoolkid always being slapped across the brain box.

Grandpa Yeats used to say, *Forget it. Forget the hurt. Stay mute. Keep your mouth shut. Never engage.*

It was good advice; the best advice. I played dumb. And it became my identity. I was *inept*. It was my new badge of honor.

The public library was my favorite place. I always carried the little notebook Grandpa Yeats gave me so I could jot down bits and pieces of information. In the library, I turned the pages of the *Webster's* to *I*. And there it was on the top of the page: *Inept*. I owned the page. And lo and behold, there I was, a portrait in definitions and synonyms: *Incompetent. Unfit. Unfitted. Incapable. Unable. Unskilled. Unprepared.*

My problem had been labeled by my schoolteachers, slapped into my head, like the mark of Cain, but now it had become my gift and my blessing. That was me. Good. Now I knew what I was. I thought it would be fun to tape a photograph of myself onto that *Webster's* page.

I was indifferent to athletics. School sports were anathema to me. What was the purpose or point in chasing or kicking a stupid ball around a stupid field with a bunch of other stupid kids? They would all cheer and screech when they scored a goal. *Morons*, I thought. Soon I withdrew from everything. I wouldn't go to my own birthday parties. My mother would throw them, but I hung around outside while inside they had games and cake.

But there was a hidden payoff to this isolation, a comfortable reward for this new identity game: I could become, without effort, a victim, a martyr. Then they'd be sorry. I'd show them.

One evening, I was called to the headmaster's study. This was the second time I'd been summoned by the Crow. The first occasion was regarding a gruesome book that my father had, a picture book of the horrors of the First World War, with the trenches and the mud and the carnage. The book was titled *Covenant with Death*. He'd shown it to me when I was young, perhaps five; I took it to school, and one of the teachers reported me to the Crow.

"Where did you get this book?" he asked me.

"My father gave it to me."

"Your father? Is he mad? This book is terrible. Doesn't he know that war is glorious?"

That was the word he used: *glorious*.

I pulled my dumb-insolence gag. It worked.

The Crow told me to get out of his office. He confiscated the book.

Round two. My new offense was to be caught reading *The Revolution Betrayed* by Leon Trotsky. I'd taken it from the Port Talbot Library and "forgotten" to return it. One of the little sneering tin-god prefects had reported me.

Once again, I was standing in the Crow's bleak office.

Outside, on the rectangular lawn, some boys were playing croquet in the fading sunlight. One lamp near the tall bookshelves cast almost no light at all into the room. The Crow was sitting at his desk. I could barely make out his face in the gloom. His bony hand rested on the cover of the Trotsky book.

"Why are you reading this?" he asked. His voice was remote. "Do you believe in Communism? Are you a follower?"

Silence.

"You do know that we are involved in a Cold War with the Soviet Union? Have you heard of Stalin?"

"Yes, sir," I replied.

"Then why are you reading this book?"

"I'm interested in the Russian Revolution. My father told me that Trotsky was assassinated by Stalin," I replied.

The only sound was from outside, the click of a mallet on a croquet ball. There was another silence. The headmaster got up from his chair, walked to the window, and watched the boys outside.

The summer light made me sad.

The Crow spoke quietly, with no sound of contempt: "You don't seem to care about anything being taught here. Do you find it difficult? Mr. Evans tells me you have no interest in math or chemistry. But here you are, reading Trotsky. Do your parents know you are reading these kinds of books?"

"Yes, sir," I replied. "My father knows."

"Have you read Karl Marx?"

"I tried to read him, sir, but it is complicated."

"Precisely. I read him at Cambridge."

Pause. He studied me as if I were an insect under a microscope.

He went back to his desk and handed me the book.

"I'm not going to confiscate this. Besides, it's a library book. But I don't want you reading it in class. You may go."

A few days later, the Crow summoned my parents to the school to receive his report. Mr. Rees was lenient, telling my parents that their son was probably "different," a bit slow and a bit of a dreamer, head in the clouds, that sort of thing. My parents were relieved. They also told me that Mr. Rees's stern, narrow face creaked into a smile as he told them what I'd said when he asked me a few weeks before why I had not seen the school production of Shakespeare's *Twelfth Night*. My response had been: "I don't think the cast is very good." He said the teachers had enjoyed a good laugh over my precocity.

During the English literature hour, Mr. Codling invited me to stand before the class and read a poem. "Let us hear from our resident critic, young Master Hopkins."

What was that?

Mr. Codling pointed at the floor where I was to stand.

"Wake up. This is your opportunity to show us how it is done."

What was he talking about?

"Come on. We haven't got all day."

There was no sternness, no threat in his voice. Old Arthur Codling knew all the tricks of sullen boys; he could see through our masquerades to our anxieties.

Reluctantly, I got up, shuffled my way to the appointed spot next to Mr. Codling's desk. He handed me a hefty book, *Palgrave's Golden Treasury*.

Then, pointing at a marked page, old Arthur Codling said: "Read that to the class."

It was the first time I had been asked to demonstrate, perform, or recite anything before a bunch of sullen boys because I always sat at the back of the room.

Keep your head down. Don't get involved. Trust no one.

The poem was "The West Wind," by John Masefield, the British poet laureate.

I knew his poem "Cargoes." But this one? I had never read it. I began, curious to see what it was all about:

It's a warm wind, the west wind, full of birds' cries;
I never hear the west wind but tears are in my eyes.
For it comes from the west lands, the old brown hills.
And April's in the west wind, and daffodils.
[. . .]
It's a fine land, the west land, for hearts as tired as mine,
Apple orchards blossom there, and the air's like wine.
There is cool green grass there, where men may lie at rest,
And the thrushes are in song there, fluting from the nest.
[. . .]
"Will ye not come home, brother? Ye have been long away,
It's April, and blossom time, and white is the May;
And bright is the sun, brother, and warm is the rain,—
Will ye not come home, brother, home to us again?"
[. . .]

*To the violets, and the warm hearts, and the thrushes' song,
In the fine land, the west land, the land where I belong.*

Boys don't cry. I wanted to. But I didn't. I gave the book back to Mr. Codling.

The boys were silent—no smirks, no sneers. Mr. Codling looked at me.

"Thank you. Rather good."

four

APRIL FOOLS' DAY

Four years later, after two boarding schools, a few brushstrokes of social isolation, and failing grades, I reached the ripe age of seventeen.

I stood with my mother and father in the kitchen behind the bakehouse, a small, square space that also served as our living room and dining room. We were about to go see a film at the Plaza. It was our Friday-night ritual, but this particular Friday evening, a shadow fluttered overhead. The shadow was my school report. As always, these reports arrived during my school holidays in a white envelope addressed to Mr. and Mrs. R. A. Hopkins, 19 Commercial Road, Port Talbot, Glamorgan.

And now there it was, my notice of doom, propped against the willow-patterned teapot on the kitchen counter, waiting to be opened and read. Why? To remind my mother and father of their son's stunning stupidity. Those little memos *always* arrived in the middle of my school holidays, and *always*, the envelopes stood there, leaving me to wonder for days:

Why am I not allowed to open these sealed death warrants?

And then I'd remind myself:

Because they are not yours to open, dummy.

And then I'd reply:

What if I smashed that willow-patterned teapot on the stupid counter to smithereens and thereby changed the reality of my world? Cause and effect. No teapot, no school report, no school—no me. There was no need to wonder about the exact contents of the white envelope. It would be the same old refrain, another rusty nail hammered into my coffin.

It was time for the ax to fall on this jolly April Fools' Day evening.

My father opened the envelope and pulled out the neatly folded report. Clipped to the report was a letter. That had never happened before. A letter? He briefly glanced at the report, his eyes moving quickly down the list of my misdemeanors, before moving over to the attached letter. He read it slowly. I watched his face for a flicker of reaction. Nothing. Ominous.

"What does it say?" my mother asked.

I'm a failure. That's it. I don't need to have it spelled out for me.

"'Dear Mr. and Mrs. Hopkins: With some regret and disappointment I must report that Anthony's grades are below the educational standard of this school. Unfortunately, he demonstrates little or no interest in the academic subjects being taught here. He demonstrates little or no interest in the healthy sporting opportunities of our establishment, be it rugby, cricket, or any other athletic activity. Furthermore, he tends to isolate himself from the other boys at the school. Yours faithfully, J. Idwal Rees, headmaster.'"

The old Crow was dead right. I did have a tendency to isolate. The school did maintain, as advertised, "a high standard of education and a matchless reputation." Everyone agreed—the problem was entirely within the dummy standing before his parents in their airless kitchen, its one window facing the gray concrete wall of the shop next door.

My father began the usual lamentations: "Who knows what'll happen to you. It worries me. Honestly, you're bloody hopeless. You'll never get anywhere, never amount to anything in life, the way you're going on. God knows, we work hard to give you an education. Complete bloody waste of money, as far as I'm concerned. What the hell is wrong with you? You should get your head examined. Can't you do anything useful? You're bloody useless. I don't know what . . ."

Right on, Pops. You hit the bull's-eye. I am bloody useless.

My mother jumped in: "Oh, leave him alone, for goodness' sake."

My mother accepted most of my defects and shortcomings. She was a stoic. "What's to be will be."

But my father, my old man? He brooded. When I was a young boy he'd taken me on his bread rounds in a delivery vehicle with A. R. HOPKINS AND SON, LTD. written on the side; I saw him only in left profile. I sometimes grew afraid sitting there, hearing the car engine and the gears shifting and the *thud-thud* of the windshield wipers because I couldn't shake the idea that there was only a left side to my father's face. Through my childhood, I had dreams where he wasn't real, just a walking profile.

I had always been conscious of shadows flickering through our house because my mother and father were both prone to depression and dark moods. They fought and wept. My father drank heavily, which only fueled his already heightened emotionality. I once heard him weeping in the back garden.

As a child, I hated the sound of sobbing, especially coming from a man. He and my mother spent days without speaking to each other. He had colossal amounts of energy that went nowhere.

"Bakers are mad," he liked to say.

I had something of my father's spirit—some vague loneliness or sorrow, or was it fear?—that I spent my whole life trying to shake. I kept running away from my parents and toward something I couldn't describe but imagined to be better than anything I'd known.

I thought of how my father had played with me when I was very little, probably three or four. He would pick me up and almost throw me in the air. I always wanted to touch the ceiling. In those early days, our town, Margam, had gas lighting. There was no electricity until the end of the war. In his games he would hold me up near the gas mantel's light bowl. I used to ask him to throw me up to the gas hard. I tried to reach the untouchable ceiling.

In the front garden were two poplar trees and a green-painted iron railing on top of a low redbrick wall. Next door was Mr. Jones's proud little collection of primroses and lupines. I spent most of my time alone in our back garden. I didn't make friends with the other kids, preferring my own company. Next door on the other side was the house of Mrs. John and her husband, Bert. They had a daughter, Mary, and a white-and-black-spotted dog I loved called Spot.

My father liked to have chats on summer evenings with Bert. Those summer evenings in 1944 were redolent with the smell of burning weeds and dried leaves. In those war years, the Ministry of Food encouraged people to grow their own vegetables in victory gardens, and the government gave allowances to people to have allotments in farm fields.

My father was always in a collarless shirt; Bert John wore the same, paired with a peaked cap. They smoked acrid Woodbine cigarettes, which they called *coffin nails*. They both grew cabbages and beans. The government encouraged co-operation; younger men were meant to offer the products of their garden patches to children and the elderly. Children's malnutrition was a concern, infantile paralysis the big threat. Harsh as I know those wartime and postwar days were, the gathering of a nation together was a great moment in my memory.

After mowing the small patch of lawn or digging up potatoes in the narrow strip of earth, my father would stop to talk to Bert, both lighting up their Woodbines and looking up at the mellow sky, chatting like two philosophers:

Yes. Another nice day tomorrow. The nights are drawing in. Soon be autumn.

Wonder when this bloody war will be over. Did you hear about Trevor Williams?

No, what?

Dead.

Never.

Yep. North Africa.

Ah, well, better turn in. I'm on the early shift tomorrow. Good night, Dick.

Good night, Bert.

I listened to these dialogues and committed them to memory. I had many people's voices in my head, and yet I didn't have a voice of my own, so I kept quiet. I played the piano, drew pictures, and lived alone in my own world, silent but for the sound of classical music. I believed that I'd put one over on everyone by becoming self-sufficient. *That'll show them. What's the point of closeness to anyone? You get ripped apart in the end.* Death was always near, and when it came to us or those we loved, it should be borne with stoic acceptance.

Miss Thomas, our gentle, gray-haired first-grade schoolteacher, had taught the motley crew of ragamuffin, restless kids the Lord's Prayer and the Twenty-Third Psalm. She encouraged us to learn the words she chalked up on the blackboard, even though many of us hadn't learned to read. They were powerful, mysterious words, and although I couldn't read well, suddenly one day the colored chalkboard words came to me, and I was able to learn those particular lines quickly.

The next day, Miss Thomas unexpectedly asked me to stand up and recite the opening lines of the Lord's Prayer. Being an all-or-nothing freak, I spoke the prayer and psalm rapidly, no mistakes. Miss Thomas was pleased, and later that afternoon when my mother came to pick me up and take me home on the bus, I overheard Miss Thomas tell her about my performance.

It was my first good review!

When we got back to the house, my mother asked me to recite the opening lines of the prayer. Again, I rattled through all of *Our Father* and *The Lord is my shepherd*, speaking quickly, parrot fashion, no intonation or expression.

My mother was so pleased. There was still a gleam of hope.

Then she asked me to do the same for my father.

"Our Father, who art in heaven, hallowed be—"

My father scoffed: "Don't believe in that rubbish. That's fairy-tale nonsense."

My first bad review!

That's the way he was constructed. He, like his father, was an atheist. There was no harm meant. That was that. Live and let live.

That evening of the school report, as the grandfather clock ticked away in the corner, my parents stood as if frozen by disappointment. I felt no sadness for myself, only sadness for them. They were silent and defeated. They couldn't look at me; perhaps they *wouldn't* look at me. It was almost as if I were a dead thing.

I stepped away from them and decided to change the rules of the deadly game.

A quiet, level voice came from my mouth:

"One day I'll show you. I'll show both of you."

The moment of certainty fused two parts of myself together. That was it! An inner click, a fasten-your-seat-belt click. The hopeless Welsh boy was getting ready for action. What sort of action? No clue. But it didn't matter. I felt like a powerful, friendly hand had gripped my shoulder and an inner voice had said, *Now you know that you know. There's no way back. You were never part of them. Ask for nothing, expect nothing, accept everything.*

Suddenly even the world of objects looked different. The small, cramped room, the ancient ticking grandfather clock, the copper and brass ornaments my mother had collected over the years mounted in pride of place on the shelves of the old Welsh dresser—none of it looked the same. Light shone through the grimy windowpanes as if they'd been freshly cleaned.

My father looked at me in a new way. It was a waking-up look of recognition, my first real contact with him, with my mother, and with everything around me. He tore both the report sheet and the letter into two pieces, crumpled them up, and tossed them into the unlit fireplace. Later, I would fetch the papers and press them into a notebook I'd keep for the rest of my life.

"Well, I hope you do show us," he said. "I hope you do."

"I know you will," said my mother. "We both know you will."

My father coughed, then looked at the grandfather clock.

"Well, are we ready? Are we going to the pictures or not? If we are, we'd better get a move on."

We were going to the Plaza to see *Woman's World*, one of those grand old Hollywood CinemaScope epics chockablock with movie stars like Lauren Bacall, Fred MacMurray, and the suave and sophisticated Clifton Webb.

We walked past St. Theodore's Church and Theodore Road, past Salmi's Italian tea shop on the corner of Abbey Road, then on to Talbot Road, with its furniture shop, insurance offices, and Young Men's Christian Association, where I was always being pressured to go and socialize but never did. A board out front advertised *The Easter Play*.

As we made our way through town, my mother held on to my father's arm. "Why do you always walk so fast?" she said. "I can't keep up with you. Slow down."

"I always walk fast," he said.

He did too. It was on the rest of us to keep up.

Everything looked bright, washed and hung out to dry in the sunshine. Something had shifted, a minuscule readjustment. I glanced at my mother and father, trotting along the pavement, and suddenly felt that I no longer knew them. They looked the same as they had always looked, spoke the same as they had always spoken. But now we were different.

Port Talbot was new and yet familiar, as if I had lived in it before, not in some other life but in this life. I felt a bit out of my mind. Seventy years later, I still often feel that way, what people describe as not right in the head—not insane, but slightly removed from reality.

My parents, too, had episodes of strangeness.

One damp Saturday afternoon in mid-September when I was a boy, my mother and I walked unsteadily on a footpath on the side of the low mountain above Bracken Road to visit a farmer's thatched cottage, a broken-down wreck of a place. An old man, Mr. Williams, had lived there for many years, and inside his cottage was a clutter of junk—copper jugs and pots and plates on the kitchen table, coats and shoes on the chairs, and a heap of newspapers on a broken sofa. Hanging on the wall just inside the front door was a pair of deer antlers and, on the opposite wall, a framed oil painting of a lake and gray mountains.

My mother gave Mr. Williams six shillings for the antlers and two shillings for the painting. For free, Mr. Williams threw in an ancient copper disk on which a black steel handle had been welded. My mother had a knack for finding junk and polishing it. She hung the painting from a picture rail above the cottage piano in our front room and the antlers in the hall near the front door. (I still have the flat copper object with the black steel handle, and I still have no idea what it was meant to be—a frying pan? A frying disk?)

That afternoon, after buying the antlers and painting, we walked back across the wet field to the farm track, and just before we reached the log-plank bridge into Ty-Fry Road, my mother stopped and asked me a question: "What would you do if I ran away and you never saw me again?"

I looked up at her. Her face looked pinched and pale as she stared across the fields at nothing. The day was overcast. There were heavy rain clouds. What was she looking at? And why would she ask me that question? If she were to run away, would it be my fault?

I felt how a dog or a cat might feel when its owner leaves, not knowing when or if that person would return. Her words fell into my tin brain box and stayed there, locked away like life savings.

When we got back to the house, my mother told me to sit and read "Hansel and Gretel" quietly and not fidget. I didn't want to read. I tried to stay in my seat but I kept shifting around. I wanted to run around and play. The German clock on the mantelpiece ticked. It was a depressing sound, the sound of hush and silence, everything still, almost frozen. I felt as if I were being watched.

When I looked up, my mother, still wearing her raincoat and brown hat, was standing in the hallway. Why was she watching me? Was she about to run away, leave through the front door and never see me again? I was overcome with a blank feeling, something like those empty outlines of farm animals on the pages of children's coloring books where you could color a cow green, a horse blue, and set them in a red field.

My father thought she was mad to have bought the antlers and painting.

"You must have been soft in the head. What a bloody waste of money. How much?"

"Six shillings for the antlers," she replied.

"Why antlers? They're no use to anyone. And this? What's this?"

"What does it look like? It's a painting. I gave him two shillings for it."

"A painting? You call that a painting? I could paint better than that."

I wanted to tell him not to talk to her like that or she'd run away, but I kept silent.

From then on, I always wondered if she might be about to bolt.

Even as I struggled with classwork, I took refuge in art, and I used to draw pictures with pencils and crayons. I knew nothing about painting, but a neighbor of ours, Bernice Evans, was an artist, and she would sometimes come to our house. Bernice lived with her parents at the corner of Margam Road. She was a gentle, soft-spoken girl who reminded me, years later, of the part-Welsh actress Glynis Johns; she had the same voice.

One afternoon, Bernice came to the house to talk to my mother about something. I was lying on the living-room carpet, drawing in my notebook. Bernice told my mother that she would like to draw a pencil portrait of me. The following Sunday, Bernice arrived at the house carrying a small bag of pencils and chalks and a pad of cartridge drawing paper. She completed the portrait quickly, and it was an amazing likeness.

Some years later, in August 1947, Bernice told me she would like to give me drawing classes in her little studio above the Port Talbot Post Office on Station Road. I was nine, and she was perhaps nineteen or twenty. I would go to her place on Friday evenings after school. One evening I went over, and she told me she could spare only half an hour because her boyfriend was taking her to the Plaza to see *Odd Man Out*, a film with James Mason and Robert Newton. As an exercise, she suggested I paint a pirate standing on the deck of his ship. The exercise was my first attempt at poster paints on cartridge paper. My pirate wore a red spotted bandanna and brown leather boots.

I concentrated on the pirate's boots and the sea behind him. Bernice was very patient with me. Soon after, there was a ring at the door. She went out and called down the stairwell for her boyfriend to come up. In walked this young man, who looked at my picture and then at me.

"I like his boots," he said. The man's blue eyes twinkled.

Bernice introduced me to him: "This is Richard. He's an actor on the stage in London." It was my first meeting with the actor Richard Burton.

Burton was the twelfth of thirteen children. His mother died soon after giving birth to his younger brother, so the two brothers were raised by a sister, a lovely lady named Cecilia, known as Cissy, on Caradoc Street in Port Talbot. I was fascinated by him. After he became famous, he would come back to stay with Cissy. Once when he was visiting, I heard about it at the bakery because the girls were atwitter. I asked someone to take me over there to get his autograph. When I arrived, he and his wife, Sybil, were finishing breakfast.

"You're Dick Hopkins's boy, aren't you?" he said. "I used to work in the shoe department across the way. Do you speak Welsh?"

"No," I said.

"Then you're not a true Welshman! You should speak Welsh." He handed me the autograph and said, "Well! We're off to the match!"

"What match?" I asked.

"What do you mean, what match?" he said. "Rugby! Wales versus France! Aberavon in Cardiff Arms Park! Don't you know anything?"

Sybil said, "Richard, stop it! Don't tease him," and they headed to their gray Jaguar.

As he drove away, I thought, *That's what I want to be.*

five

TERRAZZO. TERRAZZO. TERRAZZO.

Jack Edwards, the owner of the grocery shop next but one to our bakery shop, was a senior board member of the YMCA. Everyone in the area liked Jack because he was easygoing and generous. He was a good administrator at the YMCA, organizing table-tennis matches for the younger boys, Saturday-morning rugby practices, and the amateur drama competitions that took place every summer at the Trecynon-Aberdare Drama Festival.

My father asked Jack to take me to the YMCA.

"Anything to get him out of the house. Introduce him to some other kids," my father continued. "He doesn't have any friends. Worries me. His last school report was bloody awful. He'll end up starving in a garret somewhere. Wanders off up the mountain. Lives in a dream world. Don't know what's to become of him."

Jack laughed. "You worry too much, Richard. Anthony will find his way."

My mother had a soft spot for Jack. She liked him because he was a bit half-soaked—a Welsh term for simplemindedness, whimsicality.

"That's what I always tell him," said my mother. "Dick worries too much. He worries about everything."

"Oh, yes, it's all very well to talk," my father complained. "Someone must worry; we can't all live up in the clouds, can we? Dreaming and playing the piano all day, that bloody *Moonlight Sinatra* over and over."

"*Sonata*. Not *Sinatra*," my mother said, laughing.

"What? Who? Yes. Well, whatever it's called. I don't know. Beethoven. No wonder the man went bloody deaf. And mad."

"Stop swearing," my mother said.

"What you need is a good war," he told me. "As it is, you don't know you're born."

Six o'clock the following evening, Jack came to pick me up.

"We'll walk, OK?" Jack said. "It's not far. Twenty minutes. Get some air in your lungs."

Jack was old enough to be my father. I had never trusted adults, or anyone else, for that matter, but I'd always liked Jack. He was funny, always having a laugh, and also, he seemed to like me. He liked everyone. There'd be no scowling, growling put-downs, or slaps across the head from him.

It felt strange to be walking along the old Talbot Road with Jack Edwards like the two of us were old friends on an evening full of spring light.

We arrived at the YMCA.

In the narrow hallway, Jack introduced me to a frail, elderly man.

"Mr. Nicholas, this is Anthony. He's going to become a member."

The man gave no hint of enthusiasm. I could have been the

Invisible Man. When I held out my hand to shake, instead of taking it, he stared at it and grunted. It occurred to me that this jolly old bird could be a follower of the old adage that children should be seen and not heard. Mr. Nicholas must have been an important member of the YMCA board and therefore burdened by weighty responsibilities. Jack said, "Yes, Mr. Nicholas. Thank you, Mr. Nicholas."

Mr. Nicholas pulled Jack aside: "Something has come up, Jack. Confidential. It's about the Saturday rugby practice. Complaints from people living on Bay View. Bad language from some of the older boys."

"Oh, dear, that's not good. Really? I'll investigate it."

While both men quietly murmured and muttered away, I had nothing much to do but count the little black and white squares that made up the floor of the hallway. Then I started counting the little black and white squares that made up the floor of the short corridor that led to some inner sanctum beyond the dark green double doors. It gave me something to do.

Statistics and details often calmed me. The YMCA floor must have had several hundred thousand such details. It was called a terrazzo surface. This YMCA floor was not unlike the kitchen floor of my parents' first house in Margam.

My mother was proud of her terrazzo kitchen. Whenever a neighbor, be it Mrs. Griffiths, Mrs. Jenkins, Mrs. Hanford, or Mrs. Whoever, came to our house for a gossip, they would remark, "Lovely kitchen, Mrs. Hopkins."

Loftily, she would say, "The floor is terrazzo, you know. *Terrazzo.*"

The memory prompted me to repeat the word: "Terrazzo. Terrazzo. Terrazzo."

After five long minutes, Jack nudged me. "Hey, you. You all right?"

"Yes."

"Good. Come on, let's go up to the games room."

As we made our way up the stairs, Jack turned and looked down at Mr. Nicholas. "I'll meet you in ten minutes in your office, Mr. Nicholas? Just going to show Anthony around first."

Then, in a whispered aside to me: "He's a miserable old bugger. Big chapel-goer."

Jack Edwards was now my greatest hero and my first true friend.

I heard the general noise made by young boys whooping, shouting, and laughing. Reaching a dimly lit area at the top of the stairs, I felt edgy. *I don't want to be here! Why am I here?* I thought. I heard the *tap-tap-tap-tap* sound of a Ping-Pong ball and table-tennis paddles and froze. *Oh God, they're going to make me learn snooker.*

"Terrazzo," I whispered to myself. "Terrazzo. Terrazzo. Terrazzo. Terrazzo. Terrazzo."

Jack looked at me. "What was that?"

"Terrazzo," I said.

"Terrazzo?"

"Yes. The floor down there is a terrazzo floor."

Jack looked puzzled. "You're a funny one."

We were now approaching the Ping-Pong mayhem.

"Here we are. This is the games and recreational room."

It was a big room. There were a few chairs along one wall. In the center, two boys were playing the noisy game of table tennis. At the back of the room was a snooker table. I recognized the seventeen-year-old boy poised over the green, cue ready to pocket the ball. He was Donald Price. We had never spoken to each other. He was too cool, too relaxed for the likes of me. But now he glanced up.

"What are you doing here?"

"Watching," I said.

He pocketed the ball with one stroke.

"Hello, Donald," said Jack. "Do you know Anthony?"

A shrug from Donald Price.

Sensing my reluctance to join either the wild-looking Ping-Pong boys or the sullen Donald Price at his snooker table, Jack told me he had to see the old bugger Mr. Nicholas in his office downstairs to talk more about the scandalous rugby practice and the bad-language problem.

"I'll be back in fifteen minutes. All right?"

"All right," I replied.

"Good. Don't get into any trouble."

He left and went downstairs. I sat on one of the chairs to watch the two boys slamming a little white ball back and forth over a net.

Soon, I grew bored and I wandered off. Outside the games room, the corridor was quiet. Roaming the halls, I found something sad and empty about the place. Where was Jack Edwards? I wanted to leave. There was nothing here for me.

Looking for an exit, I went down the stairs. From behind the double doors at the end of the corridor, I heard voices.

I cracked one of the doors open and peered in. It was a large room, more like a hall. It might have been a gymnasium at some time. There was a stage with green curtains. Three people holding pages were standing on the stage. A man who seemed to be overseeing whatever was taking place stood in the center of the room. He appeared to be conducting using the manuscript in his hands. I noticed Jack Edwards across the hall, sitting next to Mr. Nicholas.

Mr. Nicholas signaled at me to leave, but the man in charge, the conductor, turned around and saw me. He came over to the door and said, "Yes? What do you want?"

"I was just watching. That's all. Sorry." I started to leave.

Jack came over. "It's all right, Cyril. He's with me. He's just joined the YM."

Cyril looked at me. "Well, come in, then, and sit down by there." He pointed at a chair next to the door. "What's your name?"

"Anthony."

Jack explained, "He's Dick Hopkins's boy. Hopkins the baker, Commercial Road, Taibach. You know his shop."

Cyril: "Good, well, sit down there. We are rehearsing."

The three people onstage had stopped doing whatever it was they'd been up to. They were waiting for their conductor.

I sat next to Jack. Across the hall, old Mr. Nicholas nodded off. No one seemed eager to wake him.

Cyril seemed likely to become another friend because he hadn't frowned at me or told me off at the door. He wore green corduroy trousers and a brown, prickly Harris tweed jacket.

I whispered a question to Jack: "Who are those people?"

"They're the YMCA Players. They are rehearsing."

"What are they doing?"

"I just told you. Rehearsing."

"Oh, sorry."

"They are rehearsing *The Easter Play*. It's on next Sunday."

"Who's that man who spoke to me?"

"Cyril Jenkins. He's the producer. He wrote the play. That's his daughter over there, sitting near the stage. That's Bob Ace, her husband."

Six more people entered from the left side of the stage. One of them was a tall man I recognized as the town council's sanitary inspector. His name was Duncan Miles. He used to drink (and no doubt drink and drink and drink) with my father in the bar of The Grand Hotel. Duncan started to speak in a rich voice full of vibrant passion and probably also beer: "The place of a skull, they call it. Golgotha—"

Cyril interrupted: "Not so fast, Duncan. Give it more weight. Like this: 'The place of a skull, they call it.' Then pause, look around, wait for Geraldine to come on. Then, when she reaches the center of the stage, turn to the audience and say 'Golgotha,' but with deep meaning: *Golgotha*. Do it again."

"Right you are, Cyril. No problem."

"Come on, Duncan, be serious."

"I am always serious. Never otherwise."

Apparently, actors were like this. They bantered. And yet they were working hard too. The rehearsal went on for another half hour, though to me it seemed like just seconds.

Jack asked me if I'd enjoyed it.

"Yes, thank you. I did."

We were about to leave when Cyril Jenkins came over. He asked me my name.

"Anthony Hopkins," I replied.

"Would you like to be in it?"

"In what?" I asked.

I really was a bit slow. It got on people's nerves. And yet, amazingly, not *these* people's nerves. They seemed to like having me around.

"This play. Would you like to be in it? We need one more male. To play a saint. Just one line."

Jack looked at me and said, "Well, here's your chance."

"Yes, please," I said. "I'd like that."

"Good."

Cyril shook my hand. "We play for three nights, starting a week from Sunday. I'll give you the script. We'll rehearse again on Tuesday night, then again on Saturday afternoon before the performance. Would you ask your mother if we can borrow a bedsheet? My daughter Marilyn will sew it into a robe and headdress. She makes the costumes."

"Yes, I'll ask her."

Cyril called Marilyn over. She was sorting out some papers.

"Marilyn, this is— What's your name?"

"Anthony."

"Anthony. Anthony Hopkins. He's going to join us. Give him the pages with the saints' words."

Marilyn had a nice smile. She went back to her papers, returned, and gave me two carbon-copy sheets of paper.

Cyril pointed to a line. "Read it now. So I can hear it."

I looked at the paper. "Which one?"

"That one, the one I pointed at. 'Blessed are the meek.'" He seemed slightly puzzled or amused, but not angry. "Go on, read it. 'Blessed are the meek . . .'"

"'Blessed are the meek, for they shall inherit the earth.'"

Brief pause.

"That was lovely," said Marilyn. "He's got a lovely voice, Dad."

"Yes. Not bad, but we don't want to make him bigheaded, do we?"

Then to me he said: "Well done. Have you acted before?"

"No," I replied.

"You'll be another Richard Burton," said Marilyn. "You'll go a long way."

"My father says I'll go a long way on a double-decker bus," I said.

My new pal Jack Edwards walked me back home.

He asked me how I felt. I thought about everything I'd seen that day.

"It feels good," I told Jack. "I wonder if I'll be nervous in front of an audience?"

"No, of course you won't. It's only one line. But it's a beginning. Your father will be happy, and your mother."

"I hope so."

"They will. They want the best for you. You'll be fine. I keep telling your father that: 'He'll be fine!' You'll be fine."

His words would echo through the years: *You'll be fine. I'll be fine. You'll be fine. I'll be fine. You'll be fine. I'll be fine.*

Walking home with Jack that night along the familiar streets, I saw the lit-up houses and the closed shops, the rumbling cars and the quiet evening buses with their passengers gazing out, no longer as my neighborhood or even as a real city. All of it now looked like scenery for a show.

The Easter Play approached.

"Maybe you'll be famous one day," my mother said. "You never know."

My father was also pleased, but out of habit, he managed to sprinkle a little cold water on good news.

"He won't make any money acting," he said. "You'll have to get a job when you leave school."

"Dick, you don't have to be so blunt," said Muriel.

"It's all very well, living up in the clouds," he said.

"You always say that," said my mother. "Change the record, for goodness' sake." To me, she said, "Who do you play?"

"One of the saints. I have to say 'Blessed are the meek, for they shall inherit the earth.'"

"Oh, well, you never know," my father said. "Maybe Hollywood next."

There was a general sense of relief and relative happiness in the air.

I was the youngest in the cast. And yet, perhaps for the first time in my life, I didn't feel nervous.

The play was a series of scenes and tableaux surrounding the Crucifixion. Doug Rees was Herod. Duncan was Joseph of Arimathea. Cyril had taken over the role of the shepherd of Golgotha, a witness to the Crucifixion. "The place of a skull, they call it. Golgotha." Rehearsals were all confusion. Cyril placed us in groups. I didn't know what was happening. But piece by piece, it all came into shape: a seventy-five-minute show.

At the dress rehearsal, I first heard the addition of music: the prelude to Wagner's *Lohengrin*. Cyril had woven the music into the first lines of the play, and suddenly the words' effect was stronger. The powerful stage lights came on and I blinked up at the rafters. The lighting and the opening strings of Wagner had transformed the makeshift theater into a palace. Cyril was standing in the wings near the record player. I stood next to the other saints.

The costumes were homemade. Cyril was dressed as a shepherd; Geraldine, playing Mary, was draped in saintly blue; and Bob, her husband, wore something equally saint-like. I wore a costume made from a bedsheet and a headpiece with a golden star on it.

Saturday arrived. There was an afternoon dress-rehearsal run-through, and then it was showtime.

My mother and father and Grandpa and Grandma Yeats arrived. I spied on them through a gap in the curtain. The four of them sat together in the back of the room, my father reading the program. My grandfather lit a cigarette; he looked nervous. The hall filled up. The performance was about to begin.

Cyril: "Quiet. House lights dim. Music."

House lights went down. *Lohengrin*. Stage lights increasing...

Cyril went onstage and spoke the opening lines: "The place of a skull, they call it. Golgotha."

Through the spyhole in the curtain, I watched my father in the dim light. His mouth was slightly open. Wonder? Who knows? He never spoke about feelings. Had the scene—the lighting, the music, the atmosphere magically created by Cyril Jenkins, hovering over the scratchy record—made the same impression on the old man as it had on me?

Enter the saints.

"Blessed are the merciful, for they shall obtain mercy."

"Blessed are the poor in spirit, for theirs is the kingdom of heaven."

It was my turn to speak: "Blessed are the meek, for they shall inherit the earth."

The play came to an end and we, the YMCA Players, stood there in a straight line and bowed to the hundred and twenty people in the audience. Cyril stepped forward to receive his share of praise.

That was it, my first acting job.

That night, back in that same dark kitchen behind the shop where, on April Fools' Day, I'd been told I was useless, my mother told me something that I never forgot.

"Your father cried when you spoke that one line," she said. "I haven't seen him like that for years."

The old man cried? That's one for the books!

"Who cried?" I asked, wanting to make sure I'd heard her right.

"Your father," she replied irritably. "Who do you think I was talking about? He cried."

"Oh, yes?" I said, trying not to sound as surprised as I felt.

"He's proud of you. I am too."

"Good."

"Your grandfather and grandmother are too. Did you enjoy it? Being up there on the stage?"

"Yes, it was OK," I said.

My father came in through the back door. He had locked up the garage for the night.

"That was good," he said.

"Yes. We are going to see it again tomorrow," said my mother, "and Tuesday."

"When you were getting changed, I saw Duncan Miles," my father said. "He thinks you are very good, and so does— What's his name? Jenkins?"

"Cyril Jenkins."

"He played the shepherd, right?"

"Yes, and he wrote the play."

"He thought you were very good. So there you are. You never know."

One evening just before I was due back to school for my last term, I was in the shop helping my parents clean up when someone gently tapped on the shopwindow. It was six o'clock. The shop had closed. The assistants had gone home. My father was checking the cash register. My mother was gathering the unsold bread to repurpose the next day as breadcrumbs. Hearing the tapping on the shopwindow, my father looked up and saw a man peering in through the glass.

"We're closed!" my father shouted, but the man persisted in his tapping. My mother went to the door. The man outside was Indian, dressed in a long black coat. On his head was a turban. There were not many Indians in South Wales at that time, although they were beginning to travel from Asia to Europe, mainly Britain. Some made a living selling trinkets, ornaments, ties, and scarves. It appeared to be a tough and lonely life for them. My mother, always kind and welcoming to strangers, opened the shop door to let the man in. He had a small suitcase with him.

"Thank you, missus. I wonder please if I could buy some bread?"

My father called over to the man, "Shut shop. No bread." Then, to my mother: "Why did you let him in? He just wants to sell you some rubbish."

My mother glared at him and told him to be quiet. She asked the traveler what he needed.

"I would like please to buy bread," the man replied.

My mother wrapped a loaf of bread in a paper bag and into another paper bag she put doughnuts. The man offered to pay, but she said, "No money. These are for you."

"Thank you, lady," he said. "You are kind. You will be rewarded."

My father: "Oh, here we go! Who's going to reward us? The bloody Inland Revenue?"

"Just be quiet," snapped my mother.

The traveler opened his small suitcase and set it on the countertop. Inside the case was an assortment of neckties and scarves and an array of small pieces of jewelry and metal trinkets. My mother picked through the brightly painted scarves and neckties.

"Did you make these scarves and ties?" she asked.

"Yes indeed," replied the traveler. "My mother taught me how when I was a boy. Also, I made the jewels, the silver elephants. They are sacred."

My mother selected two scarves, two ties, and a miniature silver elephant. She went to the cash register and took out two one-pound notes. My father watched the transaction with suspicion.

"Where are you from?" he asked the traveler.

"Sir, I am from the Punjab, India. I came to Britain through Bristol and have been traveling here many weeks." He smiled at my father, then at my mother.

My mother gave him the pound notes, and he held on to her hand.

"You are a kind lady. Most generous lady. But you must be ready for an illness. You will be ill, but you will recover and be well and live long, many years."

"That's bloody cheerful news!" muttered my father.

The traveler, still holding my mother's hand, looked at my father and smiled: "You, mister, are lonely man in your own prison and you are sad. If you do not believe, then life will be over soon."

Then he looked at me. I hadn't thought he was even aware of me being there.

"You, young man, have snake eyes, troubles, but you will be one day very known everywhere, and soon you will live in a big castle."

"He must be drunk," my father scoffed. "A castle?"

Another killer look from my mother, but the traveler just smiled at my father's comment.

"You take notice of my words, mister, they will come true. You will know." He let go of my mother's hand, bowed his head to us, raised his hand. "Blessings from my home in the Punjab."

He left. We never saw him again. But I thought of him when my mother became gravely ill with peritonitis and was rushed to the Port Talbot hospital. She almost died, but she was saved by a young surgeon, Dr. Sabir. He was from the Punjab.

All of the events the traveler predicted came to pass. Even the castle.

six

DUMB INSOLENCE

My mother cut out a square of the *Western Mail* newspaper and handed it to me with the words "Why don't you try for this?" It was an audition notice for the Prince Littler Scholarship at the Cardiff College of Music and Drama.

I sent in the application. A week later, I was invited to an audition in Cardiff Castle. I waited in the main hallway. After ten minutes, I was shown into studio B, where I met Mr. Raymond Edwards, the principal of the college. To compete for "the Prince Littler Scholarship at forty pounds per annum," I had given my all to memorizing the speech Othello gives before killing Desdemona: "It is the cause, it is the cause, my soul . . ."

I had no technique but a good voice and an instinct for the dramatic.

When I finished, Mr. Edwards smiled and asked me if I wanted to sit down. "Yes. Very good. Very good. You like Shakespeare?"

"Yes, but I don't know much about it. I can do 'To be or not to be: that is the question.'"

"Good, very good. Well, thank you, Anthony. We will let you know soon." He seemed impressed.

Two weeks later, a notice arrived telling me that I was on the short list of three and would be interviewed by the governors of the school at eleven o'clock a.m. on the thirtieth of July at the Cardiff city hall.

I thought *short list* meant my height.

My father said: "No, it's not your height, stupid. It means you are one of only three chosen from all the others who applied."

I went to the Regent that night to see *Twenty Thousand Leagues Under the Sea*, a film starring Kirk Douglas, James Mason, and Peter Lorre. Sitting in that dark little cinema, I felt, for the first time in seventeen years, a sense of some hopeful future.

My parents' bakery business was doing well. My mother was my father's savior. Her determination to make a go of it conquered my father's caution. When it came to taking chances, he was a bundle of worries, but my mother had no time for that.

"You're afraid of your own shadow," she said. "We can't live in the past forever. We must get on with life."

When she told him we were getting a phone for the bakery, he protested: "We don't want to be rash!"

A week later, a phone was installed: Port Talbot 105.

Then she told him to buy a new car. "Get rid of that old wreck. It's always breaking down."

He bought a new Rover. License plate EU 6600. In this new status symbol, he drove me up to the Cardiff civic center at the city hall for my interview for the scholarship. The smell of polished leather seats and the glittering newness of the car bolstered my hopes. The city hall was grand. Pillars and statues.

My father came into the vast building with me to make sure I didn't get lost.

In the small lobby outside the interview room, I saw two young girls, Anne Holmes and Sandra Sheffield. They were the other short-listed candidates, both friendly girls. Someone came out from the inner sanctum. Time for my inquisition. My father wished me luck.

Three men seated behind a large table—Dr. Hines, governor of the college; Raymond Edwards, the principal; and Alderman Llewellyn Heycock—stared me down.

They asked me questions about my education. Had I done well at school?

I thought: *OK, here we go. No way will I make it into this place. This is it. Given my school record, well, thank you very much and goodbye.*

I evaded the question.

Dr. Hines was an elderly man. He seemed affable. Raymond Edwards kept writing in a little notebook. The alderman looked heavy and grim.

After five minutes, Dr. Hines thanked me and told me to wait outside.

Ten minutes later, Raymond Edwards, followed by the doctor and Alderman Beetle-Brows, came into the small lobby and made his announcement.

"The scholarship goes to the male."

I thought he meant the result would be sent in the mail.

My father nudged me. "Congratulations."

"What?"

"The male. That's you."

"Oh, I thought the mail was a letter. They'd let me know."

"You're thick as two short planks."

Everyone laughed; even the alderman smiled.

My parents were proud. Back at the bakery shop, everyone cheered.

Saturday, October 1, my father brought home the evening paper. "Hey, look at you. Your name's in the paper. You're famous," he said, pointing at the *Post*'s front page. "Look at that." In a little square was this news squib: "Anthony Hopkins, son of Richard Hopkins, Baker, Taibach, Port Talbot, has been awarded the Prince Littler Scholarship for the Cardiff College of Music and Drama."

"Wonderful!" cooed my mother. "Congratulations."

"Yes. Thank you," I replied, making sure I didn't give a hint of enthusiasm. I thought of the Tyutchev poem "Silentium," in which the poet advises keeping one's dreams and feelings to oneself.

"It'll be Hollywood next," my father joked once again.

I could see that he was pleased. Then my mother pointed to another little square on the same page: "But look at this. Isn't it sad? 'Actor James Dean, twenty-four, killed in automobile collision, Northern California.'"

To celebrate my scholarship, my father managed to get two tickets to see the Old Vic touring company production of *Julius Caesar* at the Empire Theatre in Swansea. The actors were Paul Rogers as Brutus and John Neville as Mark Antony. Wendy Hiller played Portia. It was a good production. When John Neville started his speech over the body of the assassinated Caesar, my father nudged me, because it was a speech I had learned.

O mighty Caesar! Dost thou lie so low?

The performance ended, and we went around to the stage door for autographs. I had that same notebook that my grandfather had given me. John Neville signed and so did Paul Rogers.

My father told them how much we enjoyed the play. He added: "My boy is going to be an actor."

John Neville: "Oh, really? Good."

Paul Rogers and Wendy Hiller politely said, "Thank you. So glad you enjoyed the play."

The woman who'd played Calpurnia hurried from the stage door. My father held out my notebook and asked her politely if she would sign an autograph "for the boy."

She waved him away like an insect. It sounds trivial, but the moment stayed with me.

He looked a bit defeated. "Oh, sorry."

In the car, driving back home, he said: "She must think she's the bloody cat's whisker. Ah, well!"

By fall of that same year, I was living in the caretaker quarters of Cardiff Castle. Mr. and Mrs. Donne were the resident housekeeper-and-maintenance couple. They were given permission to lease two large rooms to six students for thirty shillings a week.

I was in the Cardiff College of Music and Drama for two years, and was probably too young to take it all in. I was undisciplined, bulky, and angry. There were two other male students: Ron Edwards and Charles Bryce. Both were Cardiff boys. June Griffiths taught theater history. Rudy Shelley, an Austrian who taught movement, told me I had the posture of a camel. He was right.

But I managed to lumber through the two-year course. The end-of-term reports from the few teachers were mildly encouraging. I had potential, was the verdict, but I needed to work on technique. Technique. Technique. Technique. I tried to understand but couldn't grasp what it was exactly. The main influence on so many actors back then was the late James Dean. Everyone wanted to be him.

In 1957, the college put on two productions. In *Blood Wedding*, by Federico García Lorca, I was given, much to my surprise, the leading role of Leonardo. The other production was *The Skin of Our Teeth*, by Thornton Wilder, and, in another surprise for me, I landed the part of Henry Antrobus, the son of the Antrobus family. The play, which won the Pulitzer Prize in 1943, is an examination of humans, more specifically, of how they are blessed with the ability to create great art and technology but cursed with the catastrophic ability to destroy everything. Henry was the symbol of destructive power.

The production was taken on a tour of North Wales and, eventually, to the Vanbrugh Theatre, which was attached to the Royal Academy of Dramatic Art in London. The production was a success. Some London newspaper critics gave it good reviews. *The Daily Telegraph* gave me, personally, a good review. My parents came to see it. My father was pleased but had to give me due warning, once again, that there was no money in acting.

Just before leaving the drama school, I went to Bristol Old Vic to see John Osborne's *Look Back in Anger*. Jimmy Porter was played by an astonishing actor called Peter O'Toole. He was brilliant. A genius. I'd never heard of him. I left Cardiff College of Music and Drama in July of 1957, not daring to hope I'd ever be as good as O'Toole or Richard Burton but hoping to get a job, any job, that would keep me in the game.

I was offered a job with the Arts Council of Wales touring company as an assistant stage manager; I'd also play small parts. The two plays were *Look Back in Anger* and *She Stoops to Conquer*. I was totally useless as an assistant stage manager. Because I was physically strong and hefty, I was good at changing scenery, lugging heavy canvas flats around, but the simple job of placing props on the stage, anything that was breakable, forget it. I was angered by my own incompetence.

The company was made up of fifteen people. The tour was for four months around Britain, the four most miserable months to tour: September, October, November, and December. We traveled on a bus to various cities—Huddersfield, Oldham, West Hartlepool, Wigan, Derby, Durham, Newcastle. Rain and fog and damp shoes and loneliness.

In Newcastle, I was struck down by the Asian flu, a global influenza pandemic that emerged in China and spread across the world. I had no idea then that it was dangerous, but news reports later told me that the virus could be life-threatening, and these were not vague, panic-mongering reports. Between 1957 and 1958, more than a million people died of the illness worldwide. I had never felt so ill. Mrs. McMurray, the owner of the lodging house on Lovaine Street, called the doctor. His name was Dr. Waheeda. He checked me over (I had a temperature of 102) and prescribed some pills. I was nineteen and resilient. Or just lucky. Anyway, I survived, though from a week of not eating, I lost weight and muscle strength.

Mr. Sneath, our fat road-company manager, accused me of malingering. He docked me a week's pay. I gave him Dr. Waheeda's certificate of clearance. Fatso Sneath still wouldn't pay me.

But my trusty friend dumb insolence won the day: Ask for nothing, expect nothing, say nothing, just stare them down.

I can laugh now, because I know this was not a normal way to live, freezing people out as a form of revenge. What revenge? People were not harming me. What was my problem?

Well, whatever it was, I figured a few drinks would help. Usually, I drank beer. *Not too much*, I told myself, *just enough to make me feel relaxed.*

The tour continued through early December. At lunchtime in a Middlesbrough pub—we had arrived the night before and were getting ready to set up the scenery for the evening performance—I bought myself a whiskey, which was becoming my favorite meal, and found a seat in a corner near the door. The others were at the bar ordering drinks and sandwiches. Joan Knight was holding court. Frank Dunlop, the director, was there talking to Michael Friar, the electrician. The place was rocking, filled with customers, people from local office blocks. The noise of voices. A jukebox playing.

Most of the actors on that tour were rather posh. To me, they seemed far too clever and clubby. *Darling* this and *Darling* that. I couldn't stand them. I had to get away from everyone.

I drank the whiskey fast. Then, for luck and to stay warm, just one more. Suddenly, I felt all was well. Everyone looked friendly. There was nothing wrong with me. I went back to the bar, bought another shot—my third—downed that fast, then left to go back to the theater.

We were going to start the setup for the play that night, *Look Back in Anger*. *I'll show them*, I thought. *I'll do the stage setup all by myself.* I hauled around the wobbly flats and wooden frames representing walls, windows, and doors. Because of my physical strength, quiet anger, and *Screw you all* attitude, I was able to work fast and furiously.

Forty-five minutes later, the set was ready. All the stage weights had been secured; the furniture was assembled and placed precisely on the tape marks.

At 2:15, Joan Knight and the others came back from the pub.

Actor Patrick O'Connell looked at the set. "Bloody hell! What happened?"

The other assistant stage managers and Frank Dunlop looked stunned. They checked the set to make sure it was secure. Joan Knight looked at me.

"Did you do this?" she asked.

I shrugged.

"How?" she asked.

"I don't know. I just did it. Is it OK?"

Patrick looked at me. "You're a bloody headcase. You know that? A bloody headcase."

The last three weeks of the tour, I spoke to no one. I refused to answer even yes or no questions. I shut down any trace of reaction. I knew I wasn't mad. I was calculating. *Catch me if you can.*

I thought it was a great way to get through life, to stick it to others by punishing myself. When the tour ended, I didn't even wait for my last week's wage from the fleshy Porky Sneath. It was six pounds a week, which in those days was a livable wage. I wanted nothing more from anyone. Alas, as it turned out, my country wanted something from me.

seven

SHOW UP OR ELSE

On Monday, February 3, 1958, I was enrolled into Her Majesty's Service, the British Army. It was the last gasp of the compulsory two years of national service that had been established after World War II. During that time I proved myself fairly useless at marching, and so I was sent to clerical school. I made a terrible clerk too.

And yet I wound up with the cushiest job there was, typing in the regiment office. Every once in a while the sergeant major would run his hand up the back of my head and say, "Get your hair cut!"

Sometimes he'd see what a bad job I was doing at typing, kick me out of my chair, and finish the work while I made him tea.

One Monday in November 1959, I was called before Captain Michael Witte. Captain Witte, the adjutant of the Sixteenth Regiment at Bulford Camp in Wiltshire, was a decent, well-educated gentleman, fair and just. He spoke with an upper-class, almost unintelligible accent. Consonants were absent. I liked him. And on this day, I learned that the good captain had intervened to spare me a serious charge. I stood before his desk, stoic and silent. After a few moments, he picked up a sheet of typewritten paper from his desk. Quietly he told me the contents. "A civilian in Amesbury has submitted a complaint that you have become a bit of a scrapper, a brawler, and a drunk. You were involved in two fights with someone called Gallagher, a soldier from another regiment. Is this true?" asked Captain Witte.

"Yes, sir."

"Why?"

"I can't remember exactly," I replied. "Gallagher was a soldier in the Black Watch. They like to fight. He picked the fight with me."

"Yes, well, evidently, you also like to fight. I'm not pressing charges against you, Hopkins, but I am going to cancel your weekend passes for four weeks. You seem to be an intelligent young man. Why would you want to court such trouble?"

"I don't know, sir. I just seem to cause trouble. I'm a bit stupid."

In truth, I was beginning to enjoy the fisticuffs in my life. It happened the same way every time. At pubs, I kept myself to myself. Perhaps being quiet and withdrawn brings out something hostile in others. Who knows? My old play of dumb insolence probably invited that reaction. All I really wanted was to be left alone and avoid trouble. But in my early twenties my game was no longer working. And the fisticuff skirmishes exploded in pub parking areas.

The night I got in real trouble was indeed in Amesbury. At the pub, the Glasgow character called Gallagher, a tall lout of a guy, started needling me. "Hey, you, Taffy, you bloody Welsh pit pony. Buy me a drink."

WE DID OK, KID

I was sitting in a corner of the pub drinking beer, looking at the tapestry wall coverings of hunting scenes and country settings, the brass and copper ornaments over the bar. I ignored the demand.

Gallagher came over to the table.

"Hey, you, Taffy, buy me a drink."

Dumb-insolence tactic. Blank face.

"Are you going to oblige me, Taffy?"

"Buy your own drink," I said.

I got up and left the bar. I didn't want this. Gallagher followed me outside.

"Don't you walk away from me."

He pushed me against a wall. I banged the back of my head. It reminded me of a bully in my school when I was a boy who'd also banged my head against a wall. In a split second, something popped in my brain. The memory of the school bully flashed in front of me. I felt a surge of hatred and anger. I head-butted him and smashed his nose so hard, I heard the crack.

Such anger was a form of insanity. It was ugly. And it had consequences. I never heard what happened to Gallagher, but I was not only CB ("confined to barracks") for four weeks but also made to work double duty in the HQ office. To kill time, I took a correspondence course from Ruskin College in modern philosophy. My first reading was *Treatise Concerning the Principles of Human Knowledge*, by George Berkeley.

> *MIND-SPIRIT-SOUL. But, besides all that endless variety of ideas or objects of knowledge, there is likewise something which knows or perceives them, and exercises divers operations, as willing, imagining, remembering, about them. This perceiving,*

active being is what I call MIND, SPIRIT, SOUL, or MY-SELF. By which words I do not denote any one of my ideas, but a thing entirely distinct from them, WHEREIN THEY EXIST, or, which is the same thing, whereby they are perceived—for the existence of an idea consists in being perceived.

I recognized something that had bugged me for years: the feeling of unreality, the sense of not being part of my own life. I lived with a feeling of limbo, of waiting for the next chapter of my life. Perhaps that's why I had been drawn to the theater. When I was acting, I didn't have to be me any longer. I could pretend to be another person. Much easier.

I came across a Magritte painting of mirrors and the backs of heads and saw myself in it. It was a weird experience, all those heads looking away from me into the future. It felt as if time were running backward. I walked around asking myself questions like *Have we already died, and are we going back to the womb?*

Captain Michael Witte had given me a friendly warning, although it wasn't really a warning. It was well-meant advice: simmer down.

I finally got free again and was stationed in Wiltshire, and one weekend I hitchhiked to Pewsey. It was a beautiful Saturday, and the village was quiet. I walked around and had a couple of drinks in a pub called the Moonrakers. In that pub, I felt a strange sensation of familiarity, something like déjà vu.

I don't understand anything about the mechanism in the brain that creates that sensation, but I did feel as if I had been there before, had lived in that quiet village in some other time. In folklore, the Wiltshire people are known for their innocent simplicity. The pub's name came from a tale of two farmers who, after a night on the town, both drunk and barely able to stand, stared at a reflection of the moon in the village pond and resolved to rescue the drowning moon by raking it onto dry land.

There was something about military service that interested me. It was the discipline and precision of life. There was little room for wanderings of the imagination. You had to be there, show up or else.

On February 8, 1960, after two years of service, I was booted out into Civvy Street, meaning civilian life. I could complain, I suppose, that the army had been a waste of time, but it wasn't. I didn't do much as assistant to the chief clerk of the Sixteenth Light Ack-Ack Regiment, but I'd enjoyed the routine deadness of the days. I liked that nothing was expected of anyone other than that we obey orders. Now, free to do whatever I wanted, I went back to Wales. I worked briefly with a subcontractor at the Steel Company of Wales tool store. It was a simple job, sorting tools and bits of piping, but I couldn't hack it and was told to leave. Again, I went without picking up my last week's wages.

What was left that I knew how to do? Acting? It sounded so fatuous. The idea of making a living that way struck me as absurd. And yet. Perhaps acting would be my salvation, a way through. I did long to become another version of myself. I took the train to Bristol to have a look at the Old Vic, thinking maybe I'd ask for a job.

Outside the Old Vic's box office, I studied the photographs of the actors in stills of scenes from the current play, *The Queen and the Rebels*, by Ugo Betti. They all looked like proper actors, intense and serious and very in possession of themselves. I went into the foyer and peeked into the theater. There was a rehearsal underway, a woman onstage proclaiming something or other.

A man approached me. He was theatrically dressed in a dark green shirt and yellow bow tie.

"Are you loitering?" he said.

"Loitering? No, I'm looking for work. Acting."

"You must be mad. You can't just show up and ask for a job. Have you any experience?"

"I was on a tour with the Arts Council with Colin Jeavons and Pat Healy in 1957."

He offered me some advice and told me to write letters to directors of theaters. He wrote on a piece of paper *Manchester—Library Theatre. Nottingham Playhouse.* He wished me luck.

I followed his advice and wrote a few letters to acting companies. I was groping about in an unknown desert, but to my surprise, there was a reply from someone named David Scase, the director of the Library Theatre Company in Manchester. I was to travel up to London the following week for an audition.

I found myself in the heart of the city, near Cambridge Circus. Other actors were waiting around in the theater. After an hour, I was called to the wings of the stage. A young woman went on and gave my name to someone in the auditorium.

Voice offstage: "OK, bring him on."

I walked onto the stage. The auditorium was dark. A man came forward. It was David Scase.

WE DID OK, KID

He was a unique personality, a burly ex–merchant seaman. There was something friendly and no-nonsense about him. He looked like a boxer, tough and direct. He smoked like a chimney, deep inhalations of smoke and nicotine. He didn't seem to give a damn about anything. No arty stuff about this bloke. Refreshing.

He came to the edge of the stage, introduced himself, and offered a firm handshake.

My audition piece was from a play by Maurice Maeterlinck, *Monna Vanna*. The director seemed impressed, not so much by me as my choice of play.

"Monna who?" He laughed.

"*Monna Vanna*, by Maurice Maeterlinck," I replied. "A symbolic poet."

Mr. Scase smiled. "Oh, symbolic. OK. If you say so. OK. When you're ready."

He went back to his seat and waited for me to launch into it. I walked to the center of the stage, took a few breaths, and started my audition speech. A soundtrack in my brain kept up a nonstop commentary: *Who do you think you are? Give up now.*

I couldn't make it stop, but I managed to give the audition speech my most passionate ham performance.

It was as though I had plunged my hands into a flowing stream, and withdrawn them sparkling with light, shining with confidence and sincerity. And it seemed to me that men were changed, that all I had hitherto thought had been wrong. Most of all did I feel that I was changed, emerging at last as from a long imprisonment; that the gates were opening, flowers and leaves entwining around the bars; that the snows were melting on the far horizon, and the pure air of the morning entering my soul and breathing upon my love!

I couldn't remember why I'd chosen that play or that speech.

There was a brief silence in the auditorium. A cigarette lighter flashed, and the director, inhaling masses of smoke like a reverse-motion dragon, returned to the edge of the stage. He looked at me. Nodded.

"Yeah. That'll do. Not bad. Not bad at all. Maeterlinck? Symbolist? Is that what he was?"

"Belgian symbolist. He also wrote *The Blue Bird*."

"I must remember that," he said. "What's your name again? Anthony? From Wales, correct? Like Richard Burton. Anyway. Yes. Good. We'll let you know soon. We've got your details, your address, et cetera. All right, off you go, Mr. Maeterlinck."

David Scase was one of the most kindhearted men I had ever met. He gave me a sense of confidence. But the inner commentary refused to shut up. I caught the next train from Paddington Station back to Port Talbot.

Two weeks passed. Then a short note arrived in the mail. It was signed by David Scase. Yes. I was given a job as an assistant stage manager and I'd have the occasional walk-on part.

I arrived in Manchester on a cold Sunday afternoon in September. My digs were in Wythenshawe, about six miles from Manchester City.

I took in the whole double-decker bus journey to Wythenshawe from the upper deck. I'd go a long way on a double-decker bus—that's what my father had predicted. As the bus made its way from the station and through Piccadilly, the center of Manchester, I noticed a big advertisement for *Psycho*. I'd heard reports that it was a scary film.

Forty-five minutes later, I arrived at Wythenshawe. Mrs. Hale, the landlady of the tall, dark house, was a typical warmhearted, white-haired Manchester lady. She showed me to my room. I was sharing it with a tall bloke called Adrian Talbot. He was going to be another one of the assistant stage managers. I saw him briefly. Quick hello. Then the thought of *Psycho* popped into my brain, and I headed back into Manchester to see the film.

In the lobby of the cinema stood a life-size cardboard cutout of the great Alfred Hitchcock. A looped recording of Hitchcock's plummy voice, laced with disdain, came from several speakers. "Good evening. This is Alfred Hitchcock speaking." Mr. Hitchcock then calmly issued a warning to each member of the audience: "They must not, under any circumstances, reveal the ending of the film. To do so would result in terrible punishment. Something quite unspeakable." Theaters refused to allow anyone in after the film had started. Signs appeared with photos of Hitchcock saying things like "If you can't keep a secret, please stay away from people after you see *Psycho*."

It was a great publicity gimmick that only Hitchcock could have dreamed up.

That Sunday evening, the fates must have smiled on me, because I was able to buy a ticket without having to stand on line. I waited patiently near the guarded cinema doors as the previous showing ended. Faint sounds came from inside. Murmurings and laughter, silence, and then screams.

Another five minutes passed. Then the doors opened. The audience started coming out, laughing in a way that bordered on hysteria. It was one of the greatest shocker films ever. Terrifying. Hitchcock possessed an uncanny insight into the human subconscious. The boogeyman at the top of the stairs. The sense of unease that lurks in the shadows of our lives.

After the film, I returned to the digs in the gloomy Edwardian house. The entrance hall was dark and shadowed. There was a menacing staircase. Was Norman Bates at the top, holding a big knife, waiting for me?

Monday morning, I was at the Library Theatre, where I'd been told to report to the stage director's office at eight thirty sharp. There were four assistant stage managers. The stage director was John Franklyn-Robbins, who was also the leading actor in the company. I thought he looked like a bird. It was not meant to be an unkind comparison. I just tended to see animals in human faces, and this man looked to me like a scraggly vulture standing on a perch.

We stood in the Birdman's office and were treated to a lecture on rules of behavior and attitude. It was called production protocol. We were never, ever to address the actors by their Christian names, only as Mr. or Miss. Woe betide us for the slightest breach of production protocol.

It was like being back in the army. I must have been off my head, daring to think that I could become an actor. A little microbe curled up in the bowels of my brain had convinced me that I could make a living at this acting game.

My first impulse, once the lecture was over, was to make a getaway. My father, my old man, slipped into my head. He saw everything as a big fat joke. He thought both pessimism and optimism were useless. They both needed a poke in the eye.

The first play was called *The Man*, by American playwright

Mel Dinelli. To my shock and surprise, David Scase gave me the role of an errand boy called Howard. John Franklyn-Robbins was playing the leading role, a psychopath killer.

Then came *The Quare Fellow* by Brendan Behan. I was given the role of Mickser, a thug in the prison yard. There was a moment where I had to fight someone and throw him to the ground. Then, in *As You Like It*, I played Charles, the experienced court wrestler. I was bad at both roles because I failed to master the art of stage combat and instead engaged in *real* combat.

"You nearly killed that poor actor!" Scase told me one night after I'd thrown my scene partner across the stage. "You've got power as an actor, but you're all over the place and that's dangerous."

The holiday season came. Mrs. Hale made me a big Christmas dinner.

"You've got to eat to keep your strength up," she told me.

The new year loomed on the flat horizon.

One Friday evening, I was told to report to Mr. Scase after the show.

This could only be bad news. My dumb insolence kicked in. I knew the jig was up. So what? Big deal! Nothing touched me.

After the curtain call, I went to the director's office. Scase stood up from his desk when I went in.

"Sorry, but I'm going to have to let you go," he said.

"OK," I said.

"Just OK?"

"Yes, I understand."

Scase was amused more than anything. He thought I was an oddball. "That's all you have to say—OK?"

"Yes. I don't know what else to say."

I felt listless and the old lethargy kicked in. What else could I say?

"I'm letting you go because you seem to be a bit clueless. You have a strong presence onstage, and that's good, but you have no technique. You're dangerous. You could have caused damage to poor John in that scene in *The Quare Fellow* and the wrestling match in this show. You nearly broke Rick's neck! You're a bit of a bruiser, aren't you? Bit of a troublemaker?"

"I don't want to be a troublemaker," I said.

"That's OK," said Mr. Scase. "I think the problem is a lack of experience. You need to go to one of those posh drama schools in London, RADA or LAMDA, something like that."

I nodded. "OK."

"Training and discipline. One day, we may work together again. Who knows? You've got something, I can see that, but now, you're just not ready. OK?"

"Thank you, Mr. Scase," I said. "Sorry to have caused trouble."

He nodded—a bit puzzled, or maybe amused by the young bruiser from South Wales.

"OK. Mr. Maeterlinck? Take a tip from me. Get into one of those drama colleges. You'll do OK. I think you could be a good actor. No hard feelings?"

"No."

He gave me a hug. That was weird. In those days, men rarely hugged; they shook hands. Hugs? Never.

On that same Friday night, I paid Mrs. Hale the rent, leaving the cash in an envelope along with a note thanking her for her hospitality and telling her I was leaving Manchester.

I packed my few odds and ends in the small suitcase, and on Saturday night, after the final performance of *As You Like It*, I walked out once again without my last week's pay. I didn't need their stupid money. I didn't want to be in their debt. I bade farewell to Charles the Wrestler, skipped the curtain call, spoke to no one, put on my topcoat, picked up my suitcase, snuck out the stage door, and scarpered to the station. It was raining.

What next?

I had no idea where I was going. I felt like a jailbird escaping from prison. I liked the idea of being a fugitive; it brought a great sense of freedom.

At the station, I heard a voice say over the loudspeaker, "Train for Nottingham leaving platform three in twenty minutes."

I remembered that night as a film role. *I'm a convict on the run. They'll never catch me. No, sir.* I bought a one-way ticket to Nottingham, and twenty minutes later the train, with me on board, was on its way, whistle blowing, nonstop to another city. I had a suitcase with some clothes in it and ten pounds in my pocket. Another adventure.

I didn't want them to know about it back in Wales. I was trying to make up my mind what to do. I couldn't stay at my parents' house. They'd help me out, but I didn't want their help. There would be a price: my father and mother's disappointment. The last thing I wanted was to be a bearer of letdown and disappointment.

Then I remembered a conversation I'd had a few months earlier with an old bloke named Stan, a retired corrections officer. When we were rehearsing *The Quare Fellow*, Mr. Scase had invited him to give the company a tutorial on capital punishment and its effect on others in prison. After his talk, Stan and I went out for a couple of beers at Tommy Ducks pub in Manchester. He seemed to look on me with a grandfatherly regard because I didn't know what time of day it was.

Stan told me that he had been part of the night watch at Manchester Strangeways Prison. When a man was to be hanged the next day, he and another officer would stay through the night in the man's cell. Their duty was to take him to the scaffold in the morning. In the story Stan told me, the condemned man in question was nineteen. Stan described his shock as he watched the young man drop through the trapdoor to his death. The calm efficiency of the famous English executioner Albert Pierrepoint utterly undid Stan.

"It changed my life," Stan said. "I was a young man myself at that time. I thought I knew the score. You know what I mean? But that moment, seeing that young bloke drop through the floor like that, was when I grew up."

Listening to Stan talk, I thought of a beautiful summer afternoon when Brian Moore, a fair-haired eight-year-old boy from Margam Road, told me that we would all die one day. I remember the exact spot when I heard this shocking news. We were standing at the corner of Beechwood Road and Margam Road. I could hear the sounds of Arnallt Brook burbling behind a redbrick garden wall.

One boy had recently been crushed by a boulder in Margam Wood, and another had drowned in the Betsy Pool on Margam Moors. Each time, the women in our street, my mother and the neighbors, cried as the funeral hearse carrying the small casket drove past the houses to the cemetery.

"Die? We *all* die?" I asked Brian Moore.

"Yes, we all die," he said.

Hearing that piece of news on a warm summer afternoon

changed me. I was four. That overwhelming thought, that we all vanish in the end, or at any time, really, vanish unexpectedly into the nothingness from whence we came, as if we had never been, was a hammer blow to my head, the shriek of the wailing banshee. It seemed impossible that all the splendor of life would dissolve into darkness, but there it was.

Stan told me that I should use this awareness of mortality as inspiration. "Once you leave home, you've left home," he said. "You're on your way. No turning back. You're in the big hungry world now, sink or swim. Whatever it is you want in this life, my son, you just must grab hold of that thought and give it your best shot. If it doesn't work out in the end, tough luck, so be it. One thing you can't fail at is death."

eight

JUST PASSING THROUGH

The train arrived in Nottingham about midnight. There were some large steel milk churns beneath the station clock, and I found a bench hidden just behind them. I sat there, dozing, then waking, then dozing—having odd dreams—then suddenly, it was Sunday morning, 6:15.

I looked in a phone book for a public bath- and washhouse. I remembered using one in Birmingham on the 1957 Arts Council of Wales tour.

My grandfather Yeats once told me: "When I was a youngster, before I met your gran, I was working on the railway. On Saturday nights in the bigger towns like Swindon and Reading, those baths and washhouses were the only places you could clean up in. A lump of carbolic soap for a penny, get yourself all cleaned and spruced up, wash your clothes, then afterward, a bit of a singsong with the penny-anno in the pub and a dance with your girl, and Bob's your uncle! They were the good old days."

A hot bath was five shillings. That would get me going. There was a washhouse near the station. It looked Victorian or Edwardian: White-tiled walls. Brass pipes. After soaking in a hot tub for an hour and shaving away the stubble, I felt like a new man. Yes, the pungent smell of soap stung my eyes, nose, and throat because I had used carbolic laundry soap by mistake, but the sun was shining, and there was hope.

I had a copy of the magazine *Contacts*. This was essential for actors. Repertory theaters of Britain were registered. (If you were "working in rep," that meant you had to learn a play in a week and have two or three shows at the ready at any given time. You might appear as a spear-carrier in a Shakespeare play one night and the detective in an Agatha Christie murder mystery the next. I was well suited to the work, as I was a quick study.) I earmarked a few theater addresses and noted the directors.

I found my way to Nottingham Playhouse. The theater, a triangular building, was on the corner of Goldsmith and Talbot Streets. The foyer door was open, and the place looked deserted. I heard vacuum cleaners above. There were photographs on the walls near the ticket office, portraits and names of the actors in the company.

I recognized Robert Lang's face in one of the photographs. Four years earlier, he had played Tony Lumpkin in *She Stoops to Conquer*. Oh God, that endless tour with the Arts Council! I couldn't believe that I had been involved in that nightmare.

A man came into the foyer. His face was not beaming with encouragement. "What are you doing here? Can I help you?"

"Just looking at these photographs," I replied.

"Yes, I can see that, but the ticket office is closed, so you will have to leave."

"Sorry."

I went out to the street. The man locked the doors behind me. Bells began to peal from some distant church. I was a little too warm in my military officer's topcoat, but I was proud of having found it at a Manchester secondhand shop. It had been a bargain at five pounds, even with a few cigarette burns on the right sleeve.

I felt hungry. Time for lunch. I wandered around until I came upon a small Wimpy restaurant. I went inside and ordered a hot dog. It was the first and last hot dog I ever attempted to eat. I tried gnawing through the rubber sausage while trying to plot the next move of my life, but I had no clue what to do or where to go next.

As I pondered the depths of my hopelessness, a group of theater people—three women and four men—burst upon the scene. They chose a table and gathered around it in a chatty huddle. I recognized two of the men: Robert Lang and Morgan Sheppard.

Trying not to let on that I knew who they were, I watched them and listened to their twangy actor voices. Robert Lang glanced over at me. I responded with a modified, toned-down version of the dumb-insolence look. He looked away, looked down at his coffee cup, frowned, and looked at me again.

"What are you doing here?" he asked me. He seemed to be figuring out where he'd seen me before.

A couple of his friends glanced up to see whom he was talking to. They gave me a quick once-over, then turned back to their chitchat.

Mr. Lang's face didn't register an ounce of warmth, but I was surprised that he'd remembered me at all after four years. I had been a lowly assistant stage manager. ASMs were to be seen and not heard.

I got up to leave the restaurant, and on my way out, I stopped by their table and said, "Nice to see you, Mr. Lang. We met on the Arts Council tour of 1957."

"Yes, I know that. Why are you here? Are you joining the company?"

"Yes. Well, I'm not sure. I am looking for work. But yes."

Mr. Lang looked both puzzled and amused. He noticed my suitcase.

"Sounds a bit vague. Yes and no and maybe. We are rehearsing today. Sunday, of all days."

"Thank you, Mr. Lang," I said, although I had no idea what I was thanking him for. As I was about to make my way out of the claustrophobic little bar, Mr. Lang asked me another question.

"Have you just arrived in Nottingham?"

Nonchalantly, I replied, "Just passing through, really."

"Oh, yes? Just passing through. OK."

One of the women looked me up and down and grinned. Or smirked.

"Aren't you hot in that big coat?" she asked.

I shrugged.

"And what is in that suitcase?" she asked.

"He's just passing through," quipped Mr. Lang.

"Oh, really? Just passing through. How fascinating."

I fantasized about upending their little table, but I made the sensible decision not to cause mayhem.

"See you around," I said. I smiled and left them unscathed.

Outside on the pavement, I had no idea where to go. Standing in front of that forlorn Wimpy bar on that warm Sunday afternoon in 1961, alone in a strange northern city, baking inside my cigarette-burned military topcoat and clutching my suitcase of treasures, I realized I was a lost cause.

"Where now, little man?" a woman said.

Her voice made me jump.

"Hey, you. Are you OK?" the voice asked.

I turned to see the woman with the smirking face who had asked me what was in my suitcase standing next to me on that lonely pavement.

"Yes, thank you," I replied. "I'm fine. And you?"

"Robert told me your name. Anthony? Is that your name?" she asked.

"Yes. Anthony. That's right, Anthony."

"Just Anthony?"

"Yes. Anthony. Yes. And—yes, Hopkins. Anthony Hopkins."

"And you're just passing through? Right?"

"I'm hoping to get a job. Somewhere. I was in Manchester, but then I thought I'd come here to Nottingham."

Why was she questioning me? Was I a criminal? I picked up my suitcase. "I had better go now," I said. "It was nice meeting you, very nice."

She persisted with her interrogation.

"Do you have anywhere to live?" she asked.

"No. But I'm going to start looking around. Adverts in the local papers. I'll find something. Anyway, I'd better be going now."

She gave a little tug at my coat sleeve.

"Look, it's none of my business, Anthony, but I don't think you know what you're doing. Sorry to be a busybody."

She did have a point there.

Her next question: "Are you an actor?"

"Well, sort of. I have an Equity membership card," I replied.

"Sort of? With an Equity card? OK. You're looking for a job, right?"

I was reaching inside my jacket pocket to show her the card.

"You don't have to show me your card," she said. "I believe you. But you're looking for a job. Is that right?"

"Yes, I think so," I answered. "But I don't know where to start."

"OK," she said. She wouldn't give up. "You think so, but you don't know where to start."

Was that a smirk or a smile on her face? And why did she keep repeating my answers as if I were a hopeless case, a bit touched in the head?

"No. I just thought I'd come here to Nottingham and look around."

She kept looking at me. Then she smiled at me again, but it was a kind smile.

"My name is Beth." She gave me her hand to shake. "Now, listen carefully to me, Anthony. I'm a stage manager at the Theatre Royal. I know they need an extra hand at the playhouse as an ASM. That's an assistant stage manager. You understand? Good. Go to the stage door of the playhouse and ask the doorman, Frank, for Roy Battersby. Roy is directing a production of *The Winslow Boy*. Tell Frank that Beth from the Theatre Royal sent you. Roy will be in the workshop right now. They are building sets."

I listened attentively. But Beth wanted to make sure I'd understood.

"OK, tell me what I just told you."

"Tell Frank that Beth from the Theatre Royal sent me to see Ray Battersby."

"Not Ray. Roy. Roy Battersby. *Roy.*"

She wrote her own name on a piece of paper and gave it to me.

I thanked her, picked up my suitcase, and trudged back to Nottingham Playhouse.

I met the director, Roy Battersby. He asked me a few questions, and for some reason, he gave me a job as an assistant stage manager and cast me in the role of the brother in *The Winslow Boy*.

Roy Marsden and Valerie Bland were the other ASMs. Roy had just graduated from the Royal Academy of Dramatic Art, better known as RADA. The stage director, Janet, asked me where I was staying. I told her I hadn't found anywhere. She asked Roy Marsden if there were any spare rooms at his boardinghouse. He answered that yes, there was an extra room in the same building.

And just like that, thanks to the kindness of one woman I never saw again, I had a job and a place to live.

Rehearsals for *The Winslow Boy* started a few days later. The rehearsals were followed by a bus tour of colleges and schools. We played only one week at the Nottingham Playhouse itself.

One day, out of the blue, Roy Marsden asked me if I had had any training as an actor. I didn't know what he meant. He asked me if I knew anything about RADA.

"No," I replied.

"I thought as much." He didn't hold back. He wasn't going to sugarcoat it. He told me that I was undisciplined and looked as if I had no idea what I was doing. By now, I had completely shut down. It was the feeling of absence that caused the most anxiety. I was stuck, which was the deadliest feeling.

I don't know why, but Marsden sent away for a RADA

application for me and inquired about auditions for the autumn term. He suggested I fill out the forms and prepare some auditions, and he wished me good luck.

The time at the Nottingham Playhouse came to an end. I returned to Wales. Eventually, I sent in an application to RADA. A week passed, then came a reply. I was told to bring two audition pieces—a Shakespeare piece and a modern one. In the middle of July, I took the train to London for the auditions.

I thought I'd have a go at Shakespeare's villain Iago. He was a fascinating person to analyze—a monster who was not big and scary but small and quiet. Bad guys like that—they never make eye contact with anyone, and yet they see right through you.

What was the motivation in Iago that drove him to destroy Othello? Jealousy? Envy? Envy is the most corrosive state. Not jealousy. Jealousy has an object. The cause is outside, external. But envy lives deep inside like a silent, yellow deadness. I felt, for the first time, an ability to understand a character's motivation. I believed the goal of Iago ("most honest" Iago) was to destroy everyone and everything.

> *And by how much she strives to do him good,*
> *She shall undo her credit with the Moor.*
> *So will I turn her virtue into pitch,*
> *And out of her own goodness make the net*
> *That shall enmesh them all.*

Iago is unable to explain his compulsion to destroy Othello and those around him any more than he can describe the vast desert within. In the final scene, having unleashed chaos on the world, Iago replies to Othello's question about why he did it:

WE DID OK, KID

Demand me nothing: What you know, you know.
From this time forth, I never will speak word.

I loved the way those words sounded coming out of my mouth. I said them repeatedly.

The auditions were held in mid-July—Bastille Day, which I took as a good omen—at the Vanbrugh Theatre, which was part of the academy.

I arrived in London's Paddington Station and took the Underground to Goodge Street in the bohemian district of Fitzrovia where George Bernard Shaw once lived. It was 11:45 a.m., a warm, sunny day full of the noise and smell of London. I headed for the Vanbrugh Theatre. I had it all planned. First I'd audition, and after, I'd stop by the Marlborough Arms pub for a drink.

Twenty minutes later, having identified myself to a uniformed registrar in the RADA main entrance, I was taken to the wings of the Vanbrugh.

On the stage, an overemoting actor was declaiming lines from *Henry V*. He spoke every line as if it ended in an exclamation point.

This day is called the feast of Crispian.
He that outlives this day, and comes safe home,
Will stand a tiptoe when the day is named
And rouse him at the name of Crispian.

When he came to the end of the speech, he gave a good impression of Laurence Olivier's delivery. I caught a glimpse of him as he walked off the opposite side of the stage. He looked extremely confident.

Suddenly, the hated old head chatter reappeared: *Why are you here? Are you out of your mind? Pack it in. You have no future in this business. You'll never amount to anything because you can't do anything right—*

My name was called. I glanced at the exit and thought of running away. But instead, with a sigh, I turned and walked onto the stage. The auditorium was dark except for a few lights in the center-stall seats.

A woman's rather posh voice asked me for titles of the audition pieces I'd chosen.

"*Monna Vanna*, by Maeterlinck," I whispered. "And Shakespeare's Iago."

"Sorry, I couldn't hear you. What are the pieces?"

"*Monna Vanna* by Maeterlinck!"

"Maeterlinck? OK. And the Shakespeare piece?"

"*Othello*. Iago."

She made a note. I could already tell that her hopes were not high.

"Thank you," she said. "When you are ready."

The Maeterlinck speech went well. I had memorized it so thoroughly that it was part of me.

Murmurs in the auditorium. I could make out just one word: "Interesting."

"Thank you, Mr. Hopkins."

Oh, now I'm Mr.*! That bodes rather well.*

She said, "And now which Shakespeare?"

"Iago."

She nodded.

I took a breath, relaxed, and something clicked in my head. Two parts of myself came together. The anxiety I'd felt just minutes earlier was suddenly something I knew to be universal. I was not unique. I was not alone in my self-centered obsession. Everyone experienced anxiety and emptiness. Iago felt it. That was why he acted as he did. Human behavior was beyond good and evil. Nothing was black-and-white. And so I would play one of the cruelest figures in Shakespeare with no trace of bad intent.

The speech is a soliloquy to the audience. Already, the audience knows his diabolical plan, so it is not necessary to hint anymore. Play the scene quietly, in perfect stillness. Find a member of the audience and address the opening lines to that person. Blank. Clear. *Reasonable.* On that stage, for the first time in my life, I suddenly knew how to play a diabolical villain. *This*, I thought, *is what ultimately terrifies.* Not raving but delivering a plan with straightforward logic, bringing each member of the audience, one by one, into your confidence, then sharing with them, sentence by sentence, your perfectly rational argument for terror.

And what's he then that says I play the villain,
When this advice is free I give and honest.

I gave the quietest delivery possible without being inaudible, and there was no other sound in the whole theater.

When I came to the end of the soliloquy—"And out of her own goodness make the net / that shall enmesh them all"—I looked out into the audience. No murmurings this time. No reaction. Ah, well. To hell with them! I had drinking to do. I walked offstage.

"Mr. Hopkins!" the upper-crust woman's voice rang out. "Wait."

The stage manager stopped me. "Where are you going? They want to talk to you."

I returned to the stage but hung close to the wings.

A man came out of the darkness of the auditorium to the edge of the stage light.

"What's your hurry? You've got a train to catch?" he asked.

He had a somewhat throaty voice, as if the sound had gotten stuck somewhere inside his beige suit. He seemed amused but also kind.

"No," I said. "I just thought that was it."

The man introduced himself. "I'm John Fernald, principal of the academy. We just want to make sure of your details. Address, et cetera. You're Welsh? I can hear an accent."

"Yes," I replied. "From South Wales."

"Jolly good. Well, I must say you are rather good. I've never seen Iago played like that before. Jolly good."

He was a hearty English chap, *jolly good show* and all that. The woman came out of the darkness and offered her compliments. Her name was Judith Gick. She was a teacher at the academy. She was a tall and glamorous woman, someone from the world of the West End.

"Well done," she said. "Rather frightening."

I gave the principal my details.

"You will receive the decision in the mail," he said.

All in all, it looked encouraging. Perhaps things had changed course. I hadn't been dismissed. But the mistrust was still lurking around at the back of my brain. Time for that beer at the Marlborough Arms.

The pub was packed, filled with the smoke and noise of lunchtime office people. I recognized the *Henry V* actor. He was standing at a screen that divided the pub into lounge and saloon bars. Emboldened, I complimented him on his performance. He thanked me. His name was Geoffrey Hutchings. Another young man came over and introduced himself. Alex Henry. He was from Leeds in Yorkshire. We were three hopefuls. We drank a lot.

Afterward, Alex and I, having nothing better to do, went to the Pavilion Cinema in Piccadilly to see a silly British slapstick film, *The Night We Got the Bird*. After it was over, Alex wished me luck, and we went our separate ways.

I didn't take the train back to Wales. I lay down on a park bench near the Edgware Road. Something had changed. That squeaky whisper in my brain that I was no good had gone quiet, though whether because of the drinking or the principal's *Jolly good*, I could not tell. Whatever the reason, on that hard park bench in the middle of the city, I slept soundly through the night.

nine

A DRIFTER

It was a Saturday afternoon in September at The Grand Hotel. I was having a drink with my grandfather Yeats in the saloon bar. I was twenty-three. Young and careless. Indifferent. I had some important things to get on with. I don't know what was so important, but at age twenty-three everything feels important.

I felt uneasy because I knew my grandfather Yeats was ill. I saw the haggard look upon his face. I knew he was going to die; I felt it. I told him I had to leave.

"What's your hurry?" he asked.

"I'm leaving for London tomorrow."

"Yes, I know. You're starting college. Right?"

I was irritated.

"It's not a college. It's called RADA. Royal Academy of Dramatic Art."

"Sorry. RADA. But why don't you come back to the house with me? I've got a nice piece of London haddock."

He picked up a shopping bag from a nearby barstool.

"I just bought it. It's fresh. I thought you'd like it before you leave."

Typical old man, always going on about London haddock. He was always going on with a wink and a nudge about the good times. He was like Joe Gargery in *Great Expectations*: "There'll be such larks, Pip, old chap."

I had more important things to do. I'd outgrown all that childish nonsense. I thought, *Why does he treat me like a little boy?*

"No, I've got to go."

"Your Gran wanted to give you something."

"I can't. I've got to go. I keep telling you."

That hurt him.

"OK. If you must go, you must go."

We walked out of the bar. On the pavement leading to Oakwood Lane, he asked me once more: "You *sure* you don't want to come to the house? Your Gran wants to give you something."

No. I had to get away from him. He looked at me and then smiled and shrugged.

"OK. If you must go, then you must go. So long. Don't forget to write to us."

He offered his hand. It was bony and frail. I felt him place or press something in my hand. It was a ten-shilling note.

"Thank you," I said, thinking only, *Please, God, don't let him mention haddock again.*

"Well, you'd better be off, and good luck in college. Have a drink on me."

"Thanks," I said. "Thanks for the money."

I walked away toward the Plaza cinema. It was a relief. I turned and saw him, my frail old grandfather, standing there on that pavement. He was holding his shopping bag with the stupid fresh haddock. He waved. I waved back. I had important things ahead of me.

WE DID OK, KID

That was the last time I saw him. He died a few weeks later. Cancer of the lungs.

When I heard the news from my father on the phone, I could hardly breathe. I had to shut the feelings down. No tears. No grief. Nothing. Too much agony. When you're twenty-three, there's no time for all that.

My mother believed that I had become a replacement for his younger daughter Jenny.

When I was young, I'd told him I wanted to be a drifter. He'd laughed and said, "A drifter? Well, why not? All you need is a knife and a piece of string. The open road. Keep on smiling."

In the film *Tender Mercies*, a drifter wanders through the vast, lonely flatlands of Texas. He's a drunk, washed-up. He spends two nights in a roadside motel gas station and gets into a fight with another man. Next morning, he asks the owner, a young widow, if he could do some odd jobs around her property for a few bucks. He promises her not to drink. The widow takes him on and he begins to settle in. She has a young boy, Sonny. Her husband had been killed in Vietnam. The drifter does his work, stays off the drink, and after a while he and the widow get married. All seems well until a tragedy strikes. His young daughter is killed in an automobile crash in northern Louisiana.

There is a scene toward the end of the film. He's raking a patch of ground. The woman, his new wife, asks him if he's OK. He wonders why he, a useless drifter, a drunk and nothing but trouble, why would he be treated with kindness, be taken in and given shelter, when his innocent daughter was killed in an automobile smash? Why? Why? There is no answer. The great actor Robert Duvall delivers a heartbreaking simplicity to the scene: "See, I don't trust happiness. I never did, and I never will."

I often wonder why I walked away that Saturday afternoon, knowing that my grandfather, who had been the kindest man I had ever known, was going to die. But I did. I couldn't tolerate the grief. I locked that away. Why should we get attached? It all ends in tears.

That same month, September 1961, I started as a student at the Royal Academy of Dramatic Art. My first days were confusing. I had to take classes like the psychology of movement and voice and speech. I learned sword fencing, dance, diction. I carried *My Life in Art* by Stanislavski around London like it was the Bible.

Stanislavski's system, which he developed in the early 1900s, had the actor reaching for inner motives in the pursuit of a certain task. His method required us as actors to explore our own memories and ask ourselves seven questions about each character we played: *Who am I? Where am I? When is it? What do I want? Why do I want it? How will I get it? What do I need to overcome?*

By one interpretation, the system—Method Acting—involved four processes: relaxation, concentration of attention, imagination, and emotion memory. I never fully embraced the Method in the sense of staying in character for days on end, but this version drew me in. I wound up throwing away so much of what I learned over the years and developed my own methods, but that education gave me a discipline that I'd been lacking as well as a blueprint for how to approach a text in great seriousness.

Uta Hagen always said that when you're crossing the stage, make sure you have a physical objective. Always cross the room for a reason, perhaps to pick up a drink or put on a coat. No movement should be gratuitous. Stanislavski talked about the objective and the super-objective and the resistance. Hamlet's super-objective is to avenge his father. His resistance is that he's riddled with doubt. All these ways of thinking about scripts can be useful for an actor preparing a role, but in the end you need to find your own way into a text.

I gradually created my own method for learning lines. What's key is that I reread the material again and again, hundreds of times, marking the pages up as I committed them to memory. Once I know the page cold, it gets a star. I'm sure to others, the writing looks like the ravings of a madman, but I assure you it's a very precise system, and it works for me.

At RADA I was cobbling together an approach and finding my way. Each morning, I took the train from the apartment where I was staying, the basement of a tall Edwardian house on Westbourne Grove. The owners of the house were Marjory and Frank Williams. An old Cockney bloke, Marjory's father ("the old geezer," as Frank called his father-in-law), would come over from Whitechapel to have a bite of Sunday lunch, which was usually a roast with vegetables.

One Sunday, Marjory invited me to join them. Why? I think she felt sorry for me because I didn't eat much. She told me I didn't look well. I told her I was fine. I lied—I was hungry. Not starving, just *hungry*. I spent most of my money in pubs. I thought often of breaking into grocery stores to steal food. Anyway, on this gloomy Sunday, I was invited to lunch with the old geezer, Albert. He had recently been widowed. He wore his cloth cap indoors, sitting rigidly upright in his chair at the table. He looked unwashed. I offered to shake hands with him, but he just stared at me stonily with his pale blue eyes. He asked me what I was doing in London.

I didn't have the courage to tell him I was hoping to be an actor. I mumbled something about being a student. I don't think he heard.

"You old enough to remember the last shindig, son?" he asked me.

His daughter said: "Oh, Dad, don't bring up the war again."

"Why not? You youngsters have had it pretty cushy. All of you!"

He was a belligerent old bastard. Marjory went into the kitchen to get lunch ready. Frank joined her—to help or just to get away. And that was the old man's cue to start regaling me with his story:

"I was in the Battle of the Marne, the slaughterhouse of craters and mud and decaying corpses."

Ah, this will be cheerful, I thought.

He told me about the machine-gun fire, the horror of death.

"I was a nipper," he said. "A young kid, and I was bleeding terrified. Shells and machine guns. You got paralyzed with terror. But this one night was the worst. Flares lighting up the sky like it was daytime. Suddenly I picked up my rifle and ran. You could be shot for running. Anyway, up I got and off I went like a rabbit. Didn't get far. Fell into a crater full of mud. We used to drown in that stuff. Lots of my mates went that way. Anyways, there I was, just a kid.

"Suddenly, I noticed another chap in there with me. Flares would light up and then blackness. I noticed the chap, bit older than me, was a Jerry—German soldier. He had his rifle and I had mine. We were both terrified. I didn't know what to do. Then the young Jerry put his hand into his greatcoat pocket, pulled something out, and offered it to me. I took it, and then he vanished. He'd given me a photo. Later, when the daylight came up, I looked at the photo, and it was the poor bugger's wife and little girl.

"I kept that photo for years after that bloody shindig was over. God knows who he was, or who his wife and little girl were. He was just like me. I was angry for years. All that waste. For what? When I got back, I spent time in hospital. A bunch of us, fifty or sixty of us, were invited to Buckingham Palace. Not for a medal, but to meet the king and old Queen Mary. We were all there on the grounds. Most of us had been shot up. I just had shell splinters in my legs. We waited, but no one showed up. No king or anything like that. Too busy, we were told by this uniformed equerry, the king's personal assistant. He handed us each a parchment or something. His Majesty had told the equerry to give us all his heartiest congratulations. I threw mine from the Waterloo Bridge into the Thames. Yeah, so much for the glory of war. But I'll never forget that fella, old Jerry."

Men like that stuck with me. I wonder now if listening to them as closely as I did, memorizing without effort their words and cadences, was part of how I was able to play so many different characters over the years. As you repeat the words again and again, they sink down into you and become part of your subconscious. Learning lines involves work but magic too.

* * *

I attended RADA for two years, from 1961 to 1963. There were some notable students there when I started: John Hurt, Ian McShane, David Warner, Simon Ward. But it was the old story: I couldn't fit in. I tried, but my distance kept me in a bubble. I stayed quiet and shut down. I had my own secret plan. I knew that once you revealed your secret visions, they fell apart. *Keep your mouth shut.* That was the tip my grandfather Fred Yeats had given me. And one thing that made it easier to keep to myself was drinking. Liquor was beginning to take over my life and that suited me fine. It helped me commit to the loner role I was playing.

As a result of my social withdrawal, I missed the joyful frenzy of 1960s London almost entirely. The rip-roaring decade of the swinging sixties, the birth of the Beatles and the Rolling Stones, Carnaby Street, and the Dolly Birds—it's all foggy to me. This was a time of free love, miniskirts, and political marches, and the United Kingdom rapidly became, against all odds, the hippest place on earth. Fun, fun, and more fun. And I experienced no trace of it. Even though it was just down the road, it might as well have been taking place on the moon.

I liked wandering around. The Edgware Road. Marble Arch. Hyde Park. There was a park bench opposite the Dorchester hotel in Mayfair where Burton and Taylor used to stay. I would sit and see myself going in through the revolving doors.

Key, please, I imagined myself saying. *One of these days*, I thought. *One of these days.*

I didn't have time for the free-love scene. I preferred the people who ran shops. There was Georgie Dennis, a full-blown Cockney, meaning he was born in range of the clanging of the Bow Bells, the church bells of St. Mary-le-Bow in London's

Cheapside. George had his own flower shop on Waterloo Road, across from the Old Vic. I would call in and he would make me cups of tea.

One day, George told me a story about Richard Burton when he was playing Hamlet.

"Oh, yes, I used to feel sorry for him," George said. "Make him a nice cup of tea, I would, and a nice big cheese sandwich. I asked if he was doing all right financially. I was willing to let him have a couple of quid. One day Richard says to me, he says, ''Ere, Georgie, let me show you something.' He took me outside the front door, and he pointed across at the Old Vic. 'See that gray Jag, Georgie? Over there? That's mine. I spent five thousand on that. I'll take ya for a spin in her one day.' He was ever such a nice man. Now he's with what's 'er name. What is it?"

"Elizabeth Taylor."

"That's it. Mind you, I liked Sybil, his first wife. Ever so nice, she was. Ever so nice. But today, it's all bang-wallop-and-see-you-sometime. It's Hollywood did that to him. That's the way it is now. These new blokes. The Beatles. All the girls screaming. My old mum, she would turn in her grave."

I had a flat in Randolph Terrace. Thirty shillings a week. Top floor. The bare spartan minimum. I liked it. It had a gas fire and a small kitchen alcove. But I never cooked. I'd get breakfast near the Old Vic. While around me, the Mods were tooling about on their Vespas, the men in tailored suits, the girls in miniskirts and boots, I reported to the theater in damp shoes and damp clothes. Cheap jacket, corduroy trousers, Marks & Spencer tie, a white nylon shirt. I was not a single cat's whisker.

I had a few girlfriends here and there. No attachments—just hello and goodbye. Can't even remember their names. My first real love was a RADA classmate from Spokane, Washington. The sound of that city's name at the time was as exotic to me as any tropical destination: *Spo-kane, Washington*. It might as well have been El Dorado. Then, six months into our relationship, she went home for the 1962 Christmas holidays, and when she came back, she dumped me. I was twenty-five and I thought, *I will never love anyone again. It's too painful.*

I imagined myself as Alan Ladd in *Shane*, a Western from a few years earlier. He rides off into the Wyoming desert as a little boy yells, "Come back, Shane!" I would not come back. I vowed to be on my own in the vast, lonely West from there on out.

I threw myself into my lessons. I learned how to play the opposite of what was on the page—to do a sad monologue in an upbeat way, give light lines weight—because you can always dial it back, but it's good to feel the range. And I came to believe that everything had to be full-bodied and strong. No mumbling. Just go for it. Again, you can always cut it back. Acting is a process of eliminating, uncovering, discovering, and discarding. Start at the peak and gradually peel away the leaves and the weeds until you get to a naked place that feels right.

Two great teachers—the Swedish dancer Yat Malmgren and Christopher Fettes, who was born in Edinburgh Castle—taught briefly at RADA. They eventually founded the Drama Centre London. From them I learned a theory of movement that Michael Chekhov called the psychological gesture; it was based on the theories of Rudolf Laban and Stanislavski. The idea was to find a movement that let you embody the character, perhaps hunching your shoulders to suggest defensiveness or throwing out your chest to display confidence.

Malmgren and Fettes were not the happiest teachers there. They were taskmasters, hypercritical. They could easily tear you to pieces. But I was drawn to them. I absorbed their techniques very quickly. I seemed to be, at the time, the only student willing to absorb them. RADA was a true academy, focused on technical excellence, so a lot of the students thought anything having to do with psychology was a lot of rubbish. And yet I began to pay more attention to my own perceptions, past and present, and to the way my body moved.

When I'd arrived at RADA, I was "weight-stressed," as they called it. I moved rather like a Welsh rugby player. Yat said—in a strong Swedish accent that made his advice resemble a medical prognosis—"You must develop the more *introverted* system, the nervous system. Otherwise you will become *extroverted*, and that is so boring."

I thought, *What the hell is he talking about?* But gradually, I started developing the stillness and self-awareness he encouraged us to bring to the stage.

Becoming familiar with a script was like picking up stones from a cobblestone street one at a time, studying them, then replacing each in its proper spot. Only then could I look out over the road and know every inch of it spread out before me. Only then could I navigate that route in any weather, even with my eyes closed.

The rooming-house geezer's World War II stories got me thinking back on my childhood experience of that "shindig," as he called it.

In June 1944, an idyllic summer filled with sound and heat,

American officers were billeted near us at Margam Castle, in preparation for the invasion of Europe: D-Day. They often roared past our schoolyard in their green-camouflage vehicles. One morning we kids were playing outside our school when a soldier shouted at us from the truck. He tossed a paper package into the yard, but Miss Humphries, a teacher from class four, happened to be on playground duty, and she managed to grab it quickly. We kids never knew what was in the package—probably chewing gum and candy.

One warm Sunday evening in the summer of 1944 I went out for a stroll near the castle with my parents. They were walking, peering into the woods, looking for the nightingale we could hear singing nearby. I was pedaling my little three-wheeler bike up and down the narrow path. It was one of those kiddie bikes with the pedals fixed on the front wheel. My grandfather had built it for me from pieces of wood and scrap metal. He used long strips of rubber for the wheel tires and painted the bike bright red.

Two soldiers were strolling toward us. As they drew close, one of them, a tall, burly man, asked my father if he could help with directions. They wanted to get to Swansea, they said, and was it too late to get a bus? And if it was too late to get a bus, was there anyplace they could rent some horses?

We learned their names were Lieutenant Cooney and Captain Durr, and after advising them on their options, my parents invited them over for Sunday dinner the following week. During those tough days, families were encouraged to welcome American soldiers into their homes in the spirit of hospitality, cooperation, and friendship. When those fortunate ones managed to return to their families in America, many sent food parcels back to British families.

WE DID OK, KID

Lieutenant Cooney turned to the soldier leaning on guard in his sentry post and said, "Hey, soldier, you got a pencil?"

The soldier fumbled in his jacket. "Sure, I got a pencil," he said, and he chucked it over to Cooney.

The British joked about the indolence of the American GIs, whom they described as "overpaid, oversexed, and over here." The Americans seemed to have no formality about them, which made a stark contrast with the stifling correctness of the British Army. Cooney placed his foot on the front wheel of my bike so he could write our address in the stubby little notepad he rested on his knee.

He glanced at me and winked. "That's one heck of a machine you've got there, young fella."

The following Sunday, I heard the Jeep pull up and hoped all the other kids on the street were watching, especially Peter Jones next door and Peter Murray from the house opposite. I was lying on the floor of the front room drawing, in black and red pencil, pictures of British and American planes bombing Germany, and German planes falling out of the sky trailing red-pencil flames.

I heard the clink of the front gate and then a knock on the front door. My father let them in, and someone called from the passageway: "Hello there!"

That was Captain Durr's greeting every time he came to visit in the following weeks.

Then I heard: "Where's the boy?"

The front room door opened, and in they both came.

"Well, get up and say hello!" my mother told me. "Don't be rude."

Cooney, from Texas, said, "No, he's OK. Let him be."

Durr, from Oregon, leaned down in front of me and set down a bright red-and-white-spotted handkerchief. He untied it, and out spilled a dozen glass marbles. They were the most gorgeous marbles I'd ever seen—swirls of bright yellows and greens, deep blues and reds, oranges, purples, and violets.

"Well, say thank you," my mother said. "Isn't that wonderful? Say thank you nicely."

They came to the house several times, sometimes together, sometimes alone. Durr showed me how to shoot the marbles and how to put a spin on an alley shot, what he called a *twister*.

One night, Durr came over, and I was allowed to stay up past my bedtime. He was sitting in the armchair having a cup of tea, and I was lying on the sofa between my mother and father. I was beginning to fall asleep, and from a great distance I could hear them talking, their voices drifting in and out of my consciousness.

I heard my father make a comment about Cooney: "He's a moody sort of man, isn't he? Very quiet sometimes; he hardly says a word. We don't know what to make of him."

Durr said, "He has a dread of never seeing his wife or his little boy again. He feels he won't make it home."

My father asked Durr if he felt the same way.

"Oh, sure, I get scared too. I get scared that I'll never see my wife or my two little kids again. One of them is five and the other three. We know something big is coming up, soon, I guess—it's . . . I don't know, I can't say. It's going to be a big shoot-out, I guess. Somewhere. I try to stay cheerful and put on a happy face. You have to, or you'll go nuts. Everyone is scared."

Half asleep, I saw in my mind's eye the washing lines in the back gardens of Wern Road, and I imagined Durr saying this

WE DID OK, KID

while lying there under the billowing white sheets staring up at the bright blue sky.

For days afterward I'd wonder what "something big" was coming. I'd seen James Cagney and Humphrey Bogart in a big shoot-out at the end of *The Oklahoma Kid*, and this too got mixed up and drifted in and out of the twilight time of sleep.

Not too many days later, Cooney, Durr, and another young soldier opened the gate of our house. They saw me on my bike near the front window. Durr's "Hello there!" boomed out. They went in, and after about ten minutes, the soldiers came out of the house followed by my mother and father. They all shook hands, and the soldiers started to leave. Then Cooney turned to me and said, "You watch out on that machine, young man, and take care. We're going away soon and just came to say goodbye and thanks."

They got into the Jeep, waved, and took off. My parents and I stood at the gate watching them as they disappeared around the corner onto Stallcourt Road, at the top end of our street.

In the lovely little holiday resort town of Porthcawl not long after, we came across American soldiers clearing mines. They'd say, "OK, step back!" Then: *Boom!* Then: "OK, carry on." I couldn't get enough of those soldiers. I could have watched them all day.

Our neighbor Bert and my father knocked down a section of the garden wall so that, if they needed to, Bert and his wife, Claire, could more easily make it to our little air-raid shelter. Bert and my father worked for a week, digging a deep hole at the bottom end of the garden, which butted up against the wall of the schoolteacher Mr. Thomas's garden. Mr. Thomas complained, and my father told him to bugger off and mind his own bloody business. Over the deep hole, Bert and my father placed three sheets of U-shaped corrugated steel per a War Office handbook of instructions: *Build Your Own Shelter*. These were called Anderson shelters. Simple to build, but likely not much use in a direct hit by a German bomb.

When this part was completed and secured, Bert and my father covered the corrugated roof with patches of turf and some flowerpots. On some nights, my parents took me to their bedroom to sleep between them. Then when the air-raid sirens started up, my father would pick me up and take me down the garden path to the Anderson contraption. Mr. and Mrs. John would join us with their daughter, Mary, and their dog, Spot. Once we were inside, Bert would light a paraffin lamp, and there we would sit, squashed together in that damp little hideaway, and wait for the sound of the all-clear siren.

Sometimes we would hear the thumps of antiaircraft shell splinters or shrapnel falling on the roof of turf. The sirens sounded in these areas when the Luftwaffe was out on a bombing raid. Port Talbot had a steelworks and harbor dock that might have interested the German high command, but we were never bombed. Still, my mother's cousin Bert Williams died flying for the Royal Navy's Fleet Air Arm. And we often heard the *hum-hum* of the German Luftwaffe flying over.

The German Luftwaffe bombed Swansea, home of the poet Dylan Thomas, in 1941, killing 250 people. On the following Sunday, my father drove us to Swansea to see the damage. We saw fire hoses in the streets, buildings torn up, people's furniture littering the pavement.

I was too young to take in the details of the war, but I was woken up by air-raid sirens, and I saw Hitler in cinema newsreels and heard him once on a crackly wireless broadcast from Berlin.

A friend of my father's, Mr. Ridgewell from Neath, a few miles from Port Talbot, was a representative of United Yeast Company, and he took a liking to me. As a joke, he asked me what I would do to Hitler if I met him. Sitting on the dough table in the bakery, I said, "I would wring his neck!" and mimed strangulating him with my hands.

Cheers and applause from Mr. Ridgewell, who rewarded me with a throat lozenge.

Around this time my father was delivering bread to an Italian shop in Margam, the Conti Tea Shop. Mr. and Mrs. Conti had been in Wales since the thirties and had established a small business for tea and Italian pastries. This day, some fatheaded neighbors decided that Mr. and Mrs. Conti were the enemy and took it upon themselves to make life hell for them. These knuckleheaded ignoramuses painted *Go back to Italy. Get out* on the shop's windows.

While on his rounds, my father recognized the vandals as they were attacking the shop. He got out of his van and laid into them: "I've got your names—all of you! You bloody hypocrites! These people have done nothing wrong!"

It was mandatory that my father continue to deliver bread rations to those families, but he did so under protest and never spoke to any of them again.

My aunt Lorna's husband, Uncle Billy, and my father were conscripted into the Royal Observer Corps. Their contribution to the war effort was spotting and plotting aircraft—British or German flight movements—and reporting what they saw to the headquarters in Cardiff. I learned how to spot a Junkers

88 bomber, the British Lancaster bomber, the Mosquito light bomber, and the gigantic American Flying Fortress bomber. Sometimes I was taken to the post office on Sunday afternoons.

"Tonight, Liverpool will be smashed," my father said one day. He bought me binoculars. When there were no planes, I used my binoculars to look at the moon.

Even as a little boy, I knew that those wartime voices were getting inside me, transforming me. I would plant myself in front of the wireless. We cherished the BBC Radio satire *It's That Man Again* (usually shortened to *ITMA*) with Tommy Handley, which mocked wartime hardships and bureaucracy. "Tommy kept us going," people would say. My father was always twiddling with the wireless knob, impatient with the spaces between programs.

I listened to the Nuremberg Trials. The defendants were from Hitler's closest circle: Hermann Göring, Rudolf Hess, Joachim von Ribbentrop, and others. I listened to reports of the capture and arrest of William Joyce, the American-born traitor known as Lord Haw-Haw who began all his broadcasts with "This is Germany calling. Germany calling." He was tried and later executed.

One day when my mother came home, I greeted her with "Göring committed suicide in prison. He took cyanide so he wouldn't be hanged."

"Good God, how do you know that?" she said. "How morbid! You're nine. You shouldn't be listening to the news."

All of it captivated me, and so did the voices that brought me the news. I took in Jean Metcalfe's Sunday-afternoon show: "Good afternoon, listeners. This is Jean Metcalfe introducing another round of family favorites from British Forces radio network. 'With a Song in My Heart,' Rodgers and Hart."

In the cinemas, British Movietone News gave everyone the feeling that they were up to date: Trumpet fanfare. Commentators Leslie Mitchell, Geoffrey Sumner, Donald Gray, and Huw Thomas dished out the latest. Their ever-so-British voices stayed with me.

As did the sense of peril. Millions of people were annihilated. Russia alone lost twenty-four million. The whole of Europe was devastated. And then, in May 1945, it was over. On the night of VE Day, my father and Uncle Billy set off fireworks and rockets and flare canisters, filling the air with the smell of cordite. There were street parties with bonfires and trestle tables with lemonade and blancmange pudding for the kids. My father took me along on a trip to London. We stayed at the Regent Palace Hotel and found it filled with noisy American soldiers waiting to return home or dreading a trip to the Pacific to fight the war with Japan.

(Not long after VE Day, outside a pub in Newnham, Gloucestershire, on a warm Sunday afternoon, my mother, father, my mother's parents, and I were having a little picnic of soggy watercress sandwiches and a thermos of warm, milky tea. My father and grandfather were leaning against the car, their glasses of pub beer on the car roof. I heard my grandfather read out a *Daily Express* headline about the atom bombs falling on Japan.)

Then one day in June 1945, my mother and I were sitting in a double-decker bus going back to Margam. It was raining, bucketing down, and the bus stopped at the Plaza to take on a passenger, an American soldier. He was wearing a waterproof cape over his uniform, and he hoisted a bulky kit onto a side seat and sat opposite us. The conductor, Marion, well known to us schoolkids, came to collect his bus fare, sixpence. The soldier couldn't figure out the money. He held out some change in the palm of his hand.

"Margam Post Office, please. Is that the stop for the castle?"

"Sorry, we don't go that far," said Marion. "You don't have to pay."

"Would you like to come home with me to the house?" my mother said. "My husband will be home at five. He can give you a lift to the Castle Drive."

The soldier came back with us. He hung his cape on the hall stand. My mother made him some tea and invited him to sit down in my father's leather chair. When my father came home, the GI said, "Hi, my name is Sam Arrut. Your wife invited me to a cup of tea. I'm due to report to Margam Castle."

We learned that Sam's mission was to gather as many ID tags from soldiers as possible in order to maintain correct war records. He kept track of who had been killed and wounded. My father asked about the tank brigade that Cooney and Durr had been attached to for the Battle of the Ardennes.

Sam broke the news to us as gently as he could. "It was a wipeout. They probably never made it home."

They never made it home.

What tragedy. What waste. We got a letter from Mrs. Cooney that said, "Thank you for your hospitality."

Those days were full of loss and the sound of Vera Lynn singing "We'll Meet Again" and "When the Lights Go On Again."

Gradually, everything settled back into the usual routine, the drab gray years of the postwar world. In 1946, my father took over the bakery business from his father, and they did a swap. Grandpa Hopkins and my grandmother, Nanny, moved into our

Margam house, and we moved into their house in the center of Port Talbot. The bakehouse was in the backyard, a large block of gray stone and red brick. The skies were always gray.

I missed the suburb of Margam, where I'd lived since I was born, New Year's Eve 1937. Margam had been farmland and moors for centuries. There was a Cistercian monastery, Margam Abbey, founded in 1147. Each house had a small front garden of wall and railings or privet hedges. My parents bought our house, on Wern Road, for 250 pounds. We lived at one end, in number 77, and my father's sister Miriam and my uncle Jack lived at the top end, in number 39. The next street was Bracken Road, where, at number 12, Auntie Lorna and Uncle Billy lived.

On Sundays my mother and father used to take me to the surrounding parks and fields and woods and to Castle Drive. I picked blackberries in Star Lane with my father as we wandered up into the Brombil Valley. Once we moved into town, to Port Talbot, I felt cut off from everything I'd known, even though it wasn't so far away. I longed to be back in Margam or, failing that, to go anywhere else.

On holiday in 1947, we discovered a village called Willersey, in the county of Gloucestershire. It was idyllic, like a John Betjeman poem. My father had driven us—my mother, her father and mother, and myself (I was squashed in the back seat between Granny and my mother). It was an early Sunday afternoon on a summer bank holiday. We pulled into the car park of the Lygon Arms hotel in Broadway Village. My mother had made cucumber sandwiches, which I hated. They made me retch. The early afternoon was like an Arcadian dream: strange silences and the distant hum of voices. Timeless. My father and grandfather went into a bar to buy some beers and brought them back to the car. My grandfather always let me have a sip of his beer.

Granny said he shouldn't encourage me: "He'll end up like your brother, Jim. A drunk."

I heard a church clock strike one. We sat in the car for an hour. Then my father said: "Time to turn back."

Silence.

My grandfather suggested we take a look at the area. "Why do we have to rush back?"

We drove out of Broadway and headed past fields and meadows until we came to the Cotswold village of Willersey. I felt as if I had been there before. I knew it somehow. Just one of those feelings. My father parked the car near the village pond. There was a house at the end of the road. The New Inn was opposite. It looked familiar to me. There was a bed-and-breakfast sign in the garden.

Suddenly I asked if we could stay there for one night. My father was puzzled. "You want to stay *here*?" Yes. My grandfather said, "Why not? Well, let's see if they have a vacancy."

They had two bedrooms vacant. We stayed the night. My biggest excitement was when my father said to my grandparents: "Why don't you stay here a week? We'll go back to Wales and come back next Sunday." That was the first holiday there in that farmhouse. Mr. and Mrs. Ingalls owned the house. They were both quiet people. Mrs. Ingalls washed clothes in a big copper tub.

Three Germans who'd been prisoners of war worked there, cleaning the main yard and feeding the two pigs in the wooden scratch area. One was a red-haired man in his twenties who came from Düsseldorf. He taught me weight lifting using pieces of metal he had strapped together. "You grow strong now, *ja?*"

I spent two holidays in that farmhouse with my grandparents; the wartime songs of Vera Lynn still echo in my ears.

. . . I know we'll meet again some sunny day.

ten

CUNNING WELSH FOX

As I was preparing to leave RADA, I asked my teacher Christopher Fettes, "What do I do after this?"

"Well, you learn through experience," he said. "Just keep learning, just keep going on with it. Don't worry about it—just do it. Know that you can never be perfect. Just do the best you can." I took his words to heart, both personally and in my acting. To this day, I believe in forward movement. *Let's just get on with it* is my answer to many problems, and it often works out for the best.

In 1963, the last week before the end of the school term, I applied for an audition to the Leicester theater. A letter came back: "Auditions at St. Giles Square." There I met the director, and he hired me on the spot. And so I started my first real professional acting job, no ASM duty required, at the Phoenix Theatre in Leicester.

I'd been recommended a bedsit about two miles away from the center of Leicester, and it wasn't half bad for the low rent. That's what they were called back then, bedsits: a room with a bed, an armchair, a space behind a curtain to hang clothes. Also, a gas fireplace. That was a useful contraption to warm up a room or help end it all in a moment of depression.

The Phoenix was a newly constructed establishment, a member of the Midland Group, a fortnightly repertory company. Not half bad for a twenty-five-year-old Welsh boy from Port Talbot. Our theater was a new civic building, a modern avant-garde affair, a 250-seater space with a thrust stage, intimate enough for Harold Pinter and Arnold Wesker plays.

The production for the grand inaugural opening of the Phoenix was Thornton Wilder's *The Matchmaker*, a farce about a busybody named Dolly Gallagher Levi. (The show was later transformed into a better-known musical, *Hello, Dolly!*) I was given the role of one of the waiters at the Harmonia Gardens restaurant, a part that involved a lot of slapstick.

During rehearsal, the director, Clive Perry, became suddenly hostile and dismissive of me. If I said good morning or offered any simple social greeting, I would get no response. One Wednesday morning, he pounced on me like a cat on a mouse: "What's wrong with you? For God's sake, be funny. This is supposed to be a comedy. You're nothing but a clodhopper." I plotted his demise.

During a coffee break, as I sat at a table in the theater foyer, some bloke, one of the actors, approached me. I assumed he was probably another not to be trusted.

He placed his tray on the table. "May I?" he asked.

I gave a shrug. "Suit yourself."

After a few minutes, he introduced himself: "David. David Swift. It's Tony, isn't it?"

"Anthony Hopkins."

He asked me about myself. Where was I from originally?

WE DID OK, KID

I cheered up and we had a chat. Then, from out of left field, David advised me not to be bothered by the director.

"That's his way. Directors like to choose whipping boys. It makes them feel important. But *I* think you are funny in that scene. Don't let it bother you."

After the break, we went back to the stage.

As we were going through the same scene again, the director stood up from his seat in the auditorium and started to screech at me: "How many times do I—?"

I went to the edge of the stage and gave him my dumb, insolent stare: *What?*

"Can't you get it right? What's the matter with you?" he shouted.

The quiet voice I had used to stop my father in his tracks on that evening eight years before came out, slow and measured: "Shut your nasty little moley mouth."

A nervous laugh from someone. I stepped off the stage and left the theater.

Here I go again, off to the races. I wonder where next?

The director followed me into the lobby coffee shop. There were some afternoon visitors drinking foamy cappuccinos.

"Where do you think you're going?" he demanded.

"Where am I going? I'm leaving." I started to walk away. "Get some other idiot to put up with your crap!"

"How dare you—?"

I stopped and turned. "What did you say?"

The front-of-house manager, Leslie Twelvetrees, came from his office and wanted to know what was going on. He looked like his name—a confused and gangly gentleman waving his arms about in helpless outraged shock and embarrassment at us arguing in front of the coffee-shop customers.

"How dare you speak to me that way!" The director's face had turned beet red.

I hope he keels over dead, I thought.

"Shove your little play and your precious little tin-pot theater right up your stupid squeaky little crack."

Mr. Twelvetrees jumped and danced around a bit, trying to prevent a small public-relations upset: "Please, Tony, please be reasonable."

David Swift came from the auditorium and into the lobby. He took my arm.

"Come on, Tony, it's not worth it. Leave it."

The director looked scared. Good. I knew he wouldn't mess with me again. I enjoyed causing trouble.

Time for lunch. Back at two.

The Bowling Green pub down the road was my lunch place. It was one of those half-timbered buildings, brass horseshoes on the walls. The jolly landlord and landlady were fixtures behind the bar. Each day, I'd have two pints of Newcastle Brown and a cheese sandwich.

After lunch that day, I went back to the theater. I didn't know if I had been fired. I didn't care. There were some bits and pieces of mine in the dressing room, a book and a scarf. I wasn't going to leave them there.

David Swift and Anthony Morton were still in the coffee area. Anthony Morton put on a scared and cowered look: "Here's Taffy the Welsh terrier! Don't hit me, please!"

They both laughed because, in the end, it was funny, my anger and fighting Taffy spirit.

It looked like I wasn't going to be given the sack after all.

As we walked back to the auditorium, Morton touched my

elbow. "Good for you, boy. Don't ever put up with that. Remember: *Illegitimi non carborundum*."

"Nil what?" I asked him.

"*Non. Non carborundum*. It's fake Latin for 'Don't let the bastards grind you down.' You'll do OK. Give me a hug."

He gave me a quick hug.

This was still new to me, the familiarity, the camaraderie, the hugging and kissy-smoochy-darling stuff.

I thought my old man, Dickie Boy Hopkins, wouldn't approve.

When I got back in the auditorium and on the stage, the atmosphere had changed. Dead quiet. Rehearsals proceeded. No more screeches.

I've thought of that faux-Latin phrase often over the years, and I've seen it pop up in songs and in the mouths of politicians. Literally it means, "One must not be ground down by the illegitimates." It's bad Latin but good advice. While my sudden splurges of defensive anger have gotten me into trouble at times, they've also kept me from being taken advantage of.

The mayor of Leicester at the time, Harold Heard, arrived for the opening show draped in his chain of office. The mayor-elect, Constance Elizabeth Jackson, was there as well. It was all very high-and-mighty. After the final curtain, speeches were made by local city councilors. There were canapés in the theater bar afterward. Champagne for all. Ooh la la. Everyone was there, preening and aglow with glittering self-approbation. I skipped all that and went to the Bowling Green pub.

I got well and truly drunk that night, almost legless. I don't remember how I got back to the digs. The following morning, despite a severe hangover, I arrived at the theater. There was a scheduled company meeting. It was probably a notes session regarding the previous night's performance.

I went to the dressing-room corridor. I saw a green paper tacked on the theater notice board. Was I getting fired? But no. It was the cast list for *Major Barbara*.

Hilary Hardiman—Barbara Undershaft
Mary Griffith—Lady Britomart Undershaft
David Swift—Adolphus Cusins
Anthony Hopkins—Andrew Undershaft

This was a huge role, a major promotion. I visited Foyles bookstore in Tottenham Court Road and bought a copy of the play.

When I read it, I was certain that the director had made a mistake. Andrew Undershaft? He was a man in his sixties. How could I possibly play him? I was twenty-five! *But what the hell*, I thought. *Have a go!* Wilfred Pickles, the BBC Radio personality, hosted a show called *Have a Go*. It became my private mantra.

I went back to see my parents in Wales. While visiting them, I started reading the play in earnest, and I saw something of myself in the role of Andrew Undershaft. He was a version of my father and his father—a tough, hard realist, a fanatic, uncompromising. It was a great part.

By that point I had developed my technique for learning scripts: repetition, repetition, repetition. I read the play so many times that I knew all my lines and everyone else's too. Night after night, I read and reread the script until I knew every syllable. Once you've got it down, there's no stopping you. The words are the gas you put into the tank, whether it's Shakespeare, Seán O'Casey, or Tennessee Williams. You put that into your engine and you can go anywhere. That's the power of the word. And that's when you can have some fun. That method of preparation has stayed with me throughout my life as an actor. You become a great boxer only by doing endless footwork. I go through the script a thousand times until I get to the point where I know it as well as I know my own name.

On November 1, a Monday, we started rehearsals at the YMCA Leicester. I checked the cast list again and again all week, just to make sure there hadn't been a mistake. But it always said the same thing:

Anthony Hopkins—Andrew Undershaft

The theater company had taken over a large room. Four tables had been pushed into a large square. Scripts were neatly placed around the square, with a yellow wooden pencil resting on top of each. By ten a.m., the cast had assembled. Hilary Hardiman, Gillian Edison, Richard Kay, Mary Griffith, David Swift, and others. It was all rather formal, but I found the formality strangely reassuring; it meant something of significance was underway. We all sat in our assigned places.

The director, Clive Perry, sat in the chair next to mine and said: "Good morning, everyone. The opening performance will be the eleventh of November. We'll read the play now and start blocking it at tomorrow's rehearsal here in the YMCA. OK? Let's get started."

I didn't want to show off, so somewhat nonchalantly, I feigned indifference, turning the pages of the script like everyone else. Readings of plays before the start of rehearsals are simply for the ensemble to become acquainted with the script.

But when the reading got to the entrance of Andrew Undershaft, I looked away from the pages and gave a complete performance. I sensed a few members of the cast glancing over. Was it with surprise? The director kept his attention on the script. After two hours, there was a lunch break, after which there would be brief notes on the reading. I left for lunch quickly. I couldn't stand the social chitchat. On my way to the Bowling Green pub, David Swift caught up with me. "Hey, you. You learned the whole play."

"What?"

"The whole play. You learned the whole play. Right?"

"Yes. I supposed that was OK. Or was it wrong?"

"Don't give me that *Oh, I'm ever so modest* stuff. You must have worked it all out. It was fantastic. Amazing. We are all shocked. Well, I'm not. I knew you could do it. Hilary is so impressed. She wanted to tell you, but you left. I know Clive is over the moon."

"Who?"

"Clive! The director. The one you wanted to kill."

"Oh, yeah?"

"You're a cunning Welsh fox."

David wanted to take me to lunch. I said, "Thanks, but no thanks. I'm just going to have a drink at the pub."

Sitting in the Bowling Green with my Newcastle Brown and my cheese sandwich, I recognized something I would try to carry with me for the rest of my life. Though I would never play Hamlet myself, lines from that play came to me often. On this day, it was this:

There's a special providence in the fall of a sparrow . . .
If it be not now, yet it will come. The readiness is all.

The readiness is all! That was it. The power to accept fate and, ultimately, death—therein lay strength. I first read those words way back in the 1950s in that alien boarding school, learning pieces of Shakespeare as if they were gospel. Now I was beginning to understand them. Discipline and craft. Get ready. No more putting myself down. Instead, I began to speak to myself in a new way: *Hey, you! Who, me? Yes, you. Enough! No more of that little voice. You know exactly what you're doing. So get on with it!*

Sipping my pint of beer in the Bowling Green pub, I felt my sense of failure fade away. It was time to wake up and live. After lunch, I returned to the rehearsal. At last, I had found an answer to my problem: Never give in. Never give up.

Failure was inevitable, but so was success. Death was inevitable, but so was life.

I thought of a story I'd heard about Anton Chekhov. One morning, traveling in a coach to meet a friend for breakfast, he noticed a funeral ceremony about to take place in a nearby cemetery, and he asked the driver to stop for a moment. He watched the casket lowered into the newly dug grave and listened to the bereaved saying prayers. He contemplated the meaning of it all, the great imponderables. Then, having faced the ineffable mystery of the universe, he signaled the coachman to continue the journey. His next thought was about the deliciousness of the coffee waiting for him at breakfast.

eleven

YOU'RE THE STAR OF THE SHOW

M*ajor Barbara*'s rehearsals went along without problems and the play was a resounding success. One day in the second week of its three-week run, the rest of the cast were onstage, and I was waiting in the dressing room for my call to stand by. The door was open and the stage manager, Trevor Bentham, was in the nearby scenery dock, listening to the radio. He came over to the door, looked in, and said: "It sounds like President Kennedy has been shot. Half an hour ago. News just coming in."

Over the theater speaker system, I could hear the voices of the actors onstage.

I made my way to the stage wings. Trevor's ear was close to the radio.

The volume was low; the American voices, barely audible, were crackling with static. I joined Trevor to listen, one ear open to Dallas, the other to the voices of the Leicester Phoenix Theatre's actors.

News flash. CBS News. Someone by the name of Walter Cronkite announced: "President Kennedy died at one p.m., central standard time, two o'clock eastern standard time, some thirty-eight minutes ago."

Shortly after that, I went on. No one else onstage was aware of the event. The audience was also unaware. It was an eerie experience, watching the other actors acting away, oblivious to the catastrophic news. I was the only one with that information in my brain.

After the intermission, half the audience didn't return.

Two days later, on Sunday, November 24, Kennedy's assassin, Lee Harvey Oswald, was shot dead by a man called Jack Ruby. Another great shock. Impossible to take in. The news was full of such disturbances. Later, in Washington, I would visit the grave of John Kennedy; a few feet away was the grave of Robert Kennedy. It was a cold morning, and I could hear the sound of traffic, horns honking, a police car, the general mayhem of living and the silence of the dead.

I stayed at the Phoenix Theatre for almost a year. In 1964, I wrote to the great David Scase. He'd been the director of Manchester's Library Theatre when he'd advised me to go to a London acting school. He was now director of the Liverpool Playhouse theater.

He greeted me with the words "Well, have you improved?"

"Yeah, I hope so," I said.

I auditioned again for him.

His response: "Congratulations. Yes, that's better. Big improvement. Join me in August." The discipline and training had paid off.

I started working at the Liverpool Playhouse in August

1964, playing Christy Mahon in *The Playboy of the Western World*. I was grateful to David. He gave me a necessary boost of confidence. I found the engine, the drive, and it propelled me to another theater company the next year, where I was asked to play Leontes in Shakespeare's *The Winter's Tale* and Dick Dudgeon in Shaw's *The Devil's Disciple*. In October of the same year, I was invited to audition for the National Theatre. My audition was in front of none other than Sir Laurence Olivier, the same man who, as a sad boy, I'd seen on-screen in *Hamlet*. He was no longer a black-and-white shadow on a bedsheet but a flesh-and-blood man, a bit older but still just as regal and charismatic.

As I stood on the stage before him, he said, "What are you going to do?"

"I'm going to do something from *Three Sisters*," I said.

"OK. What else?"

I said, "Othello."

"You've got a nerve, haven't you?" he said with a laugh. He'd given what everyone considered the definitive performance of that role.

I did the scenes.

"Very good," he said.

I was accepted and joined the company in October 1965. This was at a time when the company included Maggie Smith, Albert Finney, Derek Jacobi, and John Stride. Olivier was an astonishingly effective and intuitive director. When he blocked out scenes, he said, "Every move I give you, write it down. Tony, you move there. Maggie, you move there. Joan, cross this way. Tony, go upstage. Good. Right?"

By the end of the first week of rehearsal, we'd have it down, and we'd have a run-through. We did as we were told so we weren't bumping into each other. The play worked logistically. Then Olivier said, "Right, now you're free to do whatever you want." But he said he wanted us to keep his blocking. "I beg you all, dear hearts, to actually follow the moves. But if you have a better idea, I'm sure you can prove me wrong."

He was very charming, modest, gracious. I was lucky—there's no other word for it—to be in his company. And yet all I remember of that time are the gray days, the daily journeys on the Tube, the canteen coffee, and the Italian place across Waterloo Road. I stayed in various bedsits in the northern parts of London. I spent my days in stultifying rehearsal rooms with various directors screaming at the cast as rain pelted the big windows. My first part at the National was as a messenger in *Othello*. I had to run onto the stage in act 1, scene 3, and say my lines, which were:

The Ottomites, reverend and gracious,
Steering with due course towards the isle of Rhodes,
Have there injointed them with an after fleet.

Before my entrance, I stood in the wings waiting for my cue. Harry Lomax was playing the Duke of Venice, facing upstage in this rather baroque production. And there was Olivier in his white smock. Frank Finlay was playing Iago:

Despise me,
If I do not. Three great ones of the city
(In personal suit to make me his lieutenant)

But later in the show, when I ran on as a messenger again, I . . . started speaking Iago's lines from earlier in the play that had made such an impression on me.

Three great ones of the city
(In personal suit to make me his lieutenant)

Partway through, I realized what I was doing and froze.

The other actors stared at me in horror.

Then I segued gracelessly to my actual lines. After getting through the scene, I thought, *I'll never work again.*

Offstage, one of the other actors said to me, "Are you *insane?*"

Then I ran into the prompter, Diana Boddington, Olivier's stage manager, whom he called the Captain. She said, "Idiot! Sir Laurence is so angry with you. You must go and apologize!"

So I went to his dressing room at the end of the show and I knocked on his door.

"Yes, come in," he said.

I opened the door and saw him taking his makeup off.

"Laurence, I'm sorry. I spoke Iago's lines by mistake."

"Oh, yes," he said. "You are the messenger. Of course. Yes, I thought you were going to start the whole fucking play all over again. Dear boy, what is your name?"

"Tony Hopkins."

"Tony Hopkins, as that messenger, you must say, 'The Ottomites, reverend and gracious, / Steering with due course towards the isle of Rhodes . . .'"

He said the lines very beautifully, with great power and force.

"You say it that way because you're the star of the show. You're the only one speaking at that moment."

You're the only one speaking at that moment.

That floored me. He was right. In that moment, I alone was speaking on the stage of the National Theatre. For those seconds, I was the star of the show.

"But, Tony? Don't do Iago again."

With that, he dismissed me from his presence. But I never forgot that exchange. Every night during the run of that show, when I went offstage, I'd have to pass him in the narrow corridor, and night after night, he'd say, "Better. But more." Finally, one night he didn't say that. He said, "Good. You've got it."

And yet, for a long time I was given only small roles. I asked someone in the company: "Who do you have to go to bed with to get parts here?" My instinct told me that this was not the end of the road. I wanted much more. I craved big success in my life. I didn't want to stand around in wrinkled tights holding a spear in Shakespeare plays. But how could I change my circumstances? I stayed in my usual low-key mode and kept myself to myself. I wondered why I was so angry. Here I was, doing what I wanted to do, beginning to be successful, so what was the problem?

One night, my parents came to see me in a play with Laurence Olivier's wife, Joan Plowright. Afterward, they visited me in my dressing room. Sir Laurence knocked at the door and came in, and I introduced him to them. Olivier, with his unbridled charm, gave my mother a kiss on the cheek, which almost sent her into a heap on the floor. He asked my father what he'd thought of the play.

"I'll give it a fortnight," my father replied. "By the way, how old are you now?"

"I was born in 1907," said Olivier.

Without a beat my father said, "Same age as me. We're both going down the bloody hill now, aren't we?"

Olivier laughed.

"Oh, I do hope not, Mr. Hopkins. I think and hope we have a few good years ahead of us." He bowed graciously and said how charmed he was to meet them and gently eased out of the room.

My mother was appalled that Dick Hopkins the baker had spoken that way to *Laurence Olivier*.

"Well, he breathes oxygen just like you and me, doesn't he?" my father said.

That was old Dick Hopkins. Blunt and to the point.

Finally, I began to get bigger parts. Olivier cast me in his production of Chekhov's *Three Sisters* as Andrei, the brother. We rehearsed for five weeks. Joan Plowright played one of the sisters, Masha. Olivier was a meticulous director, always helpful, never dictatorial. He was a workingman and knew the name of everyone on the crew. He was humble, even though he had such profound talent—my God, what an actor.

The play opened at the Old Vic and did well. After one Wednesday-night performance, I was in the dressing room, all ready to get to the pub next door before closing time, when someone knocked on the door. It was Peter O'Toole. He was, as they say, feeling no pain—he was well and truly plastered. He wanted me to show up on Friday morning for a screen test. I had already been interviewed by him in the office of his company, Keep Films. Now I was to come back for an audition at a park in Chelsea on Friday at ten a.m.

"It's a film test for *The Lion in Winter*," he said. "Take these pages and learn the lines. It's not a long piece. The part is Richard."

Then he vanished.

Friday came, and I showed up at the small square of green park. There was O'Toole with a film crew. He gave me good advice: Speak up. ("If they can't hear you, they'll be off to the pub.") We did the test. He said the part was mine. That was my first big break, my first time seeing a real movie camera.

Olivier gave me leave to try doing films. He'd had his own success in that medium, and it had been hard won. When John Osborne's play *Look Back in Anger* burst onto the British theater scene in 1956, theater critic Kenneth Tynan gave it a rave review because it was cutting through the Noël Coward tradition without disrespecting it. Richard Burton and Claire Bloom (on whom I had a *mad* crush) appeared in the 1959 film adaptation. Olivier didn't like the film, but it made him think: *Well, I'm coming to the end of my life.* He wanted to see what else he could do.

So he'd phoned Osborne and said, "Would you write a play for me? I just want a break from the classics." Osborne wrote *The Entertainer*, in which Olivier plays a washed-up English comic named Archie Rice. It was Olivier's favorite part. Playing such a vulgar man changed his life. He became a modern actor. He went on to do all sorts of new roles.

So Olivier couldn't in good conscience stand in my way when it came to appearing in a movie, but he said, "You must come back to the theater, my boy."

"Yes, I will," I said. I intended to do both theater and film, but increasingly I liked the idea of movies—not having to do the same lines eight times a week, perhaps doing them only eight times in a morning, then moving on to the next thing.

The Lion in Winter began filming in Ireland at Ardmore Studios outside Dublin, and my first big scene was with Katharine Hepburn in the sound studio. I was impressed that I was working with her. I thought, *How amazing is this? The baker's son making a movie with Katharine Hepburn!*

I knew all the stories about her, like how the first time she met Spencer Tracy, she'd said, "I may be too tall for you, Mr. Tracy."

And he said, "Don't worry. I'll cut you down to my size."

My God. What legends they were already.

And yet I wasn't nervous. I was young and cocky. I had no nerves. Olivier had given me great advice: "Nerves is vanity. You're wondering what people think of you? To hell with them! Just jump off the edge." Being nervous, in other words, meant you were thinking about yourself. Of course, you wouldn't be human if you didn't get a little tremor in front of so many pairs of eyes, he said. But you've got to take charge of it.

Even though it was my first time on camera, I knew enough to be more economical on-screen than onstage. Screen acting wasn't taught in drama schools back then, and we all knew actors who'd been unable to make the transition because they continued gesturing dramatically and projecting their voices to the mezzanine when all they had to do for the camera was turn and whisper.

Still, I apparently had more theater training to unlearn than I'd thought, because at the end of rehearsal, Hepburn said, "I'll give you a tip."

Of course, even arrogant as I was, I wanted a tip from Katharine Hepburn.

"There's the camera," she said. "That's your bread-and-butter machine. You're good. Don't play the whole scene with the back of your head to the camera because I'll steal the scene from you—I'll probably do that anyway. Now, don't act. You've got a good voice. You've got a good, big head, and broad shoulders. You look strong. Be like Spencer Tracy, like Bogart. Don't act. Just be. Just speak the lines. You are it—you are Richard the Lionheart!"

And I thought, *That's right! I'm it!* And I held my own.

Her words reminded me of something Spencer Tracy had said to Laurence Olivier after he saw him in *Titus Andronicus*. Laurence had worn a great deal of makeup onstage to play the part, and Tracy said: "Who do you think they think you are? The audience knows it's you." We don't need to hide behind masks. We can just show up and say the lines and have confidence that our presence will carry the day.

As I'd anticipated, compared to theater, film was easy. I started to find the theater tedious. Night after night, the same thing, with almost no time off. I began to feel that acting was a by-product rather than the point of life. I wanted to find value in the rest of my life.

"Why don't you walk out of that goddamn place?" Hepburn said of the theater. "You've got to be tough. You've got to be a killer." She was fearless. During the McCarthy hearings, she walked around MGM dressed in red in defiance of the Communist scare.

Certainly it was getting harder and harder to make myself go to the theater each night. I was fielding new opportunities and I'd signed with my first agents. (I chose agents who smoked and had messy desks, as I felt more comfortable with them than with the clean-cut go-getters.) My agents were fielding offers for me for parts in films, and I wanted to take them. But first I had to fulfill my theatrical contract.

One morning in 1967, I got a call from the Old Vic's stage manager, who said, "You're going on for Olivier tonight."

Sir Laurence Olivier was in the hospital with appendicitis. I was his understudy in August Strindberg's *The Dance of Death*. The character was Edgar, a military man married to a former actress.

I reported to the theater for rehearsal. I already had the play down cold, and when I showed up, I began saying the lines quickly.

"Slow down," the director said. "You've got it. It's all there."

Hours later, I was in the costume onstage, waiting for the curtain to go up.

Stand by. House lights, please.

I heard the audience growing quiet. My parents were out there. The curtain rose. I saw the exit lights in the back. I told myself to breathe. I didn't have a god to pray to, but I said a prayer anyway: *Anyone around, please help me.*

Then the lines began to pour from me, although part of my brain held back, observing it all. One part of me was speaking the dialogue. Another part was saying, *This is ridiculous. Tell the audience to go home.*

As I said one of my lines, I followed the stage direction to cross over and pour myself a glass of whiskey. I was on automatic pilot. Something was taking me and guiding me through it. Call it God if you want. Perhaps part of the subconscious mind is the foundation of being.

That night, I got a standing ovation.

The next day, I learned that Olivier had been in to see me.

In his hospital gown, he stood there in the back with his doctor and caught some of the show. He phoned me and said, "I saw the first ten minutes. Well done. How do you feel?"

"I went through three shirts because I was sweating so profusely."

"Well, that's called tension," he said.

"How long will it take me to get over it?" I asked.

"About twenty-five years," he said.

Olivier later said that I "walked away with the part of Edgar like a cat with a mouse between his teeth."

We went out for drinks one night, Olivier and I, and I got to hear some of his old theater stories. I was always struck by his formality. Olivier arrived at rehearsals in his business suit looking like a bank president. He did run the National Theatre in addition to being one of the greatest actors of all time.

I was in awe of him, and I listened with rapt attention to every story he told me about his career. I will never forget his recounting over drinks how his iconic Richard III performance came together.

At age thirty-eight, Olivier had not only played the difficult part of Richard III but also come up with the concept for the entire production.

"I want the stage to be very solid," he'd told the set designer, although they didn't have much building material because of the war effort. "And I want a pair of big doors at the back of the stage with a big lock and an iron key. I don't care how much it costs. Just build it."

So the cast started rehearsing, and he walked around with a hump on his back. "I was doing it, but I couldn't *get* it," Olivier told me. "Actors were walking away because they thought that I couldn't do the part. And I thought perhaps they could be right. I couldn't find the stupid thing that would make it work. I'd say, 'Now is the winter of our discontent / made glorious,' while I thought, *What am I doing?*"

Opening night arrived. Olivier sat in his dressing room. His friend John Mills came backstage and said, "Good luck tonight. We're coming to see you."

"Don't bother," Olivier said.

He put his wig on, and he thought it made him look like a schoolgirl. The hump on his back, the twisted arm with the false hand... all ridiculous. He heard "Places, act one, please!"

"Oh God," Olivier said to his dressing-room mirror. "This is going to be a disaster."

He just knew it was going to be a failure, the end of his career. He'd be the laughingstock of London. The city had put him on a pedestal; how far he would now fall in their estimation. He had all that going on in his mind as he walked to his place onstage. His stage manager, Diana Boddington, on book that night, said, "Good luck, Larry. You'll be wonderful."

"No," he said. I loved that. No long arguments, no false humility. Just defeat and dismay: "No."

Then he got on the stage. As the audience quieted, he thought, *Well, I just want to go home and get in bed, but I guess now I have to have a go at it.*

House lights down. House curtains up.

For the opening scene, he stood with his back to the audience, holding a key in the lock. He felt the lights on his back. With that: "A chill went down my spine, and I turned the key."

Clink! The sound was deafening.

He realized in that moment why he'd had the stage built

that way, why he'd wanted to begin the show that way: "I'd locked them in the room with me, the audience," he said. "I turned around. I came down the stage. I began, 'Now is the winter of our discontent / made glorious summer by this sun of York; / And all the clouds that lour'd upon our house / in the deep bosom of the ocean buried.' I had them like *that*."

He held up his glass and clinked mine. He hadn't known what he was going to do until he did it. But once he knew, he *knew*. I understood exactly what he meant.

While working with Olivier, I achieved another milestone: I found a woman to marry. Petronella Barker was the daughter of Eric Barker and Pearl Hackney, who were BBC Radio stars during the war years. Radio had been the only form of entertainment then, and so to me they were essentially royalty. Petronella and I were very different from each other, but we were in love. We married on September 2, 1967, and Olivier gave us luxury bedsheets as a wedding present. What followed were the worst two years of my life. They are a Dead Sea Scroll to me now. Suffice it to say, our opposing personalities and my alcoholism doomed the relationship from the start.

We lived in a little apartment in the Kings Arms near Putney Bridge. In the evenings, I bought bottles of whiskey at the off-license and took them back to the flat. My depression was boundless; the booze was my pacifier. I brooded. She raged.

By the time we realized how awful a match we were, Petronella was pregnant. We tried to rally for the sake of the child we were about to have, but it was no use. The marriage was a disaster, full of tensions and jealousies. I began to get more acting work, which caused resentment. And I felt huge pressure to pay our mortgage and provide for the family.

Into this mess, on August 20, 1968, a girl was born. Abigail. She was a beautiful baby. My parents came up to London from Wales to meet her. Petronella loathed my parents, so she made sure to be out of the house when they came. ("So you're off to see *Mommy* and *Daddy*," Petronella would say whenever I visited them.) My parents cried when they saw Abigail. They adored her. And they were worried for me. When I took them to the station, pushing Abigail ahead of us in her pram, my father couldn't even say goodbye. He and my mother knew that I was in big trouble, both in my marriage and with my drinking. And they were sad for themselves. At last they'd become grandparents, but the circumstances seemed destined to keep them from their grandchild.

Whenever Abigail saw me, she lit up and laughed. I marveled that such a lovely creature had come out of such a destructive union. How powerful, I thought, that even in the midst of the horror that was that marriage and my own failures, there were those tender moments with her.

Her nursery was a haven. Unfortunately, there were other rooms in that house, and those were hell. Petronella told me how horrible I was. I drank as if to prove her point. I was impossible to live with; I have no doubt whatsoever of that. I didn't know how to be good. I didn't know how to cut through, how to become human, how to keep myself from slipping into darkness.

Petronella and I had frequent rows, but one night the fighting reached a new pitch. I returned from working on location in Scotland. Exhausted after endless days on set and the long trip home, I set down my suitcases in the hall. Before my coat was off, Petronella was mocking me. Staring at me with utter contempt, she said, in a voice dripping with sarcasm, "Oh, it's Mr. Lord High and Mighty! Welcome, lord and master!"

"I'm so tired, Petronella," I said. "I've been traveling all day."

"Oh! His Majesty speaks!"

I had never been physically violent, but in that moment, I was filled with such revulsion that I became afraid for both myself and her. Without a word, I walked past her into Abigail's room, where she lay sleeping. She was one. She'd just started to walk and was learning new things every day. Everyone remarked on how much we looked like each other; she had my blue eyes. I looked down at her and whispered goodbye. Then I walked back to the hall, picked up my suitcases, and left the house without ever having removed my coat.

I'd been with Petronella for two years. I'd almost left many times. But that was the night I knew I had to get out for good. Otherwise, God knows what the consequences would have been. As I ran down Richmond Road, I heard a voice in my head say, *Keep going, keep going, never look back.* When I passed the river, I briefly paused to consider hurling myself into it.

As I ran, I wondered why it had all come to this. I had a wife and child. Our apartment was comfortable, full of antiques. My career was going well. And yet I fled that life like it was a barn on fire. I was scared and confused. My restlessness had been a great gift in some ways and caused havoc in others. Now it was causing others great pain. But I believed it was a matter of survival.

That night, I walked fast and kept walking. I didn't know where I was going. Finally, I reached a pub. I arrived out of breath.

"Do you have a phone?" I panted to the woman behind the counter.

"Are you on the run from the police, darlin'?"

"No, from my wife."

"Well, God bless you."

I called a friend, David Swift, who had been the best man in my wedding. Then I got a cab back to North London and spent the night at his house.

I'd made that break a few times but always went back. Now I knew I would never return. The last day of that marriage for me was that day, Saturday, October 25, 1969.

The next morning, David and I had breakfast together. "Please don't try to talk me into going back," I said.

"Into going back?" he said. "Tony, I'm here to persuade you not to return. You did the best you could, but I beg you—my wife and I beg you—don't go back. Petronella will kill you or you will kill her or you will kill yourself."

I phoned my parents. My mother picked up the phone.

"I've got some news," I said. "I've left Petronella."

"Oh, thank God for that," my mother said.

They saw that there was no other way, in spite of the devastation that resulted. Aside from sending financial support, I didn't have contact with Petronella and Abigail for a few years after that. It is the saddest fact of my life, and my greatest regret, and yet I feel absolutely sure that it would have been much worse for everyone if I'd stayed.

Summer 1938: Me getting a suntan on the back lawn in Margam.

August 1939: My father, Richard, me, and my mother, Muriel.

My parents' bakery on Commercial Road, Taibach, circa 1910.

1942: My mother, Muriel, me, and my father, Richard, outside the house in Margam.

1943: In my house in Margam (I was still learning how to smile).

1943: Me, age five, at 77 Wern Road.

LEFT: Saddest time of my life, 1947: Me and my mother, Muriel. The grim years.

BELOW: January 25, 1949: Eleven years old, primary school in Port Talbot (confused).

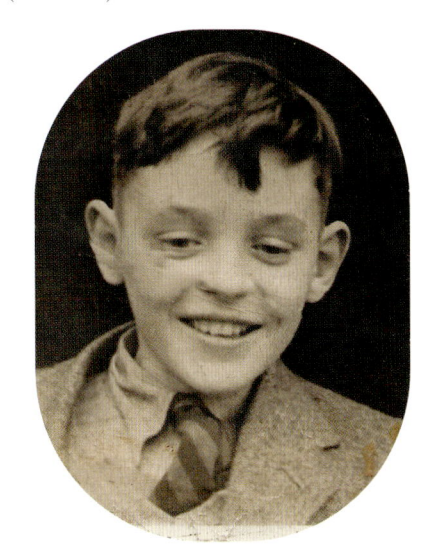

Port Talbot YMCA.

My father, Richard, me, and my grandfather
Fred Yeats, 1951, Weymouth, Dorset.

In the gardens of Cowbridge
Grammar School, 1953.

My mother, Muriel, Uncle Eric,
and Aunt Jenn, circa 1924.

December 1959: Army days, the draft.

1943: Muriel, me, Aunt Lorna, and grandfather Fred Yeats in Maudlam, Port Talbot.

The beautiful Brombil Valley, Margam: Bill, Lorna, Bobby H.

Aunt Lorna, Jack Hayes, Mimi, Grandmother Emmy.

December 30, 1948: Cousin Bobby, Cousin Rosalie, Cousin Bernice (bottom left), me, Cousin Roger (bottom right), the night before our grandmother died.

October 1958: Me at my parents' new house, Laleston, Bridgend.

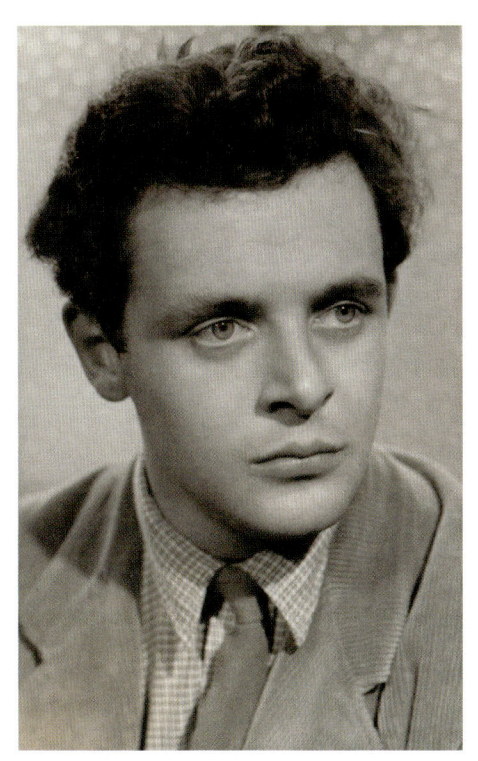

1960: My Dylan Thomas stage.

1961: Llandrindod Wells Lake.

1961: Lake at Laleston, Bridgend.

LEFT: The Ship Inn, 1970: My father, Richard, and my mother, Muriel.

BELOW: August 1972: My father, Richard, me, and my mother, Muriel.

twelve

THE DAYS OF WINE AND ROSES

Our life is a dream. We are asleep.
Occasionally we wake up enough to know that we are dreaming.

—LUDWIG WITTGENSTEIN (attributed)

In the late sixties, my father sold the bakery. He was too young to retire, fifty-four, but he had no choice. The steel industry was collapsing. The engineering geniuses got together to build a freeway—a necessary evil, but as a result, small businesses were cut off and went bust.

For my father, retirement was like suffering a slow death, so he began to cast around for a new opportunity. He had always wanted to run a pub. Though not a wide reader, his favorite author was the Edwardian English novelist Warwick Deeping, who wrote romantically about pub culture. So my father applied to several pubs for the post of manager. He had to have that connection to people. In 1968, he landed a job at the Ship Inn, one of those nouveau half-timbered bars, in Caerleon, Gwent.

Finally, he'd found his niche. He was happy in his own way. Both my parents ran the business, my mother preparing lunches and my father behind the bar. His drinking gave him courage and he would entertain his customers by telling tall tales about his life. The customers thought he was hilarious.

"You should have your own comedy show, Dickie Boy," the regulars would say.

"Too bloody late for that now," he'd reply, wiping down the bar.

Slowly, though, his mood darkened. At times, he would suddenly break down and cry. Toward the end of his life, his restlessness and depression agitated him more and more, and when the drinking became more obsessive, he talked more and more about death. He looked at me as a stranger. We were strangers, really, to each other, both distant. Kept apart by something unspoken.

"How the hell did you learn all that stuff?" he often asked me of my acting.

"Oh, I don't know how," I said. "I just did."

"You're a strange one. You were as thick as two short planks in school. That's for sure. Your head always up in the clouds."

One Sunday morning, we were in the bar of the pub just before opening time. I was helping him set up. He was tired, feeling down and anxious, and having a difficult time breathing. His breathing was all I could hear besides the noise of the cars across the bridge outside.

He never took time off. My mother worried about his health. She pleaded with him to take a break. "You can't go on like this. It'll kill you," she said.

He'd already suffered a few bouts of breathing difficulties. Those gave him a shock. But he wouldn't give in. He wouldn't even consider a medical checkup.

"There's nothing wrong with me," he insisted. "All doctors are a bunch of bloody quacks."

This cold Sunday he was sitting at a small table by the window. Outside, it was a damp, cloudy morning. I asked him if he was OK. He nodded.

"Yes, I'll be all right. Just need to sit down. Getting bloody old, that's all."

He turned to look out the window at the heavy gray sky, the fields and the river and the misty trees beyond. There were some cyclists with yellow rain capes passing. That seemed to add to the gloom.

"Sundays, Sundays, and another bloody Sunday," he muttered. "I've always hated Sundays. What the hell are we doing here? I thought it would be the answer. Years ago, I wanted to own a pub."

He turned to me.

"Do you remember that time in that Cotswold town? Was it Broadway? Or Chipping Campden?"

"Broadway."

"Anyway, there was a pub for sale, and Auntie Patty was going to help us buy it?"

"Yes, I remember. It was in July 1949."

"How the hell would you remember that?"

I shrugged.

"God knows why she was sticking her nose in," he said.

"Who?"

"Auntie bloody Patty, that's who."

He turned to watch the cars passing by.

"Anyway, it looked like it might work out. But it didn't. She made up her mind that there was no profit in a pub. She was just a bloody old Bible-punching skinflint. That was 1949? And you remembered that?"

"Yes. It was July 1949. The pub was at the top end of Broadway. It was a small country pub. You and Aunt Patty and Aunt Rhoda went inside to look it over. I stayed in the car. When you came out, you looked disappointed."

"Anyway, they're both bloody dead. So much for their wealth." The old man kept looking out the window. "Bloody strange, isn't it? I'd always wanted a pub, and here I am, running a pub in this God-forgotten place, and it's the same old thing. Getting up in the morning, looking in the mirror. Same old face, getting older. Bloody feet killing me. What the hell are we all looking for? It's like facing a big blank wall."

He looked over at me: "Say that piece again, what was it, about the skull... Yorick? *Hamlet*, right? Yorick the fool, right?"

I'd never liked reciting poetry, especially Shakespeare, on command, although I remembered many pieces and sometimes found myself spontaneously performing them when legless with booze. Even in my schoolboy days, I'd memorized several long speeches by Shakespeare and some poems by T. S. Eliot and Dylan Thomas, not as an intellectual badge or swagger but to prove to myself that my brain wasn't as useless as everyone said.

Alas, poor Yorick! I knew him, Horatio: a fellow
of infinite jest, of most excellent fancy: he hath
borne me on his back a thousand times.

Once I reached the end of the monologue, the old man stood up and went into the stockroom. I heard him crying, but when he returned, he pretended he hadn't been.

My mother was worn out by his restlessness. She was devoted to him, but sometimes she swore she would end up in an asylum because of him. "Honest to God," she said, "it's like living in a house with five people."

She was often embarrassed by his bluntness. After the burial of my grandfather, we turned to leave the cemetery. My father looked at my mother's frail uncle Hugh and said: "It's hardly worth you going home, is it, Uncle Hugh?"

Uncle Hugh laughed.

"You don't pull any punches, do you, Richard?" Then he laughed again and said, "We are all heading that way: the Alone to the Alone."

Uncle Hugh died about a year later.

And Dick Hopkins's time seemed to be coming closer.

My father almost never left home, and yet he knew all the major roads everywhere: in Wales, in Timbuktu in Mali, in Sidi Barrâni in Egypt. He longed to travel. Just anywhere. He cherished his battered AAA road atlas. It was a book that fascinated him. But he never put it to use. He dreamed instead.

On one of our rare expeditions, one sultry Sunday afternoon when I was a boy the three of us went to the Church of St. Giles in Stoke Poges, Buckinghamshire, where the poet Thomas Gray had penned his epic poem "Elegy Written in a Country Churchyard."

My mother, of course, uttered her usual complaint: "Oh, Dick, why does it always have to be so depressing? Poems about death and Hitler and the war. It's so gloomy."

Thanks to his maps, he knew the location of the Church of St. Giles and the surrounding streets as if they were part of his hometown. In the churchyard, he knew just where the grave of Thomas Gray could be found.

A few people were standing at the poet's grave, mostly typical English tourists, quiet and polite, barely speaking above a whisper. A middle-aged American couple were standing slightly apart. We knew they were American by the way they were dressed. The man wore a green-checkered jacket and gray-framed glasses, and he held a camera. My father, never afraid to ask questions or start conversations, asked them their names and where they were from.

The man's name was Dale Leigh, and his wife was Betty; they were from Muskogee, Oklahoma. Dale gave my father a business card and went on to say that he had been with an infantry outfit in the final days of the war. He'd been stationed near Windsor, getting ready for D-Day. His wife and my mother started talking. The woman told my mother about her husband's longing to come back to England to visit the villages of Buckinghamshire. She said her husband loved the Thomas Gray poem. My mother laughed and said: "Oh, yes, my husband is just the same. He loves that poem. It's just so gloomy."

Mr. Leigh overheard that and politely corrected her.

"Oh, no, I don't think so, ma'am. It sure helped me during the tough times. I learned that poem before the war and had gotten great comfort from it, yes, sir, and despite the misery of war, it kind of got me through. Yes, ma'am."

Then Mr. Leigh and my father started reciting their favorite lines. They were like a double act, alternating the lines, the two dialects Welsh and American.

The curfew tolls the knell of parting day,
The lowing herd wind slowly o'er the lea,
The plowman homeward plods his weary way,
And leaves the world to darkness and to me.

It was late in the afternoon; the sun was beginning to fade. The few English tourists who had listened to the two men reciting the poem politely clapped and said, "Well done. Excellent. Thank you."

It was my old man's quiet moment of glory. He had so few of those that it stands out in my mind as a national holiday of sorts—the day the baker and bartender got to play the poet.

Another love besides poetry I inherited from my father: alcohol. Drinking was a family tradition. The black sheep of my mother's family, Uncle Jim, was one of my childhood heroes. He worked in the Glasgow shipyards, and he was the real deal. My grandfather told me all about him as a warning: Uncle Jim was a drifter and a scoundrel, a bad egg.

Suddenly, I wanted to be a scoundrel.

I told my grandfather that I wanted to be like Uncle Jim.

"When I grow up, I want to be a drifter."

"A drifter? You want to be a hobo? A wanderer?"

"Yes. Just like Uncle Jim."

My grandmother was horrified but my grandfather understood. "Uncle Jim was a bit of a mystery man and was never to be trusted, but he was also a lot of fun, and what a laugh."

Uncle Jim died in an asylum in Glasgow. He drank himself to death.

I was sure I could take the fun parts of drinking and leave the bad. I hoped so. Because the only way I could feel normal was to drink. That was my solution for just about every problem: Get mellow, get buzzed, or get smashed. Booze made everything better. Well, almost everything.

I'd started drinking seriously in the early 1960s. I'd had booze before, a few beers here and there, now and then a bar fight in the army. But at some point I began to drink like so many others drank in the acting business—actually, not just in this profession but everywhere in those days. Three martinis at lunch was normal. In the creative fields, it was considered necessary.

Besides, it was fun! Humphrey Bogart sneered, "Never trust anyone who doesn't drink. The whole world is three drinks behind." He said if the world's leaders would just loosen up, we wouldn't need the United Nations.

Cops in Beverly Hills pulled Bogart's car over one night. He was driving around with two other actors, all three of them sloshed. One of the officers leaned into the open window and—no doubt bowled over by the stench of scotch and cigarettes—asked, "Have you been drinking, Mr. Bogart?"

"Sure," he said. "What in the hell else would I be doing at three in the morning?"

He didn't go to jail. This was LA in the 1960s, and he was Humphrey Bogart.

"Just drive slowly," the cop said, and waved him on.

When anyone pressed me to tell them why I drank so much, I'd say, "You want an argument? Ask me that question."

The truth was that every bit of news, good or bad, was an excuse to drink. During my early moments of small triumphs, I felt the energy of a new life force that called for a drink: *Let's celebrate! We deserve it!* When I felt lonely, the only way to break down the barricades between myself and others and begin feeling connected to the world was booze: *Let's loosen up and have fun!*

In one production, an assistant on the show was given the unpleasant task of getting me from the stage back to my hotel without stopping in a bar. Well, I would take that assistant with me from bar to bar and I took great delight in getting him drunk. He eventually went on to become a famous theater producer, Scott Rudin. Back in those days, though, he was just an assistant who failed at an impossible task—keeping me sober—and he got yelled at by the higher-ups as a result.

Just like Uncle Jim, I became one of those good old looking-for-trouble drunks. Whatever alcoholism is, with its symptoms and its quirks, I had them all. I was loaded and ready to go, full steam ahead, *Tugboat Annie*, I'm Popeye the Sailor Man, and I am what I am what I am, and I'm Tony the Tiger Man, the Tiger, the Tiger, the Tiger burning oh so bright in the Welsh forests of the night, I'm holding the Tiger by the tail. Blaze the trail!

Occasionally, I'd decide those who were "concerned" about my drinking were right and that it might be more sensible to drink moderately. Why not try it? Self-discipline was the key! Moderation in all things. Slow down. Take it easy. Fantastic. I'd have one drink at a party, then two, then I'd think about stopping. Then I would have a drink to congratulate myself on my reasonableness.

Most actors in those days were known as piss artists (belligerent drunks). The notorious ones were the famous top-ranking actors, the movie stars: Peter O'Toole, Richard Harris, Oliver Reed, Richard Burton, Nicol Williamson, Robert Stephens, Wilfrid Lawson. They were the legendary glory boys, the noisy heroes of sixties theater, all of them extremely gifted. I fell down the same rabbit hole. But I wasn't a party drinker. I preferred drinking alone.

In 1963, *Days of Wine and Roses*, an earnest, melodramatic, and rather sentimental film starring Jack Lemmon and Lee Remick, was released in Britain. I had always enjoyed watching Jack Lemmon. He made me laugh, especially in *Some Like It Hot* with Marilyn Monroe and Tony Curtis. Knowing nothing about the plot of this film, I took a date to the local cinema in Leicester. I thought it would be nice to see a Jack Lemmon performance and have a good laugh.

It was a drizzly Sunday afternoon. The opening song seemed a bit too romantic for a comedy—mushy Hollywood music made even mushier by a chorus of voices. The score was by Henry Mancini with lyrics by Johnny Mercer. *Classy*, I thought.

I always checked the music credits of films, more names for my filing-cabinet-like brain already filled with pieces of useless information.

The film opens in a crowded city bar. Joe (Jack Lemmon) is a hustler and party man working in some corporate business, mostly hiring young women as escorts for a bunch of old businessmen. He meets a beautiful woman, one of the escorts he'd hired, Kirsten (Lee Remick). The romance begins, and right away it becomes clear that this is a tumultuous love story.

Uh-oh, I thought. It began to remind me of a film called *The Lost Weekend*, which I'd seen with my father when I was nine. (Not knowing that the film was about the dangers of alcoholism, I'd just enjoyed the hallucinations coming out of the wall.)

I wanted some laughs, not a gauzy romance. Joe and Kirsten get to know each other. In a later scene, both are standing at the edge of a San Francisco wharf. It is late at night. Joe is pretty wasted. Kirsten is romantic and dizzy. I was waiting for the comedy bits: *Come on. Make me laugh!*

Joe checks his almost empty bottle of Jack Daniel's, takes the last drop, and lets it fall into the water. They both watch the bottle sink. Mancini music. Kirsten, dreamily, quotes some lines from a poem by Ernest Dowson: "They are not long, the days of wine and roses: / Out of a misty dream / Our path emerges for a while, then closes / Within a dream."

The lines were unfamiliar, but somehow I knew the truth of them. I had always known that life was a dream. Perhaps it was sentimental hogwash, but it pulled at something deep inside me.

In the last scene in the film, Joe has managed to stop drinking, but Kirsten is trapped in the nightmare. She begs Joe to come back to her, to drink again. To her, the world looks dirty without a drink. Joe refuses to go back. He must let her go. Kirsten leaves, and that is the most excruciating moment. Joe watches her from the window as she walks down the street, the neon sign reading BAR flashing on and off. The film fades to black. More sad music.

I knew that was also my problem, and yet I was still on Kirsten's trip, not Joe's. Sometimes I would stop for a week or two. Three weeks was my limit. Any longer, I felt I was going mad. It was the drag of lost energy that made life miserable. Perhaps it was a will to die. I have no idea. It took another twelve years for me to cut the knot and enter a new world. Twelve more years of one bottle after another falling out of my hand into the water.

thirteen

THINK. BE SENSIBLE

I met Jenni Lynton on December 5, 1969. She was a film producer's assistant working at Pinewood Studios, the vast British soundstage twenty miles from Central London. I was there filming an Alistair MacLean movie called *When Eight Bells Toll*. I was becoming known and starting to make a little money, but I was anything but a catch.

Why someone as kind as Jenni spent any time with me is a puzzle. She was everything I was not: stable, quiet, patient. My opposite. When we went to her parents' home in Epsom, Surrey, for Sunday dinner, there would be one bottle of wine on the table—for all of us! One bottle! One!

Let's just say we painted with different colors. They were stable, decent people. Why they didn't see through me is a riddle. They had never met an actor before. Her father's only observation was "He's a bit wild, isn't he? He certainly likes the drink. You sure he's for you?"

You sure he's for you? I believe was polite code for *Dump him now!*

And yet she not only stayed with me—she agreed to marry

me. And she stayed with me for twenty years. I did not make it easy on her. She'd caught a tiger by the tail.

On a Monday morning, January 8, 1973, five days before my wedding to Jenni, a voice came to me in a dream: *You don't have to put up with it any longer.*

My eyes shot open at six in the morning and I sat up in bed at the flat I shared with Jenni in Barnes, London. Finally, I had a clear sense of what I needed to do. I'd been appearing in Shakespeare's *Macbeth*, directed by Michael Blakemore. Diana Rigg and Alec McCowen were also in the cast. They were the establishment gang, the able and thoroughly professional darlings of the theater world. I stuck out like a sore thumb. I didn't belong in their company. But what made the show intolerable were the vicious snipes from John Dexter. His jabs were not going to stop, so what was the point in my sticking around? The show would be better off without me.

"That's it. I'm done," I said to Jenni. "I'm not going to rehearsal today. I'm done, finished."

"Finished?" said Jenni, still half asleep.

"Yes. Finished. I don't need to be in this stupid idiot's game. I'm giving it up."

Silence. Then: "But we're getting married on Saturday," said Jenni, now fully awake. "Are you going to stop working completely?"

"I don't know. I'll find a job somewhere. I can work in a pub or rob a bank. Who knows?"

One thing I was certain of: I hadn't come into this acting business to be punished by some nasty, twisted little sadist like John Dexter.

I called my agent, Jeremy Conway, at his home number. Get

it done now. Better to start the ball rolling. Procrastination kills. Why live with unnecessary angst when, with a clean surgical flick of a knife, you can end the discomfort once and for all?

Naturally, Jeremy was upset, and not just because it wasn't far past dawn.

"Tony, think carefully about this," he said. "It's madness."

"Jeremy, I have thought about this. Very carefully. And it is *not* madness."

"Tony, listen to me," Jeremy pleaded. "Think. Be sensible."

"Too late for me to be sensible now, Jeremy. I've never had a gram of common sense in my head ever. At least, not as far as I can remember."

"Come to the office and let's talk," said Jeremy.

"OK," I said. "But I'm not going to change my mind. Just phone them and tell them I've left. Gives them time to regroup." I started to hang up the phone.

"You'll never work again" was Jeremy's quiet and sensible response.

"*I. Don't. Care,*" I said. "I'll drive a truck or something." And I hung up.

At nine a.m. I took the Tube to the Green Park station and walked to Jeremy's office in Hay Hill. I felt free. It felt good. I had no intention of reversing my decision.

In Jeremy's office I took two phone calls from the National Theatre's administration. Michael Halifax was the first to call. Michael was the theater company manager. He was a highly sophisticated man, always generous and kind. He said, "Tony, think carefully about this. You can't just walk out of a theater company. It's madness. What about the other actors?"

"What about them?" I said. "Recast. If other actors or

long-suffering minions of any establishment are willing to endure a toxic environment where certain power-hungry bully boys are at liberty to abuse actors, and anyone else for that matter, then fine. Good luck. But not for me, old sport. I've been in the army. I'm not in the army anymore, and I won't be screamed at as if I'm back in the military."

Another familiar pause, and the same warning, now from Michael: "Tony, you will never work again."

"Fine. So be it," I said. "Thank you, Michael."

Next call: Laurence Olivier himself. He spoke bluntly: "You're being quite foolish. On your own head be it, dear boy."

"Thank you," I said. "Much obliged."

It was eleven a.m. when I left Jeremy Conway's office and walked across Green Park. It was a glorious winter morning. I could hear the faint rumble of distant traffic, the jingle-jangle commerce of life. Other people in the park looked like they were going places. Work. Offices. Shopping. The stuff of life and death. Make hay while the sun shines. I felt free to live or die. Nothing mattered much. Or was I fooling myself yet again? Was I back to square one, starting all over again with my old man's monotonous portents of gloom and doom for his troublesome son?

I no longer cared. I'd broken the spell once more and stopped the Dance of Death into hell. *Illegitimi non carborundum.* Don't let the bastards grind you down.

I began singing to myself.

Here we go round the mulberry bush,
The mulberry bush
The mulberry bush

Here we go round the mulberry bush
On a frosty Monday morning.

Upon arriving home at lunchtime, I sang out to Jenni, "It's over!"

When I saw her ashen face, I realized that she thought I meant the wedding.

"No, no," I said. "Not the wedding. The job. I finished. I walked out."

I told her that this was good news. Never again would I tolerate bullying or being put down. There seemed to be an unwritten code for some people that certain others were merely lower forms of life and therefore deserved punishment. Not me.

"That's it?" she said.

"Yep."

"But we're getting married on Saturday," she said.

"I know. Something will turn up. Have no fear."

The wedding took place in Barnes. At the wedding reception, the dreaded John Dexter showed up, though he didn't say a word to me. The director Michael Blakemore, and a few actors from other shows too. Why any of them came was a mystery. Probably support for Jenni. A few had warned her about me. Several actors got well and truly smashed even though they were due to be onstage for a 2:30 matinee of Olivier's *Long Day's Journey into Night*.

"Good luck there, my friends," I said as they stumbled blearily out into the sunshine and over to the theater.

For our honeymoon, we went to the glorious Lake District in North West England. Jenni drove us there. I didn't drive. I had never taken a driver's test. That's right—I was an unemployed wretch who couldn't drive. Why she married me, God only knows. She was made of strong fiber.

About a week later, Jeremy Conway called. Could I get to London to meet an American casting director named Renée Valente? She wanted to offer me a leading role in a TV series called *QB VII*.

"I thought you said I'd never work again," I said. "What is this? A joke?"

"Well, you were born under a lucky star," replied Jeremy. "Do you want to meet this woman? She's a casting director from Screen Gems."

"Screen Gems? What's that?"

"Do you want to meet her or not?" asked Jeremy.

"OK."

"They'll send a car to the Lake District, pick you up, and bring you to London. The Dorchester hotel. Meet Renée Valente at three, and then they'll drive you back."

"Is it a good script?" I asked. Arrogance personified. The drunk staring down at the world from the gutter.

"Very good," Jeremy replied. "Yes or no?"

"Yes, OK."

The next day, a grand-looking car arrived at the Lake District hotel, and I was driven to the Dorchester in Mayfair, London. Very grand. I was taken to an impressive suite. Renée Valente was a down-to-earth, tough-talking woman in her forties with a husky cigarette voice.

"Sit down," she said. "Anthony, right?"

"Tony."

"OK, Tony. Drink?"

"Whiskey."

"Whiskey coming up."

She got to the point: The series, called *QB VII*, was based on a book by Leon Uris, a story of a war-crimes investigation. She wanted me to play Adam Kelno. The cast included Leslie Caron, Ben Gazzara, Lee Remick, Jack Hawkins, and Robert Stephens.

Not bad, I thought. *Quite a cast.*

Renée handed me a thick tome of a script to read and told me that ABC would give her an answer to her casting recommendations within a week.

I was driven back to the Lake District.

A week passed. No phone call. Then on Saturday, January 27, the call came through. The role was mine.

fourteen

THAT'LL KILL YOU

Filming started at Pinewood Studios and then moved to Israel. The story centered on a libel suit brought against the author Leon Uris. In his major book *Exodus*, Uris had mentioned a Dr. Dehring who had worked at the Auschwitz-Birkenau concentration camp and performed seventeen thousand surgeries without anesthesia.

A Dr. *Dering*, a practicing doctor in London, sued Uris for defamation of character. He said that he had been arrested by the gestapo in 1940 for being part of the Polish underground army and had operated on ninety people in the camps, removing their sex organs. Dering, who was not Jewish, made it through the war alive and arrived in England in 1946. The case went to trial at Queen's Bench Seven (QB VII) at the Old Bailey.

He won the case on a technicality, but he was awarded only one halfpenny damage because the truth was that he had worked in the experimental unit under Nazi doctor Mengele. The name Dering was changed to Kelno by the screenplay writer Edward Anhalt, so any further trouble there was avoided.

I was shown a rough cut and found that the voice of Jack Hawkins, a childhood hero of mine and a great favorite of my father's, had been dubbed. He played the judge, but his voice was weak from surgery for throat cancer. The issue was that they'd used an American actor. I objected, so they asked if I would do it. I knew Jack Hawkins's voice as well as I knew my own, so I did the dubbing for the whole film. My father was more impressed with that than nearly anything else I'd done—and he actually got to meet Jack Hawkins to boot.

Once *QB VII* was finished, in 1973, I wasn't sure I'd be offered any more work. Certainly not in Britain. But then, out of left field, I was called about a role in a film called *The Girl from Petrovka*, starring Goldie Hawn and Hal Holbrook. The filming started in Vienna, then moved to Hollywood. The only glitch? Vladimir Radzhenko, a Russian dialect coach on the film, introduced me to tequila. I found it to be the answer to all my problems—that is, until I began to hallucinate and go slowly mad. One shot and I'd feel the monster start to cross the room toward me. Two and the invisible monster would creep up my legs into my body. And then this other personality would come out, a vindictive, cynical, insulting, horrible man who burned bridges and hurt feelings.

And yet somehow, good fortune still seemed to come my way. I worked a lot in the early 1970s, and usually my slight wildness paid off with performances of which I was proud.

In 1973, I starred in *A Doll's House* with Claire Bloom, over whom everyone on set would fawn. There's a scene late in the film where I'm supposed to go berserk. On our set, there was a Christmas tree with glass ornaments on it.

"May I break an ornament?" I asked the director.

"Break what you want," he said. No interest. "Do you want to rehearse it?"

"No—why don't we just shoot it?" I said. "Where's the camera angle?" I gathered some more information about the blocking.

Rolling.

I threw the Christmas tree onto the piano and smashed every ornament on the tree.

Claire screamed—a genuine scream, I believed, of shock and alarm.

Cut, print.

I got a round of applause.

One of the props guys said, "God, that woke everyone up."

With every role I took, I felt that I was growing as an actor and becoming more comfortable on camera. And yet there was still so much about my real life that I was unable to face, even when the universe was hitting me over the head with it.

In *The Arcata Promise*, a televised drama with a cast of three, I played Theodore Gunge, an alcoholic actor. The other roles were played by the great Canadian Kate Nelligan and the wonderful British actor John Fraser. It was my last acting job in Britain before taking off to New York, and the similarity to my own life was uncanny.

The actor, Theo, lives alone in the shabby basement of a London house. His once successful career as a classical actor is over. Alcoholism has wiped him out. Theo's invisible companion is his own delusional voice, his split self. The voice never stops berating him, attacking him for his willful self-destruction. A woman he loved has dumped him. Theo blames everyone but himself. He is not the culprit. The world is out to get him. Alcoholism is the dictator that drives him to self-pitying despair. In a violent argument about his drinking, Theo shouts: "I can stop drinking any time!"

His companion yells back: "Then why don't you stop?"

"Because I don't want to!"

Those two lines hit me in the head.

That's me! I thought.

During rehearsal, I looked at the director, David Cunliffe, and said, "This is kind of close to home."

"You're right, Tony," said David. "This is your life. Good luck."

A moment of recognition. Something was wrong. But I had no idea what to do about it.

We began shooting on a Friday in the ATV Studio in Leeds. At 9:00 a.m., I took my first slug of scotch. At 9:15 a.m., I took my second. I learned later that the producer Peter Willes had placed a hundred-pound bet with David that I wouldn't get through the performance. Peter lost the bet. I got through the whole recording session without a hitch. The defiant willpower of the insane.

Looking back, I take no pride in this. I feel only deep sadness. How many lives are destroyed and damaged by drunks? To think now about how many other people—my costars, the director, the producers, the gaffers, my agents—were counting on me to get through that shoot. How cavalier I was with their time and talent. How, for lack of a better word, *rude*. The appalling arrogance of the alcoholic is matchless. But my ability to deny reality was coming to an end.

This is from the film's final speech:

LAURA: I stayed with you because I loved you. I endured you because I couldn't imagine life without you. I feel battered. Ignored. Belittled . . . You drink. You talk. You dominate. You rant. You rave . . . I admire your acting and respect it as much as anybody else does. But I'm not just a servicing arrangement to your needs. I'm something else. And I'm going to find out what that is. [*Laura turns to leave.*]

That would be a foreshadowing of many conversations soon to come in my own life.

One night in London before I moved to New York, the chaplain of the studio saw me in a bar by the set. As usual, I was drinking alone.

"Cheers," he said, and pointed at my drink. "I used to drink that stuff."

"You did?"

"Yeah. What is that?"

"Whiskey. Want one?"

"No, no. I used to drink that stuff, though."

I looked at my drink and saw my own reflection in it. I was an egotistic brute—young, atheistic, arrogant. The padre, kind and calm, gestured again to my whiskey and said, without any evangelism but as a statement of fact, as if talking about the weather: "That'll kill you."

Then he walked away. I took another sip and put him completely out of my mind.

One afternoon when I was in Vienna, Jenni called me at my hotel to tell me that a person was coming to Austria to see me.

"Who?" I asked. "Why would anyone fly anywhere to see me?"

"John Dexter," she replied.

"John *Dexter*?" I couldn't believe it. "Is he coming to arrest me?"

"He wants you to be in his New York production of *Equus*."

"Why me?" I asked. (*Equus*, in which a boy who blinded six horses with a metal spike is sent to a psychiatrist, is a play about insanity. Once again, I could relate to the material.)

"He's arriving on Saturday. He wants to talk to you. That's all I know. Will you meet him?"

"OK. Where?" I asked.

"A restaurant near the opera house."

On Saturday, I went to the restaurant and met the sinister Dexter.

His first question: "Why did you walk out of my production?"

"Because you were a nasty little bastard. That's why," I replied.

"Yes, dear, well, you need a nasty little bastard like me to direct you."

"Why?"

"Because you are a much better actor than you think you are. And you can be much better than anyone. You just have a head full of Welsh saboteurs. They're all eating away at you. They make you the drunk that you are. You'll end up like that other Welsh lunatic Dylan Thomas or your buddy Richard Burton."

"How many times do I have to tell you—Burton's not my buddy! Why must everyone always—"

"Yes, well, you're all bloody mad. Larry told me to say hello. He says I'm insane to even think of casting you. Maybe I am.

So, are you interested? New York next year. Start rehearsing in September."

He made no promise that he would be less spiteful. He was the same man he'd always been. But by then, I knew I wouldn't tolerate disrespect, and so did he. And the truth is, he was a great director. I'd learned that I far preferred the tough directors who knew what they wanted to the arrogant and incompetent. Dexter had vision and he worked extremely hard. His frequent greeting to actors who came to audition for him was "So, what are you going to thrill us with today?" It was sardonic but also genuine. He longed to be thrilled by a great performance.

As I came to know him better, I discovered that he'd suffered a great deal in life. He'd joined the army at the age of fourteen to serve in World War II, suffered from polio while a soldier, and had health troubles his whole life. (He died at the age of sixty-four during heart surgery, leaving no known survivors. In a memoir published posthumously, he complained of how hard it was at times to find work because he was "difficult, British, homosexual, expensive—and whilst I can, with modified rapture, admit to the first three charges, the last is deeply wounding." I found him to be troubled and quick to anger but a big softy underneath.)

"OK, I'll do it," I said.

We shook hands, and the dreaded Dexter returned to London the next morning.

A week later, shooting of the Goldie Hawn movie moved to Hollywood's Universal Studios. It would be my first trip to California. I kept thinking back to when I was four and had a severe case of pneumonia. (One little kid down the road had died from it.) And while I was lying in bed, the radio played Bing Crosby's "California, Here I Come." In my hallucinations, I imagined being there. Little did I know that one day I'd actually go.

A big limo picked Jenni and me up at the airport in LA. It was raining and I couldn't see the city very well through the fog. The driver dropped us at the Sunset Marquis hotel on Alta Loma near Sunset Boulevard.

The next morning I got up and went down to the pool area for breakfast. I had never seen sunshine so bright.

"Where's Grauman's Chinese Theatre?" I asked someone at the front desk. "I'd like to see the Hollywood Walk of Fame."

He pointed to Sunset and told me to turn right and walk about an hour. I left Jenni back at the hotel and went walking alone along Sunset. Even with sunglasses on, I was blinded by the brightness of the place. I stopped into the Brown Derby and got a tequila. I looked at all the stars on the Walk of Fame and the handprints of my heroes. On my way back, I heard the sound of cop cars and saw lights flashing.

I saw a bunch of officers swarm a man in a parking lot just ahead of me.

"Drop the knife!" shouted one of the cops.

"Keep moving!" another shouted to the people on the sidewalk. So I kept walking by, and then I heard *pop, pop, pop!* Gunshots. Screams.

"What just happened?" I said to an officer who'd cordoned off the area.

He shrugged. "Where are you from?" he said, noticing my accent.

"Wales by way of England," I said.

"Welcome to the United States," he said, and smirked.

That was California in the 1970s. I couldn't get over the sunshine and the madness of it all. Everything looked like something from an acid trip. I was in paradise.

Once when I had a day off, I took a tour of a theater in Pasadena, and none other than Bing Crosby was sitting on the stage, rehearsing with some kids. He looked more like my father than ever. (That same afternoon, Crosby fell through a trapdoor; I later heard Bob Hope joke that he fell off his wallet.) So it all felt very much like a fever dream.

A block away from my hotel was Dean Martin's classic bar, Dino's Lodge, on the Sunset Strip. I sat there most nights drinking my tequila until they kicked me out. I kept hoping Dean Martin would come in and have a drink with me, but he never did.

One day, a successful publicity man took me out to lunch at a very fashionable place in West Hollywood. He was everything I could not stand, and he told me that my career needed a boost.

"It's a small town," he said. "You've got to be seen at the parties. You're not on the circuit. You've got to be seen around. You know, you've got to meet . . ."

I began to feel ill.

Outside, a star passed by in his Rolls-Royce.

"Going to parties is how you get that car," the publicity man said. "You're not seen on the scene," he said. "You should be seen in the places where people matter."

By the end of the lunch, I was depressed. Was that really what I had to do to make it in Hollywood—go to swank parties and be photographed at high-end restaurants? It was the last thing I wanted to do. The thought of going to parties and premieres . . . I'd rather have my fingernails pulled out.

That afternoon I had to take a script to ICM. Sybil Williams, Richard Burton's ex-wife, was there. She'd become a literary agent after divorcing Richard.

"How are you?" she asked. "You look glum."

I told her about the publicity man.

"Oh God, what did he tell you?" she asked.

"That I should go out more."

"Don't," she said. "Richard did that. He was drunk all the time. It's a terrible life. Hollywood's a nightmare place if you play the game its way. It'll kill you. Play the piano, go home, be with Jenni, write, draw, whatever you want to do, but don't listen to that man. Phone him from me and say you're not interested in his help."

I did, and I was flooded with relief. And the next day I was offered a role in David Lynch's *The Elephant Man* with John Gielgud, Anne Bancroft, and John Hurt—without ever being "seen on the scene."

I phoned Sybil and I told her about the work I'd gotten.

"There you are," she said. "See? You let go of what other people tell you to do, and suddenly work comes to you on a plate."

fifteen

NEW YORK

New York in 1974 was hardly in its heyday, but to me it was a wonderland. The magical bars stayed open until four in the morning. And when I went to buy cigarettes and asked for Benson & Hedges, I was told, "We have sixty-six versions. Which one do you want?"

I got to sit in on a class taught by acting guru Lee Strasberg; he was guiding Shelley Winters (of *The Poseidon Adventure* and *A Place in the Sun*!) and Eli Wallach (of *The Misfits* and *The Magnificent Seven*!) through a scene. I also met one of his rival acting teachers, Stella Adler. She told me over drinks one night at a bar that I had to be a tyrant. "You have to be a killer in this business. You have to know exactly what you're doing." It was a refrain I heard again and again. Kate Hepburn and Peter O'Toole at various points each said, "You've got to be tough in this business." To paraphrase what a certain guy said two thousand years ago, you need to be as gentle as a lamb but as cunning as a serpent—or they'll get you.

I'd never felt surer of myself as an actor, although I was also going to increasing extremes to feel in control of myself as a person.

One day when I was in New York on the way to *Equus* rehearsals, the actor Michael Higgins saw me and witnessed a weird ritual of mine. Every morning, as I went from my apartment on Fifth Avenue to the Lyceum Theatre, I felt compelled to walk on the curb. Sometimes I'd step off the curb to walk in the gutter.

"I noticed you this morning stepping off the sidewalk into the street," Michael said later. "Are you nuts? You could get killed. Why don't you walk on the sidewalk?"

My reply was equally nuts: "I prefer it that way. I'm not good in crowds of people."

Michael asked me if I suffered from agoraphobia.

"What's that?" I asked.

"Fear of open places," Michael replied.

I could never confess the real reason—I thought someone might have me locked up—but it was this: I was afraid that someone would do a suicide jump from a high window, fall on top of me, and kill me. As with any phobia, it made no sense logically. The odds were strongly against my being crushed by a falling body. And yet versions of this same fear had been with me since I was little. When I was three, I often became afraid that our house was collapsing on top of me and I would flee to the garden.

Now, though, I was a full-grown adult living in a major city and starring in a major play. I had to keep it together.

The four-week rehearsal process for *Equus* took place at the Lyceum Theatre, and the play would be performed at the Plymouth Theatre; it opened on Thursday, October 24. The cast was Peter Firth as the boy who blinds the horses, Marian Seldes as the magistrate, and Frances Sternhagen and Michael Higgins as the boy's parents.

John Dexter was in peak form, lacerating the cast with his vicious tongue. The American cast members were shocked, but they got used to it. And I knew the drill and how to handle it. I retreated into dumb insolence. He couldn't get at me there. Plus, he knew I'd walk out if he pushed me too hard. Peter Shaffer, the creator of this strange play, was all smiles. He enjoyed the spectacle. The first few days went swimmingly.

Marian Seldes of the so-called New York theater aristocracy was full of professional grace. She offered me a tour of the Metropolitan and Guggenheim museums. All the culture-vulture stuff. I reciprocated by showing her my favorite drinking dens. She protested that she never drank liquor. I worked my Welsh charm on her and she agreed to try it. In no time, she got plastered on sake and lost both her shoes. After that, John Dexter warned her: "Don't go with him anywhere. And I mean *anywhere*! He'll get you killed."

The play opened and the audience loved it. There was a big party at Sardi's, the traditional place where actors wait for the New York press to say yea or nay. Clive Barnes, the capricious god of the *New York Times*, the Robespierre of the press corps, could behead any promising show with a slash of his guillotine pen, even close a play on its first night.

In that cavernous restaurant, a few of us got tanked up and legless. Other opening-night audience members were there—Sybil with her new rock-star husband, Jordan Christopher (whom she married after Richard Burton left her for Elizabeth Taylor), and her pal Lauren Bacall.

My mother and father were there. This was their first trip to New York. My father got weepy. He couldn't believe his wayward boy had come this far in life. My mother and Sybil greeted each other with loud Welsh warmth and tears.

"Mrs. Hopkins, who would have thought it possible!" Sybil said to Muriel. "I used to come into your shop on Commercial Road to buy cake. Richie loved your doughnuts and jam tarts."

More tears and wonder.

Also in attendance was another Welsh woman by the name of Rachel Roberts. She had been married to Rex Harrison and never recovered from their divorce. Rachel and I got smashed. (That was my only encounter with her. Years later, I heard of her painful suicide at her home in Los Angeles.)

A copy of the *New York Times* arrived, hot off the press. Our director hushed us all. As he read, the room gradually grew more and more excited. The show was a triumph! We were guaranteed an eight-month run on Broadway. Cheers went up around the bar. We had job security for more than half a year. Cause for a round of drinks! We drank almost as much as we would have if we'd been panned.

In January 1975, during the *Equus* run, I found myself suddenly unable to walk due to a severe pain in the calf of my right leg. A doctor examined me at Mount Sinai Hospital. Diagnosis: thrombosis.

"Is it serious?" I asked the doctor as he sat behind his desk jotting some notes on a pad.

"Oh, yes," he said. "It can kill you." He continued his jottings and, without looking up, told me calmly how close I was to death. "One stray blood clot to the brain can paralyze you, and a clot to the heart can kill you."

He looked up, saw my shocked look, and smiled. He checked his notes. "I'm going to confine you to this hospital for at least a week, probably longer," he said.

"But you can't do that," I protested. "I'm in a play on Broadway."

He smiled at me again. "Yes, I know. My wife and I came to see you three weeks ago. *Equus*, right?"

"Right."

"You were quite good. We thought the young boy was excellent. What was his name? Peter . . ."

"Firth."

"Firth. Yes, of course." The doctor picked up the phone on his desk and called someone. "Nurse? It's Dr. Rosenthal. Yes, to my office . . . Yes, a patient. Thank you, nurse." He replaced the phone. Another smile.

"Yes, my wife and I are keen theatergoers. Well, at least my wife is. So we go to various plays. After the play, we sometimes go to Charlie's on Forty-Fifth Street for a light meal. Of course you know Charlie's, don't you? My wife pointed you out to me. You apparently enjoy the atmosphere in that noisy bar. It seems to me that you are quite the social drinker."

I had no idea what this conversation was leading to.

Dr. Rosenthal looked back at his notes. Then he gave me yet another smile.

"I see here in your records that you are thirty-seven."

"Correct."

"Born December thirty-first, 1937, in Wales. Correct?"

"Yes."

"It's interesting, because even brief physical tests on your reflexes and heart and lungs indicate the physical condition of a man of fifty or perhaps even sixty-five years of age. How about that?" Another smile.

"So what does that mean?" I asked the good doctor.

"Well, you are now a statistic. Men and women who live the social life that you seem to enjoy rarely make it to sixty. Some do. But this is a medical statistic. You get my drift?"

I nodded.

There was a knock on the office door.

"Come in, nurse."

A young woman came in. She was British. Fair-haired and smilingly pleasant.

Dr. Rosenthal introduced me to Nurse Blakely.

"I was just explaining to Mr. Hopkins that we all enjoy social events—a little fun and celebration here and there—and why not? But an excess can be dangerous. Would you agree, nurse?"

"Agreed, Doctor." The woman nodded and smiled at me.

What was this? A conspiracy?

"Yes, of course. Nurse Blakely will tell you from her own experience in the medical profession about the numbers and the alarming toll of premature deaths from smoking, overeating, and drinking."

They both smiled at me as if I were half-witted. This *was* a conspiracy. They were both ganging up on me. The story of my life.

"So, Nurse, everything is ready?"

"Yes, Dr. Rosenthal."

Ready? Are they going to strap me into a straitjacket?

Dr. Rosenthal told me that the *Equus* producers had been given the news that I was not fit to continue in the play for a week or two. Jenni had also been given the report. I heard she took the news calmly, as if she'd known it was inevitable. It wouldn't have surprised me if she had wished upon me an early death. I couldn't blame her for any ill will she had toward me. I was no use to anyone, and that wasn't self-pity but something even worse: a terrible depression that felt terminal. Lying in the hospital bed, I recalled the scene from *Days of Wine and Roses* in which Lee Remick says that the world looked so dirty without a drink.

The following afternoon, Dr. Rosenthal checked in on me. He was wearing a white raincoat, probably on his way home to his theater-loving wife. Rain started to fall and began pattering on the windows. The room was bathed in a faint yellow light.

I had been placed on an intravenous blood thinner. My full test results were in, and there were no more smiles from the doctor.

"You have the beginning of liver problems. Could turn into cirrhosis. Also inflammation of the pancreas, and your lungs are becoming congested. I strongly advise you to stop smoking immediately. Smoking is deadlier than alcohol. It causes stasis in the arteries and veins. Alcohol in excess is also a killer. I don't need to tell you that. You already know. So, my friend, it's up to you."

He paused and stared at me.

"What puzzles me and what puzzles so many of my colleagues in this business is why people who seem to have everything in life—success or wealth or fame or whatever it is; I don't know, but something that most people would kill for—why do the lucky ones start ripping themselves apart?"

There was a silence. It was now raining heavily outside and that added to the Manhattan gloom.

"Sad, but there you go," the doctor said to end the conversation. He checked his watch.

That was the last I saw of the good doctor.

My memories of that time are foggy. During my drinking years I had caused a lot of pain. I never had any idea that I was an alcoholic. Rarely does a heavy drinker wake up to that without an intervention of some kind, and even then it takes a while to sink in. Denial is the greatest killer. And I was still in the grips of my addiction, though it was getting harder to deny it.

Mary Doyle was in the cast of *Equus*. She was an Irish New Yorker and lots of fun. She laughed at my irreverent attitude to everything. I didn't know anything about Mary's history. She told me she had once been a falling-down drunk, along with her husband, Jack, who also had a bad case of the devil's brew. Both had stopped drinking and been dry for five years. I noticed that *sober* was the word they used.

Toward the end of my contractual eight-month run in *Equus*, I'd decided to quit New York and go elsewhere. Universal Studios in Los Angeles had made me an offer, and I felt I couldn't turn that down. Keep moving. The Grim Reaper can't catch a moving target.

Six weeks before I was due to fly off to California, the production organized a party for the cast and crew at a swank Manhattan club. I didn't remember a minute of it. Mary was at the party. The next day, waking up with a pounding hangover, I asked her if we could meet. I needed help. She agreed, and we met for lunch. Mercifully, Mary didn't push anything on me.

There was no holier-than-thou rhetoric or preachy stuff, just the bare truth about alcoholism.

I told her that I couldn't believe she had ever been a rip-roaring drunk. She laughed and promised she wasn't lying. She and a few of her acting buddies had always been in trouble—fights with the police and lockups and jail time. I thought Mary's account was an exaggeration, some bravado bending of the truth.

"You'd better believe it. It's all true and even worse."

She described the nature of alcoholism, how it worked and how powerful it was once it got a grip on the sufferer.

"It sounds like you're talking about the devil or some invisible beast," I said.

"Oh, yes, it is," said Mary. "That's a good image. Hold on to that. It *is* a beast."

As far as she knew, there was no cure, and, worse, it was progressive and terminal. *If there is no cure*, I thought, *why am I sitting in this cramped little coffee bar asking her for help?*

"I'm confused," I told her. "Totally confused. What is it? A disease?"

"Yes. It's a threefold illness," Mary replied. "Mental, physical, and emotional."

It sounded dramatic, and this was something *I* had?

She went on to explain the nature of compulsions and obsessions. I knew all about those. They were more than familiar to me—anxious fixations on details, times, and dates in any year, clear and anxious memories of conversations and situations. They were irritating but I didn't think they were harmful. On the contrary, they were productive! I could memorize poems and recite them at rapid speed.

It was at RADA that I realized my ability to note details—a mechanical process, a photographic memory—was not common to all actors; it was special. Where did a certain person live? What day of the week was April 1, 1955? I could tell you all of it. How many steps were there in my apartment building? It was a technical mechanism, something like having my very own calculating machine. I was grateful for any opportunity to quiet down my brain, and I think that was what made me so enthusiastic about drinking. Not that I needed a reason. Everyone drank. It was the national pastime!

I told Mary all this. She talked to me about our incurable and insatiable need for peace and freedom from unidentified fear and anxiety. I vaguely caught on to that idea. I had read Carlos Castaneda's books on peyote. I understood that sort of tranquility in an intellectual way, but beyond that, I was not convinced.

I told her that I didn't think I was an alcoholic, that I could stop drinking anytime I wanted to. Mary never pushed it further.

"Fine. Maybe you're not an alcoholic. But anytime you want to talk, just say the word."

"Thanks a lot. I'll be fine."

But the things she'd said haunted me. *Terminal?* Was that the word she'd used?

No. Impossible. I knew so many people, especially in this acting business, who drank all the time, even more than I did. Were they all alcoholics? Of course not. They functioned beyond well. They were hugely successful and highly gifted. So much for Mary Doyle. After all, Mary Doyle was Irish, and the Irish were notorious drinkers. I'd never known an Irishman or an Irishwoman who didn't drink. Come to think about it, I'd never known a Welshman who didn't enjoy a tipple occasionally. It was all part of the creative process.

Still, it wouldn't do me any harm to stop drinking for a few weeks. Well, perhaps not give it up totally. *Cut out the whiskeys and tequilas. Stick to beer. That's the spirit. Common sense. Yeah. I'll show Mary and her husband and the rest of them. Bunch of Bible-thumpers. How can I be part of such a group, or any group? I'll do it my way.*

The last night of my involvement in *Equus* was the end of June. The actor Anthony Perkins—Norman Bates himself— had rehearsed to take over. I was invited to producer Kermit Bloomgarden's Central Park West apartment for a farewell party for me and a welcome party for Mr. Perkins.

I had been what is called "white-knuckled" dry, no drinking for two weeks. That was proof enough that I was not an alcoholic! Mary Doyle was at the party. She noticed me hovering around the table of liquor. She came over to me.

"Are you OK?" she asked.

"*Yeah, I'm fine!*" I replied aggressively.

"Just asking."

Reformed alcoholics are a pain in the ass, I thought.

As she walked away, I looked down at my sad glass of Coca-Cola. *Why not pour a bit of scotch into it?* I thought. *Pep it up a bit. Let's have some fun! I've been dead long enough.*

And that was the last thing I remembered of that party. The rest of the night was a total blackout. Next morning, Jenni and I were in a cab on our way to JFK Airport. We were flying to Los Angeles. I'd been given a part in a TV film called *Dark Victory*, a remake of the old Warner Brothers classic. I stared out the window of the car in shock from the extent of the blackout. *What did I do? What did I say? How can I not remember?*

Next to me, Jenni was silent. I wondered why she put up with me. I thought about asking her to tell me what had happened at the party but then I thought that perhaps I did not want to know.

Laura's speech from *The Arcata Promise* came back to me. There were no more excuses. I was a deadbeat. I had always been a deadbeat. Why not jump out of the cab and onto the Van Wyck Expressway? End it all.

It would be some time, though, before I hit bottom. That came once we'd relocated out West. Booze is fine if you can keep it in check; I believe it can help you through certain awkward situations, be part of a joyful life. But there's a cost. The fun of drinking is a scorpion—its tail is lethal.

C. S. Lewis said, from deep within himself, "We may ignore, but we can nowhere evade, the presence of God. The world is crowded with him. He walks everywhere incognito."

Well, He was with me one Saturday night when I drove my car in a drunken blackout through Beverly Hills. I'd driven that car all night from Arizona without knowing what I was doing. I could have killed someone. I could have taken out a whole family. I found out what I'd done when I went to my agent and said, "Someone's stolen my car!" and my agent said, "Nobody stole it. We found you on the road. You would be in jail right now if we hadn't."

As I sobered up, I looked up at the eucalyptus trees and thanked God no one had died that night. I imagined my parents back in Wales hearing that I'd killed someone or myself. I saw their hopes smashed. I heard a voice ask me, *Do you want to live or do you want to die?*

WE DID OK, KID

I want to live, a voice answered from somewhere deep inside me.

Then I heard the voice say, *It's all over now. You can start living.*

The craving to drink left me. That was eleven o'clock on December 29, 1975. What grace the universe showed me in that moment. How lucky I am to have found clarity at last, to say that I would do everything in my power and call on all other sources of power to never again have a night I didn't remember, to never again get behind the wheel and endanger others, to never again let that monster creep across the room and up my leg, making me cruel and cold.

"I'm an alcoholic and I need help," I told my agent. He got me the time off I needed to focus on getting treatment.

The tradition I belong to suggests that it's much better to change lives one person at a time by helping them one on one rather than by crowing to the world about having found a cure for one's affliction. This is known in the rooms as attraction rather than promotion. And so I will say only that if you're starting to wake up to the ways in which alcohol is ruining your life, as I did to the ways it was ruining mine, there are people out there who will take you out for coffee. You can find them in every city and town at every hour of the day. I still go to meetings now myself, almost fifty years after getting sober.

The day after my revelation, I went out for lunch with my friend Bob Palmer, who brought along his friend George. They were going to take me to my first Twelve Step meeting.

I was in a state of shock because the urge to drink had gone.

I saw a waiter carrying a tray with a glass of red wine across the room. *How strange that I used to drink that*, I thought.

"How are you feeling?" Bob asked.

"Inadequate."

He said, "You are."

That floored me. He explained that I had so little power, I was unable to predict what would happen in the next three minutes. Therein lay terror but also freedom if we accepted it.

At the first AA meeting I attended, I was moved by the speaker's story. *He's just like me*, I thought. He was a truck driver, not an actor, but we were the same. I had something in common with everyone in that room: We were drunks, and we didn't want to drink anymore. I thought, *They're all misfits like me. Like all of us. We feel we never belong. We feel self-hatred. All of us are the same. I'm not alone.*

I sought Bob's advice often. He told me, "Just stay calm. Keep it simple. Go to meetings. Stay in contact. Phone me every day if you want. Avoid the gurus and the mystics. You're just human with lots of faults. So are we all. Take your time with the steps. Enjoy the work. Enjoy the coffee. Enjoy this moment."

The message clicked at last. I wanted to fight my weakness. I didn't want help. The old ego was trying to run the show. But then the other side, the sensible part of me, said, *Just lie down now and shut up. Let somebody help you up.*

I thought of an old gag: A shark says to a fish, "Isn't the water a bit warm today?" And the fish says, "What's water?" Because I was suddenly learning so much about what was around me that I'd never noticed before. And once I accepted it rather than staying in denial, everything in my life changed.

On one of the early days of my recovery, I was driving through Los Angeles when I felt called to pull over to a Catholic church. There I found a young Black priest going into his office.

"Can I talk to you a minute?" I asked.

He said, "Yeah, come in. How can I help you?"

I said, "I found God."

"Congratulations," he said. "It's called grace. You had to choose between life and death, and you chose life. God was there all the time asking you that question. He was just waiting for you to make up your mind."

That was a message I needed to hear, and I was so grateful that I found people to tell me the same thing again and again.

A friend of mine in the rooms told me, "Alcoholics are the worst. We will fight to the end for victory over the booze. Once you give up *fighting* everything, you can live again."

If you *fight* alcoholism, it'll kill you. You have to accept that you are an alcoholic and you are flawed. Once you accept that weakness in yourself, you can breathe. And you gather a support group around you of damaged souls who, like you, are trying not to drink. Some of them have been trying to stay sober for a day, others for decades. Together, we help one another make it through another day of sobriety.

When such people sit across from you at a diner or a coffee shop and tell you what they know, at first they may infuriate you, as Mary did me. When you are a drunk, you will very likely find it extremely irritating when people try to save your life.

I went back to Mount Sinai years later to thank Dr. Rosenthal for setting me on the path to sobriety, but I couldn't find him.

Wherever you are, Dr. Rosenthal, you have my thanks and gratitude.

sixteen

THE SHIP INN

Getting sober changed me as an actor. Before that, I thought I was the boss. But admitting that I needed help was a humbling experience. My first sober job was in Europe, playing Lieutenant Colonel John Frost in the World War II film *A Bridge Too Far*. In one scene, German soldiers try to surrender to Frost, and he tells them to go to hell. In another, my character politely commandeers a house. The whole time we were filming, I was having an out-of-body experience, thinking, *How the hell am I still alive?*

In 1978 I was cast in a BBC TV film called *Kean*, by Jean-Paul Sartre. Sartre was one of my favorite authors and I was thrilled. I flew to London and found a place to stay. On Monday I took the Tube to the North Acton BBC rehearsal room and met the director and cast. We gathered around the usual reading table. I took notice of one of the other actors, Julian Fellowes. He was a studious young "actor chap." He barely spoke and appeared indifferent and mildly disdainful, and he was obviously extremely smart.

The reading turned out to be pretty good. After lunch we started to work on the first scene. Blocking is the director's moment to take control of the cast. It is a vitally important operation; without blocking, there is a chaos of traffic jams and collisions.

Within three minutes I picked up on something that was profoundly depressing: The director had, as far as I could tell, neglected to do a jot of preparation. He seemed to have no notion of directing anything.

I had traveled five thousand miles, paying my own way, and now I had a quick decision to make: Walk out and fly five thousand miles back home or stay and adopt the British stiff upper lip.

After rehearsal, as I was walking out of the building, Julian Fellowes offered me a lift. When he dropped me off at my new digs in Redcliffe Gardens, I asked him if he'd like to come inside to meet Jenni.

Over coffee, he asked a probing question: "So what do you think of this outfit? The read-through this morning and this afternoon's so-called rehearsal?"

Jenni asked Julian, "Why? Did something go wrong?"

Julian laughed. "Yes. It was a disaster. The director is one of those lazy con men who cherish their precious fatheadedness—you know, 'Let's all have some jolly fun.' Your husband looked as if he might kill the man." He turned to me. "True or false?"

"Yes, true," I confessed.

"I don't know you, Tony—may I call you Tony?—and you can tell me to leave if you don't like what I am about to say, but do you know why this whole thing is a mess?"

"No. Why?"

"You."

"What do you mean?"

"Why do you play Mr. Nice Guy? You are so polite and tolerant. The director hadn't done his homework, there was no preparation, and his job was to prepare and create a semblance of order. He does nothing, and you, you just go along with it as if afraid to rock the boat."

"Do I come across like that?" I asked.

"Yes, and you know you do," replied Mr. Fellowes. "It's a game. You can't play those games. You are too good an actor for that. I don't know you but I've watched you in the theater and in films. You are not what you pretend to be. False modesty. You're a killer. You can't pretend otherwise. Own it and claim it and enjoy it.

"As for this charlatan director we are meant to be working with, either walk or change the rules of the game. He's playing by his rules, the utter-indifference game. And you have every right to walk away, or you can start playing by your own rules. Don't forget, actors are generally despised, some perhaps for good reason, but most are despised due to other people's envy. It's your face that's been up there on the film screen and not theirs. You know what I mean. Anyway, it is rather bold of me to offer unasked-for advice."

I knew in that moment that I wanted us to be friends for life.

The chaos at the theater prevailed, but I spoke up for myself. Things got better. After getting sober, I noticed the difference. No fights this time. No tantrums. Just a quiet leave-taking and a relieved flight back home. And when I got back, I felt that I no longer had any time to waste.

In those years after getting sober, I had a lot of reckoning to do. And I faced constant reminders of how bad it had been. I met a former waiter who said, "When you came in to the restaurant, I always gave you half measures because you drank so much. I was trying to help you."

I can't imagine how I didn't notice my drinks were watered down. If I had noticed, I surely would have started a fight. I had very few friends and I could turn very nasty. And that's the ugly side of alcoholism. It brought out a brutal monster side of me. I am not proud of it at all. And I take full responsibility for it because I had no idea what was happening to my unsettled self.

And yet, that same propulsive energy was part of what helped me to succeed. I just had to get it under control and direct it toward the good or it would have killed me, and it surely would have continued to make life hell for other people. I've worked with some brutally talented actors who are wonderful but who killed themselves drinking. And the ones who lived, you could see on their faces the toll drinking took. The dissipation.

Richard Burton, my hero, was one person who struggled with it. Amazingly, he took over for Tony Perkins after Perkins took over for me in *Equus*. I was in New York in 1976 doing publicity for an NBC TV show about the Lindbergh kidnapping (I played the alleged kidnapper). I'd been living in Los Angeles for about a year, and it was strange to be back in New York. I asked the *Equus* stage manager, Bob Borod, if I could stop by to say hello to Richard and wish him luck.

"Yes, Richard knows you're in town," Bob said.

A few hours later Jenni and I called at the stage door of the Plymouth Theatre. Bob greeted me and introduced me to Brook Williams, Richard Burton's loyal assistant. He was warm in his welcome to Jenni, and seemed pleased to meet me. As we were going up the stairs to the familiar dressing room, Brook muttered: "Elizabeth is in the front of house tonight and Richard is nervous. The paparazzi are everywhere. The play opens tomorrow night. This is our last public preview." Richard Burton and Elizabeth Taylor had married not long before for the second time.

We were shown to Richard's dressing room. It was the same one I had occupied for eight months. Richard graciously greeted us. He looked drawn and haggard. He had sworn off liquor a few weeks before. Sitting in a lotus position on the dressing table was a tall, beautiful woman who looked as if she were mummified by coils of white fabric from head to foot.

"This is Susan," said Richard. "She is Brook's lady."

The mummified woman made no response other than a slight nod. I took her to be looking down her nose at us.

How weird these people are, I thought. *What is wrong with them? Are they all unhinged? Do they really believe themselves to be of any significance? They are actors. Clowns. Entertainers. Nothing more.*

"You're from Port Talbot?" Richard said.

"Yes," I said. "I came to see you on Caradoc Street."

"Good God, what a memory," he said. "I remember you. Yes, from the baker's shop. Good Lord, why haven't we worked together?"

"I don't know," I said.

"I want to ask you something. How the hell did you learn all those rhymes?" he said, referring to our part in *Equus*. "Good God. Are you coming to the show tonight?"

"I can't get tickets."

"Thank God for that," he said. "My wife is coming. Elizabeth. Let's get together sometime and make a film."

He gave Jenni a hug and shook my hand. His hand felt frail.

As we were leaving through the stage door, Elizabeth Taylor

came in with Kate, one of Richard's daughters with Sybil. They were escorted to their seats.

I later heard that was the night Taylor put two and two together about Suzy Hunt. The mummified lady was not Brook's lady; she was Richard's, and she was destined to be, at age twenty-six (about twenty-five years younger than Richard) the next Mrs. Burton. Taylor was tough. She knew something was going on, and that night she said, "Have a champagne, Richard."

He'd been off the sauce for a few weeks. He'd later say that his performance in *Equus* was the first time he was sober onstage. He had a bad problem. He'd started drinking at the age of eleven and would often drink a fifth of booze in the course of a performance.

"Alcoholism is a dreadful disease," he once said on *The Dick Cavett Show*. And yet he said he wasn't sure that he himself was an alcoholic. He died less than a decade later at the age of fifty-eight, and alcohol was a major contributing factor.

I knew many actors whom we called working alcoholics—they would be blotto drunk, but when they got jobs, they would dry out enough to do them. And as soon as the work ended, they'd start drinking again. I was surrounded by people who, whenever they were unemployed, were blotto drunk.

Sometimes the line between working and not working could get fuzzy, though. There's one movie I did, a terrible early 1970s film. I was talking to an actor who'd been in it with me and I said, "I don't remember doing that scene."

The other person said, "I don't either."

We concluded that no one in that movie could remember a minute of doing it; we'd all been blackout drunk.

When I kicked the booze and sobered up, I knew I owed

apologies to those I'd hurt. There were many cases in which I'd bitten the hand that fed me. I got in touch with former directors and colleagues. I was sick and tired of myself. I was sick to death of my cruelty. I couldn't change what I'd done, but I could at least do my best to acknowledge the behavior and vow not to do it anymore.

I wrote Laurence Olivier a long letter detailing my indiscretions, my bad behavior while I was drunk. He and Joan Plowright, his wife, wrote back to me, and I'll never forget one of the lines in their response. It was *Be so happy*. I would later talk to Larry about drinking. He loved the stuff so much that he asked me in awe, "How did you *ever* stop drinking?" He seemed genuinely mystified.

Kate Hepburn had hated all the drinking around her. It made her crazy in Humphrey Bogart and Spencer Tracy. Looking at everyone wasted during the filming of *Lion in Winter*, she'd said, "Goddamn, what's the matter with you English people?" So when I phoned her to say I'd stopped drinking, I was not surprised by her response: "Thank God for that."

Of course, the greatest apology of all was the one I owed to my only child and my first wife. In 1977, I contacted Petronella and Abigail, then nine, to try to make amends to them. They agreed to see me, and I flew to London.

The meeting was awkward. We put up a good front, but obviously so much damage had been done. They didn't want me there. Throughout the meal, they kept catching each other's eye and making faces.

Later, as a teenager, Abigail came to stay with me now and then, though she kept her hoodie up over her head much of the time—as teenagers will, I suppose. I helped her get small acting parts and I tried to make her feel as welcome as I could. I bought her an apartment. But she drifted away.

Abigail never seemed able to forgive me for leaving the family when she was a baby. She had her reasons. I can't blame her for that. That's life. But it was and is a tremendous source of pain.

Whenever my grandfather was asked about his daughter Jenny, who'd died as a little girl, he said, "The memory is too painful. I don't want to go back there."

I feel that way about being estranged from my daughter. It broke my heart. When I think about it, which I do as little as I can, I remember my grandfather teaching me to keep moving and not to dwell.

And yet, though I've avoided talking about it, the estrangement has shown up in tabloids in horrific, untrue ways. Some tabloids said I got her into drugs or rejected her as a child. It is true that I have spoken about her in the press coldly, saying in one regrettable interview that after twenty years of not hearing from her, I no longer knew where she was or if she'd ever married or had children, and that at that point I did not care. Though it's no excuse, I know that was the coldness of my grandfather coming out: *Move on! No use crying! Onward! Don't waste time in the past!*

That hardness is my default. As Charles Bukowski wrote, "We're all going to die, all of us, what a circus! That alone should make us love each other but it doesn't. We are terrorized and flattened by trivialities; we are eaten up by nothing."

I hope my daughter knows that my door is always open to her. I want her to be well and happy. Until the day I die, I will never forget the sight of her in that crib, laughing up at me when I walked in the room the first year of her life, sleeping soundly the night I left. I will always be sorry for hurting her when I left the family, even as I believe to this day that I had no choice.

In 1977, my parents came out to California and I was able to apologize to them for all the unhappiness and worry I had caused them. I was grateful for the chance to show them that sobriety had given me some peace at last and that I was doing OK—better, indeed, than I had any right to be doing.

I did my best to show my parents a wonderful time. They had both worked hard and I wanted them to have a break. I took them to Disneyland, the full tourist deal. I brought them to film locations to see movies being shot. We went to all the hot spots. They loved Grauman's Chinese Theatre, with the footprints and handprints of the old movie stars. At the Beverly Hills Polo Lounge, they met Roger Moore and Liza Minnelli.

One night, my agent, George Chasin, invited us to Chasen's chili restaurant on Beverly Boulevard for an informal fundraiser. George met us there. Standing next to him was John Wayne—the Duke himself. Mr. Wayne was gracious. He offered his hand to me: "Hey, kid, you're a heck of an actor." He looked at my father. "You're his dad? And you're Mrs. Hopkins?" He shook their hands. My father's eyes filled with tears, at which John Wayne gave him a one-armed shoulder hug.

More and more as he got older, my father became emotionally overwhelmed and broke down in tears. The Pacific Ocean filled him with awe. To my father, California was the impossible dream, and his only son had achieved it.

Dick and Muriel had thought I was useless and would never amount to anything. I'd showed them. As I spent more time with him, I began to see the ways in which I was my father's son. Dick had the same restlessness I did.

Each time I went to see him at the Ship Inn, I found him more easily agitated. As he got older, his moods became increasingly erratic. There were highs of manic energy followed by tearful remorse. He often felt lost and depressed and ashamed for feeling like that. He'd make a joke: "Look out, the crows are coming."

My father always felt lost and like a loser.

"Strange, ever since I was a boy, fourteen, working with my father in the bakehouse, I felt I'd never get it right," he told me.

"Get what right?" I asked him.

"Anything. You know what I mean? Just bloody get on with it. Don't look back, just keep rolling along, kicking the stupid rusty old can down the road, the same bloody old road. What's it all about, anyway? The whole bloody business. What the hell is it all about? Let's have a drink. Oh, right, you don't drink anymore. Don't you miss it?"

He resented my quitting and for good reason. Your drinking friends will often resent you for stopping. You're no fun anymore. And they feel that your choices are a silent judgment of theirs.

When he was in one of his upswings, my father saw the pub as his new lease on life. He was the star of his own show. His customers were his audience. He told them stories. He sang for them when he'd had a few drinks. He was a showman. He ignored the licensing laws by serving booze well after closing time, reciting verses from *The Rubaiyat of Omar Khayyám* for the die-hard drinkers who stayed late.

WE DID OK, KID

Come, fill the Cup.
What boots us to repeat?
Time is slipping beneath our feet.
Unborn tomorrow,
Dead yesterday.
Why fret about it, if today be sweet?

The Worldly Hope men set their Hearts upon
Turns Ashes—or it prospers, and anon.
Like Snow upon the Desert's dusty Face,
Lighting a little hour or two—is gone.
Come, fill the Cup, and in the fire of Spring!
Your Winter-garment of Repentance fling:
The Bird of Time has but a little way
To flutter—and the Bird is on the Wing.

There was a door to which I had no key.
There was a veil through which I could not see.
Some little talk awhile of Thee and Me,
And then no more of Thee and Me.

The last verse usually made him weepy. Through tears, he'd start goading the bar patrons: "Come on, drink up!"

My mother would say, "Oh God, here we go again. Dick, that's enough!"

He would ignore her. "Drink up! Come on, you bloody layabouts! Make the most of what we yet may spend before we too into the bloody dust descend! Whose round is it?"

My mother was afraid of his drinking and heavy smoking—two packs of cigarettes every day. When he got into the hard stuff like whiskey, he became unpredictable and argumentative.

"Hey, come on, Dickie Boy," she'd call out to him from down the bar, "you've had enough. Let these people go. They've got homes to go to."

Behind his cynicism, the old man was frail and sentimental. He drove my mother mad by playing two scratched old records over and over. One was Louis Armstrong's *What a Wonderful World* and the other was a selection of 1950s favorites by Jackie Gleason's opulent orchestra with Bobby Hackett on trumpet. A particular favorite was "I'll Be Seeing You."

My old man told me over and over: "Never complain. You lot, you young kids, you don't know you're born! You have nothing to complain about. Watch animals. Dogs and cats and birds don't sit around wondering about the purpose of life. They just bloody get on with it. We should too."

seventeen

DEATH WILL COME WHEN IT COMES

At last it came time to shoot *The Elephant Man*. The film told the story of Dr. Frederick Treves (played by me), who rescues a congenitally deformed man named John Merrick from a sideshow where he's being tormented. Director David Lynch had a great cinematographer, Freddie Francis, and they filmed in black-and-white; the Elephant Man's elaborate prosthetics would have looked too garish in color.

To shoot in black-and-white in the late 1970s was extraordinary. The only time it had been done on that scale before was in Peter Bogdanovich's 1971 masterpiece *The Last Picture Show*. Freddie Francis was a genius of camera angles and art direction. He could backlight a set and make it look translucent. We filmed in East London surrounded by crumbling docks, creating a dark and claustrophobic atmosphere full of haunting images.

John Hurt, a British actor, was cast as John Merrick, the Elephant Man. I felt for him, having to sit through several hours of makeup each day to become the character. I didn't know John personally, even though we were both at RADA in the early sixties, but I knew him to be an extraordinary actor. He had created fascinating performances in films like *The Naked Civil Servant* and as Caligula in the TV series *I, Claudius*.

The first day of my involvement was at a grim-looking location near the dock area of London. The black Victorian buildings were oppressive. I was just asked to walk through the streets. David Lynch had decided to film many takes, as he, Stanley Kubrick, David Lean, and other "visual" directors were known to do. But I didn't mind. My job was easy. Back then I never minded waiting. Actors in the film business are paid to wait. I read a few books on that film set and the toughest battle I fought was my temptation to eat doughnuts from the food-service truck.

I pushed back on some of the sentimentality of my character, and yet one day I found myself having a strange emotional experience.

In the scene, Treves is looking for Merrick, and a boy says, "I can take you to the place." And I go to where this man is being kept. It's a dark, somber, awful part of London with rotting warehouses many hundreds of years old. I go into his dark cellar, a nightmare place, to find a man with a sack on his head behind a curtain.

As the boy and I walked down the corridor, I happened to hit a step and almost fell. David continued filming and we kept it in. That shock sent something into my brain. It touched some core of terror that went back to childhood—the dark room, the shadow on the wall, the nightmare. I felt real fear of being in this pitch-black place. It was a supernatural feeling. In my brain, I began to chant the Twenty-Third Psalm, "The Lord is my shepherd . . . " And I kept my eye on a spot on the wall. Suddenly a tear started falling down my cheek. They kept the camera on my face, then David said, "Good, cut. Do you want to do it again?"

I wiped the tear away and looked at him as if waking up from a dream.

"No," I said. "I don't think I can do it again."

The film company took a break for the holidays. Jenni and I drove to Wales to spend Christmas with my parents.

On Christmas morning my father invited some new neighbors over for a drink. There was the usual clatter of "Merry Christmas!" being shouted amid a cacophony of laughter and conversation. I heard my father's usual boisterous noise and noticed his high color. His face was red, bright red. The neighbors left for their Yuletide lunches. My father had looked confused through the lunch but mumbled his usual depressing lines: "Well, that's another Christmas gone! The end of another year. It's all a commercial racket."

My mother recited her part of the eternal scene on cue as well: "Why does everything have to be so gloomy? Every year the same old thing."

Suddenly, as we were cleaning up after the crowd, my father cried out. He grabbed his arm in pain. I knew right away that he must be having a heart attack.

"Call the doctor!" I cried. "Now! Call the doctor!"

The doctor was called.

An examination. *Get the old man to bed. Next twenty-four hours are vital.* Tranquilizer injection.

"It is essential that he lie still," the doctor told me.

The next morning, I went into my father's bedroom. His face was ashen. He looked at me in shock.

"I never expected that," he said. "Heart attack, was it?"

"Yes. That's what the doctor said."

He made a move to get up.

"What are you doing?" I asked him.

"I'm getting up. I can't stay in bed all day."

"Are you crazy?" I asked. "Didn't you hear the doctor? You have to stay in bed."

"What am I going to do?" he said indignantly. "Lie still and die?"

The doctor arrived to check on his patient.

Examination. Tranquilizer shot.

I followed the doctor downstairs and out to his car.

"Is it serious?"

"Deadly. It's only a matter of time."

"He wants to get up."

"Then he's mad. Rest and medications are the only way. Has he always been like this, tense and excitable?"

"Always."

"Well, he's paying the price now. His energy is the killer. The next few months, he should rest and sit back, but the damage has been done. Sorry to be so blunt. But that's the way it is."

The problem was an enlarged heart caused by a lifetime of hard work along with all the smoking and drinking.

My mother couldn't believe it.

"Do you think he's going to be all right?" she asked me.

What could I say? "Yes, as long as he rests," I said.

I returned to London to complete my role in the film. My

father seemed to have recovered. My mother was relieved that things were back to normal. But the doctor had told me that it was only a matter of time.

Indeed, he survived another year, but the decline was awful. The last few months in 1980 were the old man's worst days. He told me he could feel the shadow of death creeping closer. He had been an atheist all his life but would suddenly mutter to himself snippets of the Twenty-Third Psalm and ask why the good Lord had sent this suffering upon him and then say, "Ah, well, Thy will be done." He grew distant. At the Royal Gwent Hospital in Newport, I'd sit at his bedside, but he couldn't, or wouldn't, look at me. My mother believed right up to the end that he would recover.

He's looking much better today. Don't you think? Oh, yes, much better. Oh, yes, he'll be right as rain soon.

But I could tell that he would not leave that hospital alive.

The ward matron called me into her office one morning. She said, "I just want you to know, and I'm sure you are aware, that your father is dying. I know your mother believes he will get well. It's pointless letting her know the truth."

I thanked the matron and told her that I'd already guessed the end was soon.

"Good. It's best to know the reality. It's really days before the end. We have him sedated and comfortable."

It was a waiting game. Death will come when it comes. Each morning, I had to get out, away from the shadow of my poor mother's house of sorrow. I had to breathe again. Any excuse would suffice.

One day, he sat up and stared at a corner of the room.

"What?" I said.

"Look over there!" he said.

I saw nothing.

"It's my mother and father standing there," he said.

On one of his last days alive, my father said, for what would be the last time, "Recite *Hamlet* for me."

As I spoke the words, he closed his eyes, rested his head back, and mouthed the first few familiar words along with me.

To be or not to be: that is the question.
Whether 'tis nobler in the mind to suffer
The slings and arrows of outrageous fortune . . .

I carried on reciting pages of the play from memory. When I stopped, he lifted his head up and looked at me, still baffled by his son who was so dense in so many ways but so surprisingly bright in this one.

"Good God," he said. "How did you learn all those words?"

On the morning of my father's final day, March 30, 1981, I walked again down the hill from Hove Avenue toward Newport Road. I noticed the yellow laburnums on the avenue and the first cherry blossoms sprouting on the trees. In the park, a dog was chasing a ball and barking at the kids playing on the grass. Women on their way to the shops were hurrying down the paths, some to catch the buses into town. This was the mundane, humdrum buzz, the shouts and yelps of life. How was it possible that soon my father would not be part of this world?

At eleven o'clock that night, the phone rang. It was time.

WE DID OK, KID

My mother was stone-faced as we drove to the hospital. Not a word. Everything was still. The streets were bathed in a yellow haze of sodium light from the streetlamps. A cat ran across the road. He was just getting on with it. Surviving.

When we reached the silent ward, the duty nurse asked us to wait a few minutes.

A young Indian doctor came into the room to tell us it was over. He took hold of my mother's hand. His kind platitudes, instead of being comforting, only enlarged the horror.

"He passed peacefully, Mrs. Hopkins. He's in a better place."

Oh, really? In a better place? I began to get angry, as my father and grandfather surely would have, but I held it in. I could do that now that I was no longer drinking. Rather than storm out, I just nodded and said, "Yes, thank you."

We were taken into the dimly lit curtained cubicle to see my father's body. My mother sat on the chair at the bedside, leaning in, stroking his cold forehead. I stood at the foot of the bed. I touched his foot. It was cold. I felt cold too.

My father used to comment on the death of anyone: "Ah, well, he's finally learned the Big Secret, hasn't he?"

And now he, too, had learned the Big Secret. The silence in that ward was palpable. His death was something like a slow-motion grinding of a massive object into the chest. The vast emptiness.

I was reminded of my loneliness as a little boy, when I felt all the other kids were smart and I alone was inept. I used to go for Sunday walks on my own. And on one of these walks I found an old Norman church called St. Hillary up on the Great West Road outside Cowbridge. The church was abandoned, full of autumn leaves and the smell of rotting hymnbooks. In those days, I listened to my father and I didn't believe in anything.

I wonder if they've got any communion wine here, I thought as I explored. No wine, but there was an old visitors' book. I looked around. Heard a dog barking. I opened the book and wrote, *"For what are men better than sheep or goats that nourish a blind life within the brain?" —Alfred, Lord Tennyson.* And then I sat there and just felt the loneliness, the deepest isolation. Over time that loneliness has been, in its own way, a gift. I thought of the last moments of *Casablanca*, when it turns out that all along, Humphrey Bogart was the lonely hero. In the final moments of the movie, off he strolls into the mist.

The morning of my father's funeral, I walked Christchurch Road to Holy Trinity Church. The casket was on a trestle in front of the altar. I sat in one of the pews. I think I was still trying to come to terms with my father's death. I didn't feel anything, really. No grief. I tucked that far away into some corner.

My mother kept a few of my father's books. Some were battered relics from his Left Book Club. One was by Maurice Dobb, the preeminent Marxist economist. Arthur Miller's *Death of a Salesman*. It was the only play my father read. He identified with Willy Loman. Also, there were three novels by Warwick Deeping, his favorite author. *Sorrell and Son*, *Old Pybus*, and *Sincerity*. Another novel was A. J. Cronin's *The Stars Look Down*. The one book he treasured most, a book that had become his bible, was Dale Carnegie's *How to Stop Worrying and Start Living*.

Sadly, Mr. Carnegie's words didn't have enough dynamite power to dislodge my father's grief. On its inside cover my mother wrote a eulogy to her husband, a bit of *The Rubaiyat of Omar Khayyám*, even though in life she'd often teased him and his father for reciting it so often. "Oh, why do you go on and on? It's so depressing and so morbid. Gloomy Omar whatever his name was!"

Now she was writing it out in all somberness.

The Worldly Hope men set their Hearts upon—
Turns Ashes—or it prospers; and anon.
Like Snow upon the Desert's dusty Face,
Lighting a little hour or two—is gone.

"He was a good man, your father," she said to me, "but when we met, he had no sense of his own value. He was afraid to stand up for himself. I had to make him stand up and fight. He didn't want to hurt people, so they took advantage of him. He was full of bluster and cursing this, that, and the other, but I saw right through him. He was lonely. I shall always miss him even though there were times I could have killed him. He drove me mad sometimes, but I loved him."

I recalled how when Grandpa Yeats died from lung cancer I got on the train from London to Port Talbot. It was a bitterly cold afternoon, and the burial took place in the cemetery at the top end of the Dyffryn Road. There, in the same grave, Old Grandpa Yeats was finally reunited with his adored daughter Jenny.

Outside the cemetery gates, two elderly men waited to see me. They were two of my grandfather's workmates, Charlie Blower and someone called Smiley.

Charlie offered his condolences. "We liked your grandad," said Charlie. "He was a good man but a real lone wolf."

"He never took a day off from work," said Smiley, "even after his girl died."

That was the way of the men in my town and in my family: Head down, work hard, never let emotion get the better of you. When my grandfather and father died, it struck me how meager their dreams and pleasures had been compared with mine and how much they'd likely wanted to do and see but never had. They'd made do with so little.

That day my father died, I collected his personal effects from his hospital room: his reading glasses, his pen, his book, and a road map of America. He'd underlined exotic-sounding destinations like Nebraska and New Mexico. He'd spent his last days dreaming of how he and I would go on an incredible adventure together, a drive from New York City to Los Angeles, just the two of us.

eighteen

HE'S HUMAN, AND THAT MAKES HIM SCARIER

A man alone on the stage begins: "You are born into a tragic culture. Tragedy is bred in your bones. A country of almost impossible beauty. From the very moment you are born, the sadness infects you."

Good God, I thought, *what a script.*

The extraordinarily gifted playwright and director Dave Hare had sent me a play called *Pravda*, a satire of 1980s tabloid culture, written with Howard Brenton. I instantly knew that I wanted to play the part of Lambert Le Roux. Le Roux was an unscrupulous white South African media mogul somewhat based on Rupert Murdoch.

I phoned David. "God Almighty, what a mesmerizing part!" I said.

"Why do you want to do it?" he asked.

"Le Roux is certain and he's a thug, but he gets things moving," I said. "He says all the things we dare not say. He says all the things we dare not think."

"Any suggestions for the script?" he asked.

"No," I said. "It's perfect. The writing is so good. Though now that you mention it, I was going to tell you about something that occurred to me. I read that Hitler had more than a thousand books, but he never read any because he was so sure of his beliefs. Perhaps Le Roux could say something like 'In my house, I have a thousand books. But I don't need to read them. My mind is made up.'"

David agreed and it went into the script.

That's the peculiar psychology of demagogues. On my way through the inner fractures we all experience in childhood, I caught some of that everyone-for-himself attitude. I know how to reach that very quickly. And I'd lived through World War II as a child. I'd seen the fall of Germany—a colossus of destruction brought by madness. And madness is the thing that galvanizes us. The play begged the question: What does it take for any of us to resist calamity?

But taking the part meant returning to the National Theatre, to Olivier's stage. I was kind of paranoid because I'd been a bad boy. But they invited me back, and into such wonderful company. As the table read began, I realized that David was a terrific director, and he had cast the play perfectly.

When my scene came, I said in a South African growl, "You are born into a tragic culture." I'd worked hard to make the villain appealing, even in his monstrosity. Though perhaps I'd gone too far, because one of the other actors piped up, offering to follow me into battle: "Can I get on the same horse as Tony?"

Everyone laughed.

"You fucker," David said to me. "This guy's an *antihero*."

"No, he's a hero!" I said. "The way he says things we are terrified of is hypnotic."

"He's a monster!" David said.

"No, he's human, and that makes him scarier. He's a monster, but not a monster in the sense that he's evil. He is *certain*. And he knows that everyone has a price."

Of course, that's the dangerous territory. But I think that's what the play reveals: The weakness in our psychology. You get a juggernaut of a personality, a thug who says in a strong voice, "Do you want to live or die? Follow me if you choose life." That person can rule the world.

Look at Napoléon. Look at Stalin. He gets called a pen pusher. Oh, yeah? He galvanized Russia. He smashed German Nazis through sheer willpower.

There's a wonderful scene in *The Spy Who Came In from the Cold*, the film adaptation of the John le Carré novel starring Richard Burton and Claire Bloom. The great actor Oskar Werner as Fiedler yells at Richard Burton as Alec Leamas: "Just who the hell do you think you are? How dare you come stepping in here like Napoléon ordering me about? You are a traitor! Does it occur to you? A wanted, spent, dishonest man, the lowest currency of the Cold War? We buy you, we sell you, we lose you. We can even shoot you! Not a bird would stir in the trees outside. Not a single pheasant would turn his head to see what fell."

That was the sort of intensity and ruthlessness in *Pravda*, but *Pravda* was also very funny, and I had no patience with any complaints about the roughness of its message.

I remembered what John Osborne said to some piss-elegant journalist from the *London Times* who asked him if he thought his play *Look Back in Anger* caused offense.

Osborne's reply: "My dear lady, life itself is offensive."

Doing *Pravda* was fun, and a series of good gigs followed:

Antony and Cleopatra, with Judi Dench, *Great Expectations* (where I got to play my favorite character in the book, Magwitch!), *Othello, The Bunker.*

Then news came: Richard Burton was dead at the age of fifty-eight, less than a decade after I'd seen him in that *Equus* dressing room (the marriage to Hunt had lasted just six years). What a sad end. He'd died in Switzerland of a massive brain hemorrhage, though alcohol abuse had certainly been a factor. There but for the grace of God I would certainly have gone too by then if I hadn't gotten sober.

After Richard died, I went up to Bel Air to see Elizabeth Taylor. In 1976 we'd done a made-for-TV movie together, along with Kirk Douglas and Burt Lancaster, called *Victory at Entebbe,* about a terrorist hijacking. I was a big fan of hers. She'd made *Giant* in 1956 when she was twenty-three. The film is three hours long and her character ages twenty-five years. I'd always been impressed by what a natural actress she was; it was too bad that the tabloid fodder of her marriages so often overshadowed the public's awareness of her talent.

When I went to see her at home, she'd been quite ill with serious back problems and so she'd been watching a lot of TV while on painkillers. To greet me, she sat up in her bed in a brace. Even in her older age and despite her infirmities, she still had those gorgeous violet eyes and managed to carry herself with a regal bearing.

"How long did you know Richard?" she asked me.

"Well, I didn't really know him well," I said.

"People were so mean to him," she said. "They said he sold out. Bollocks! He touched the fucking ceiling."

"I'm sorry he died," I said.

"Yes, it's very sad," she said, "but of course he was a bad boy."

Years later, I was visiting in Port Talbot and ran into a miner coming home from work who recognized me. He was Burton's brother-in-law, and he invited me into the house. He said, "We never knew which wedding photo of his to put on the mantel when he came back to visit. We lost track of his marriages. Oh, he was wicked with the women."

Not long after, when I was in Rome shooting *Mussolini and I*, I found myself thinking about the men who'd come before me and the way I wanted to be a man in the world. I had tried not to be quite as stoic as my grandfather but also to be less volatile and more self-aware than my father. I wanted to have the presence of Richard Burton without the wickedness.

At the time, I'd been complaining about the script and about everything, really, when suddenly I realized that I was in Rome, and I was working, and I was at a beautiful hotel, the Hotel de la Ville, above the Spanish Steps, sitting in a lush garden in the sunshine. *How can I be dissatisfied? What is wrong with me?*

It was in that state of searching that a sort of mantra came to me. I fell asleep and when I woke up, a string of lines popped into my head that I repeated to myself every day for many years to come.

It's none of my business what people say of me or think of me. I am what I am and I do what I do for fun and free. Because I love it. It's all in the game, the wonderful game, the play of life upon life itself. There's nothing to prove. There's nothing to win; there's nothing to lose. No sweat, no big deal. There are no big deals. Of myself, I am nothing, and of myself I can do nothing. It is the presence within that transforms and does everything. Of myself I am nothing. And so I go about this business doing the best I can with what I've got.

I said it to myself over and over again, and I found that my new attitude opened me up to new roles and new experiences that enriched my life.

In the mid-1980s, I filmed a movie in London called *84 Charing Cross Road*, based on a very popular book published in 1970. It's about a platonic epistolary romance between a bookseller in London and a reader in New York City. The writing is funny and touching, and in the end, the reader goes to the bookstore, only to find that the bookseller has died. The film is very English, another tale of the unfulfilled and proper, of people who live quietly and then die. I think those are the films that really crush one.

One afternoon around this time, I was taking a cab through London. The taxi stopped at a pedestrian crossing, Birdcage Walk near Buckingham Palace, the royal household. The Queen's Guards were on duty. People were returning to their offices or places of work after lunch. A beautiful warm day. The taxi driver's window was down. He was humming a tune. Suddenly he called to me through the sliding-glass window between the seats. He didn't turn, but he talked so I could hear. Great East London accent.

"Look at this lot here in front of us. They all look very serious and important, don't they? All busy and full of themselves and the rest of it. Look at that bloke just in front of us, young and all dressed up, very important, and that young woman, nicely dressed—fancies herself a bit—pretty, and that lot in there, the old palace. They've got business to get on with, yes, but the funny thing is, sometime, sooner or later, they'll all be gone, like you and me, and we'll all be replaced. That's life.

WE DID OK, KID

"I've been doing this job thirty years now. Know London like the back of my hand. I was a youngster—in my twenties—in the war. Born in Whitechapel. Couple of grandkids now. Retiring next year. I watch people every day. I like to chat with people. My dad was a youngster in the First War, a kid. He was smashed about, you know, shell shock—Battle of Ypres. He was a young nipper. For king and country. He came back, married my mum. Tried to get work like all those blokes who came back. Unemployed, thank you very much. He was never the same. Drank himself to death. Yes. Funny thing is, I always stayed cheerful. My missus, she's the same. She wants me to pack it in. Settle down somewhere."

"'Death, a necessary end, will come when it will come,'" I called to him.

"What was that?"

I repeated, "'Death, a necessary end, will come when it will come'!"

"Well, that's bloody cheerful. Thanks a lot for that, mate. But, yeah, you're right. Who said that?"

"It's from Shakespeare's *Julius Caesar*."

"Oh, yes, 'Friends, Romans, countrymen, lend me your ears.' That was my dad's favorite. He read a lot of stuff. Rudyard Kipling was his favorite."

Eventually, we arrived at Sloane Square. I paid him the fare and added a nice tip. He laughed.

"Thanks, mate. You're an actor, right? I think I've seen you somewhere. On the telly?"

"Yes, could be."

We shook hands.

"Good luck, mate," he said. "I'll keep an eye out for you.

Until we meet again. So long, keep smiling, and don't forget to wash behind your ears." Then he drove away.

Just like that, it was as if I were back at the corner of Beechwood and Margam, the bubbling sounds of Arnallt Brook audible just over a redbrick wall, hearing about death for the first time from Brian Moore. How much I had changed since then. Now when I spoke about death, I could quote Shakespeare, shake hands warmly with the Grim Reaper, and make him laugh.

nineteen

FAVA BEANS AND A NICE CHIANTI

Nearing the end of an eight-month West End run of the play *M. Butterfly* in September 1989, I was out-of-my-skull bored. One morning before a matinee, I went to see *Mississippi Burning*, starring Gene Hackman, and walked out of the theater thinking, *I sure would love to do a big Hollywood movie.* I wondered if it would ever happen. I thought it probably wouldn't. I'd shot a little thing with Mickey Rourke and when he grabbed me too hard around the neck in a scene, I shoved him and said, "Touch me like that again and I'll smash your face right into the back of your head!"

Bored and irritable—that's the mood I was in as my contract with the play was ending. Then one Thursday afternoon, I got a call on the theater phone.

"I have a film script here in the office," said my London agent, Dick Blodgett. "It's interesting. Do you want to read it?"

"Yes. I'm in the theater right now."

"I know. That's why I phoned you there. Are you going to be there for the rest of the afternoon? I can send the script to you right now."

"What's the film about?" I asked.

"It's called *The Silence of the Lambs*. An American is attached to direct, Jonathan Demme. He's good."

"*Silence of the*—what was it?" I asked.

"*Silence of the Lambs*."

"Is it a children's film?"

"No, it's a kind of crime film. The part is called Lecter. It's not a big role, but Demme seems keen on you playing him. He's interested. I think Jodie Foster is the star."

"She's good. Didn't she get an Oscar?"

"Yes. You want to read it?"

"Yes. Send it over."

The *M. Butterfly* reviews had been mostly indifferent, although some were savage. Audiences had been dwindling throughout the summer. I couldn't wait for the end of the run. I'd figured out by then that the theater really was not my cup of tea. Doing the same thing night in and night out had become boring. *Why did I choose this game?* I often asked myself.

But film? That's a different game altogether. Very little repetition. Travel. Money's good. And I enjoy it. You keep moving around a lot. You're rootless. This Silence *film might be interesting. Jodie Foster? Can't be bad.*

Within half an hour, the script arrived. On the front Dick had scribbled *Lecter*.

I made a cup of tea and sat down to read. I stopped at page 15. I called the agency.

Dick said, "Hi. So? What do you think?"

"I don't want to read any more," I said. "Is there a firm offer?"

"What's the problem? You don't want to read but is there an offer? Sounds weird."

"It's the best part I've ever read. I don't want to read any more in case there is no real offer."

"OK. I'll get back to you."

That sounded promising, so I read the rest of the Ted Tally screenplay, which was based on the bestselling Thomas Harris novel. Then I took a walk outside and bought a sandwich and coffee.

The call came through: "Jonathan wants you to play Lecter. The offer is real. He's flying to London tomorrow. I got him a ticket to see the play on Saturday, and he wants to take you out for a meal and talk after. OK with that?"

"Great. Fantastic."

"Good role, this Lecter guy?"

"The best. A life-changer."

"It's a small role, but if you think it's great, go ahead. Congratulations."

Saturday came. There was a note for me at the stage door: *See you after the show, Mr. Hopkins. Jonathan Demme.*

After the show, we met and went across the street to an Italian restaurant. He never stopped asking me questions: What did I think of the screenplay? Any ideas about Lecter? How did I plan to play him?

"Like HAL the computer in the Kubrick film *2001: A Space Odyssey*," I said. Quiet and intimate.

In the film's opening scenes, FBI trainee Agent Clarice Starling has been given a dangerous mission by her superior, Jack Crawford: to interview a vicious criminal, a former psychiatrist now serving a life sentence for murder. The series of interviews by Starling are to be conducted in a prison for the criminally insane.

Crawford tells Clarice to stick to specific questions and avoid any closeness. In other words, take full charge of the interview. Do not let the interviewee make the rules.

"Who is the subject?" asks Clarice.

"The psychiatrist Hannibal Lecter."

"Hannibal the Cannibal."

Crawford warns Clarice not to tell Lecter anything personal. "Believe me, you don't want Hannibal Lecter inside your head."

When I read those lines, I knew the character instantly. The pattern of his personality clicked in my mind. Lecter is described as a monster. That was my clue. *Do not play the monster. Play a quiet, friendly version. Create a "romance" with Starling. Seduce her. Take full charge of the interview. Cat-and-mouse game. Fun. Draw the audience into the game.*

When Starling shows up to interview the serial killer Hannibal Lecter, he sees right through her, and every word he says causes her pain. His attention is light, direct, and sustained. Penetrating. The penetration is not sexual but psychological. The myth behind the story is Beauty and the Beast.

When Lecter meets Clarice for the first time, he is impressed by her professional courage. A young woman against an older male serial killer. She seeks Dr. Lecter's help and guidance, but first Lecter plays with her. He tests her. He knows how to bore a tiny entrance into her brain. He unsettles her, commenting on what she's wearing and what it means about her.

"You're so ambitious, aren't you?" he says to her, and as I

read the script, I could hear myself saying the words in a cold, menacing, deeply reasonable voice. "You know what you look like to me, with your good bag and your cheap shoes? You look like a rube. A well-scrubbed, hustling rube with a little taste. Good nutrition has given you some length of bone, but you're not more than one generation from poor white trash, are you, Agent Starling? And that accent you've tried so desperately to shed—pure West Virginia." Clarice challenges him to turn his "high-powered perception" on himself. Lecter responds, "A census taker once tried to test me. I ate his liver with some fava beans and a nice Chi-*an*-ti."

The following month I met Demme and some members of his production team at the Hotel des Artistes on the Upper West Side of Manhattan. Jonathan was a rare species of director, consistently full of goodwill, enthusiasm, and bonhomie. He spoke excitedly about how Jodie Foster was going to play Clarice Starling and said that they'd actually be shooting at the FBI Academy in Quantico, Virginia.

Some of Jonathan's colleagues were clearly a little nervous about him hiring me, but he began the meeting by saying that he'd seen me as Frederick Treves in *The Elephant Man* and was convinced that I'd be perfect for Hannibal Lecter.

"But Treves is a good man," I said. "Mild-mannered."

"Yes," Demme said, "but, like him, Lecter is a highly developed, cultured man—Lecter is just trapped inside an insane brain."

He had a point. And Treves wrestled with his goodness. There's a scene in which he says, "What was it all for? Why did I do it? Am I a good man or am I a bad man?" And he spoke those words in a neutral voice of the sort that I imagined for

Lecter, the way HAL, with flat, controlled certainty, spoke to the spaceship's crew: "Hello, Dave."

Even the *clickety-click* of the name Lecter gave me the image of that black-box machine. No emotion. No empathy. No need for sensation or appetite. Lecter isn't going anywhere. He's a specimen in a glass box. Being devoid of feeling and sensual need makes him a pitiless and terrifying presence, an incarnation of the devil.

"Don't you want an American actor?" I asked Jonathan Demme.

He laughed and said, "Don't you want to do it?"

"Yes, I do," I said. (*Don't ask questions, dummy!* I told myself.) "I really do."

A producer at the table confessed, "We did have our doubts about an English actor playing this American killer."

"Well, that's OK, then," I said. "I'm not English; I'm Welsh."

I knew they had nothing to worry about because I instinctively sensed exactly how to play Hannibal. I have the devil in me. We all have the devil in us. I know what scares people. The key is to embody two inner attitudes at the same time that don't often coexist—he was at once *remote* and *awake*.

I'd encountered those two things in one entity once very early in my life, and it became part of my childhood subconscious. I suffered from a terrible fear of spiders, and unfortunately, ours was an old house with crawling and skittering creatures everywhere. One night I switched on the light in my father's bakery, and right next to the switch was a huge black spider—patient and still, yet completely alert at the same time. I almost jumped through the roof.

That was the effect I wanted to have as Hannibal. I wanted

to be the spider in my father's bakery so that as soon as the camera was on him, he was revealed to be all readiness and all stillness too. Staring at people for a long time makes them very uneasy. Remoteness draws the witness—or victim—forward and into the circle of the predator's personality.

I thought of what I'd learned about the psychological gesture, and I intuited the inside structure of Hannibal Lecter's head. The blueprint: Remove to the background the motion factor of weight and sensing—or intending. Lecter's main power was his penetrating thinking and sustained intuiting. That would come across, too, in the perfect clarity of his speech.

People find perfect diction arresting. Mumbling is thought to be sexy, and yet the greats whom we think of as mumbling often aren't mumbling when you watch them closely. Marlon Brando was a great technician. He was a classical, romantic actor. All the great actors have that clarity. You have to know the effect you have and project yourself out to the audience. In film, the stiller you are, the better. I have heard so many stories of actors competitively bragging of a costar, "I'll act him off the screen," only to see the dailies and think, *Oh no—by doing less, he was totally in control of that scene. By working so hard, I just look insane.*

Once I began acting on film, I worked hard to become still, because it's not really in my nature to dwell for a long time in direct, sustained attention. And for this role, I had to cultivate that disposition to the most extreme degree. Hannibal had to be both awake and remote in order to create a spellbinding charisma. The way to that is through stillness.

On the day of the first table reading, I didn't get a chance to talk with Jodie Foster before we began. We just flew right into it.

I loved the accent she was using. I could imagine her in the scene where she's at the FBI and gets into the elevator surrounded by all these big men as she heads out alone to meet the monster. She radiated an inner strength and a vulnerability at the same time. *It's no wonder*, I thought, *she's considered among the best actors of her generation.*

Even though I don't usually give a full performance during a table read, I wanted to show what I could do, so I was as scary as I could be. As it turned out, this was *quite* scary. You could have heard a pin drop in the room. A couple of seconds after I started to speak as Lecter, I saw Jodie grow tense. She later confirmed that she had been petrified. And that slight distance between us remained throughout the filming. "I stayed a little bit afraid of him, I think, for the whole film," she said later.

For my first meeting with Clarice, Jonathan Demme asked me what I wanted to be doing when she came down that dark hall to interview me in my cell.

"Do you want to be painting? Reading?" Demme said. "Sleeping? Sitting on your bunk?"

"No," I said, thinking of the spider on the bakery wall. "I want to be standing calmly, waiting for her."

"Why?" he asked.

"Because I can smell her coming down the corridor."

"Oh my God, you're so sick, Hopkins," said Demme, and he laughed.

He thought that was very creepy and exactly right.

I went on to explain that Lecter had to present as extremely civilized. I insisted the costume designer give me a slim-fitting prison jumpsuit rather than a baggy one, for example. I said that Lecter would have paid someone to tailor it, because he cared about such things. And so when Clarice comes down the corridor full of lunatics screaming at her and throwing things, here Dr. Lecter is at the end of the hallway, standing politely in his tailored jumpsuit, greeting her with his full, unblinking attention. He's a monster, but he's a monster who moves silently through the night.

For that role, I also called on my childhood experiences of doing impersonations of Bela Lugosi at boarding school. As a kid, I went to see him in *Dracula*. That had been one of the first big books I ever read, even though the language was a bit over my head. In the book, the protagonist Jonathan Harker nicks himself with a razor and senses Dracula's rapt attention. The sound I imagined Dracula made in that moment, thirsting for Harker's blood, was a very particular combination of hissing and slurping. That's where I got the sound I made with my lips as Hannibal, the one that gets imitated so much. Thank you, *Dracula*.

I thought, too, of how when I was a boy playing a lonely game of dumb insolence, I heard the cold, assessing inner tone of Lecter. Does that make me a psychopath? Probably. Aren't we all psychopaths to some extent, and it's just a matter of degree? My dumb-insolence game was a game of manipulation. The game of silence and stillness can make people uneasy, because in behaving that way, you are subtly amputating your humanity.

I tried to read a book about Ted Bundy as part of my preparation but it was too terrible, so I put it down. I did read a book about Stalin, whose daughter said that there was no one lonelier than her father." There was a lot of space around him, she wrote, because people were terrified of him. He never said much. When he lost his temper, you were OK. When he smiled at you, you were dead.

Another inspiration for Lecter: my RADA teacher Christopher Fettes. Christopher was a brilliant teacher, very charismatic and extremely perceptive when it came to people's psychology. He spoke crisply and stared at you with a penetrating stillness. He didn't waste a single gesture or word.

At my audition, he entered the room and said, "Good morning. How are you?"

"Good," I said.

"Good. What is your audition piece?"

I told him.

"Good."

I performed.

A pause. "Yes, very good."

Like Christopher, Hannibal could be ruthlessly critical. He had a way of addressing people as if he could easily kill them. And yet he also had a deep respect for Agent Starling. He was still going to torture her, of course. But he respected her.

After shooting at Quantico, the film crew moved to Pennsylvania for the prison scenes with Lecter. The sets were constructed in the old Westinghouse building in the Pittsburgh suburb of Turtle Creek. In January of 1990, I arrived in Pittsburgh and met with Jodie, Jonathan, producer Ed Saxon, the director of photography Tak Fujimoto, and the crew. Jodie had already filmed her scenes in Virginia. Now the rest of the film started.

We spent a lot of time on the prison set. I enjoyed the glass-box cell. The atmosphere was dour, but there was nothing dour about Jonathan Demme. He laughed and talked all the time, and he plainly liked the Lecter character.

Several of the scenes between Clarice and Hannibal are eight or ten pages long. And in each one, there's the thick glass barrier of the cell between us. We had to shoot one person's side for a day or half a day, and then we'd turn and do the other part, because the camera couldn't shoot through the barrier. It took about twenty minutes to get me in and out of that set, so I wasn't really able to chat with Jodie or anyone else in those times. When I was shooting, I was looking straight at the camera, and she was off to the side in her street clothes saying her lines. It was a strange form of communication—Jodie later told me that the way Hannibal's dialogue reached her felt "intravenous." And I think it shows in the film.

The rest of the time, we mostly kept away from each other. Then, on our last day of shooting, we had lunch. It was freezing cold in Pittsburgh. Jodie put down her tuna sandwich and said she had to confess something: She'd been scared of me.

"I was scared of you too!" I said.

We had a big hug, and we both admitted to feeling a strange sense of distance during the shoot, due no doubt to the power of that script, which had us playing a cat-and-mouse game. Since then, we've always greeted each other with great warmth.

We've often reflected on how unprecedented that experience was. Jodie once said, "The extraordinary thing about *Silence of the Lambs* is that every single person who participated in that film feels like it is the best work they ever did. The perspective of the film is not the monster's perspective. It really is the perspective of somebody who's good and who's trying to save the world." Then she smiled that knowing smile of hers. "That being said, the monster in the movie is the best part."

I suppose it was inevitable that there would be sequels, but it's hard to recapture that kind of magic. I didn't blame Jodie for wanting to leave it alone and not return for the others.

About two years after *Silence* came out, Christopher Fettes, my old RADA teacher, called. He and my other favorite teacher, Yat Malmgren, wanted to take me out to dinner.

I wasn't sure what they would say. They'd been so hard on all of us as students. And I was proud of playing Hannibal. That role was a turning point in my life, not just my career, because it helped me reach a new level of self-assurance. It was a role I instinctively knew how to play. I worried that they'd tell me I'd missed the mark.

After we sat down at our table, Christopher looked me in the eye and said, "What a *fantastic* performance."

Yat agreed. "You've at last developed the introverted system! Hannibal is very camp, but he's a wonderful personality. You've used your understanding of the dynamics of human personality."

"On whom did you base the character?" Christopher asked.

"On you," I said. "Hannibal is part Dracula and part Christopher Fettes. I used you as a blueprint for someone who had a knifelike, hypercritical precision along with a deep understanding of human psychology. When you gave us notes in class, it could be like an ice pick impaling us."

Christopher was delighted to have inspired an iconic monster. The night was meaningful for all three of us. Those teachers who had taught me so much and who had been so strict now had no notes, only praise.

To hear from my favorite teachers that I'd done well—done *very* well—made me feel like a little boy being patted on the head and told, at long last, that perhaps he was not such a dunce after all.

twenty

LIFE, LIFE, LIFE!

In 1952, I went with my parents on a Sunday afternoon to see Charlie Chaplin in *Limelight*, which he made while being persecuted in the press due to the Red Scare. The film begins with a dramatic swell of music, the theme of the film's ballerina heroine, Terry, played by Claire Bloom, and these words: "The glamour of limelight, from which age must fade as youth enters." Something about that movie touched the loneliness in my heart.

The film is set in the London music halls Chaplin knew so well. Chaplin's character, an aging clown named Calvero who's lost his audience, saves Terry the ballerina from her suicide attempt. "Why didn't you let me die?" she says.

Calvero replies, "What's your hurry?" He tells her, "There's something just as inevitable as death, and that's life! Life, life, life!" He also says, upon being asked if he hates the theater: "I do. I also hate the sight of blood, but it's in my veins."

Such pain he called up in those scenes! I became obsessed. It struck a chord in me. I wanted to be him.

"Are you going to see it *again*? Good God," my father said

several times that week, as I returned to the cinema as often as I could to watch *Limelight*.

At the end of the film, Calvero regains the love of the crowd and dies on the same night. He tells Terry, "The heart and the mind, what an enigma."

My father bought me a little projector so I could screen bits of Chaplin's old films—*The Gold Rush, Modern Times*. I can still remember the smell of the heat from the lamp inside the projector and the way the light hit the sheet on the wall as I sat transfixed. I wrote Chaplin a fan letter about *Limelight* and sent it care of the post office in his Swiss town, and he sent back a polite, typed thank you.

Then, forty years later, at the invitation of Chaplin's daughter Geraldine, there I was sitting in the garden of that same house in Switzerland where Chaplin had received my letter. Robert Downey Jr., with whom I was appearing in the 1992 movie *Chaplin*, went too. When I sat down to play Chaplin's piano, I suddenly felt that I'd dreamed my life into being. After that visit, I went back to the *Chaplin* set, and there was a knock on the door of my trailer. Richard Attenborough came in and said, "You've just been nominated for the Oscar."

If somebody had told me in 1952 when I was a teenager with that little projector that forty years later, I would be in Charlie Chaplin's garden and that, further, on that same day, I would be told I'd been nominated for an Oscar, I'd never have believed it. But *Silence* turned out to be hot at the box office, and it received several Oscar nominations.

I certainly wasn't expecting to win. I tried to get out of the ceremony. If nothing else, perhaps I could arrange to be delayed in downtown traffic. My agent called and told me I could not get out of it, that I mustn't even try. He was right. It would have been disrespectful to the Academy and ungrateful. I didn't want to be disrespectful. Still, I had a strange anxiety about those sorts of events. It wasn't the people; it was the razzmatazz and glitter. Why I'd chosen to be an actor beats me.

"You're not going to get out of this," my friend Bob Palmer said.

"I know, I know," I said quietly.

"And be ready in case you win."

I got all dressed up in black tie and clobber. My wife also was dressed and ready. She'd given up battling my peculiar resistance to social events. But that night I made the effort. *Take a deep breath. What's the problem?*

My father, long gone the way of all flesh, paid me a spectral visit: *You'll end up alone. No friends. Is that what you want?*

Shut up, I thought. But I feared he was right. I'd made a little progress escaping the past, but not much.

A limousine picked us up at the hotel. Bob Palmer and his wife joined us. Long drive downtown to the Dorothy Chandler Pavilion. We all climbed out of the limousine.

"Smile, Tony. Smile."

Gritted teeth. "I am smiling!" Flashes and quick interviews from journalists. "How does it feel to be here at the Oscars?"

"Yeah, it's not bad." Smile.

There was a lot of babble in the inner reception area. Kisses and hugs and dresses and neck craning. *Who's in; who's out? Buzz-buzz.*

A woman came over to me and said, "You're going to get it."

"What?"

"The Oscar."

She vanished into the mayhem.

The ceremony started. Emcee Billy Crystal got a big round of applause when he was wheeled onstage strapped to a gurney wearing the Lecter mask. I didn't know what to make of it. The show went on and on. Then the Best Supporting Actor award arrived. Jack Palance won for *City Slickers*. The next awards were for best actors in lead roles.

Jodie Foster picked up the Best Actress award for Clarice in *Silence of the Lambs*. Then Best Actor was announced. Kathy Bates came onstage to open the envelope.

"And the Oscar goes to Anthony Hopkins for *The Silence of the Lambs*." Later that evening, the film won Best Picture, the first horror film to do so and only the third film to sweep the Big Five categories.

I remember getting up onstage. Kathy Bates handed me the Oscar. Apparently I gave a speech. Later I was told that one of the things I said was "My father died eleven years ago tonight, so maybe he had something to do with this as well, I don't know."

Then I was taken backstage. Questions by journalists. It all went well. I'd made it through with little or no anxiety. That was new. I made a phone call to my mother in Wales. It was about four a.m. UK time. She was at her close friends Eve and Gene's house.

"You watched on telly?" I asked. Stupid question.

"Of course I did. Why else would I be up at four in the

morning? Your father would have been proud of you. Boy from Wern Road in Port Talbot."

"Yes, I guess I did OK."

And that was it.

I'd beaten my anxiety.

Equus, 1977
Courtesy Everett Collection

The Elephant Man, 1980
THE ELEPHANT MAN © *1980 Brooksfilms Limited. All rights reserved.*

The Lion in Winter, 1968
Courtesy of STUDIOCANAL

ABOVE: *Magic*, 1978
United News/Popperfoto via Getty Images

LEFT: *Pravda*, 1985
Anthony Hopkins in Pravda (1985), courtesy National Theatre. Photographer: Nobby Clark. Nobby Clark/Popperfoto via Getty Images.

ABOVE: *The Silence of the Lambs*, 1991
Ken Regan/Camera 5

LEFT: *The Silence of the Lambs*, 1991
Ken Regan/Camera 5

The Remains of the Day, 1993
THE REMAINS OF THE DAY ©
*1993 Columbia Pictures Industries, Inc.
All Rights Reserved. Courtesy of Columbia
Pictures.*

*Legends of the
Fall*, 1994
LEGENDS OF
THE FALL
© *1994 TriStar
Pictures, Inc. All
Rights Reserved.
Courtesy of
TriStar Pictures.*

Meet Joe Black,
1998
MEET JOE
BLACK © *1998
Universal City
Studios, Inc.*

Me and Stella at the 81st Annual Academy Awards (Oscars).
WENN Rights Ltd/Alamy Stock Photo

Me and my mother at the hand and footprint ceremony at Mann Chinese Theater, LA, 2001.
ZUMA Press, Inc./Alamy Stock Photo

March 1, 2003: Stella and me on our wedding day, Malibu, CA.
Copyright Berliner Photography, LLC

Playing the piano at home in 2004, Malibu, CA.

On our honeymoon, 2003, painting.

The Grauman's Chinese Theatre handprint ceremony, 2001.
Copyright Jan-Erik Blondell

Me at the score recording for *Red Dragon*, 2002.

Concert of my music performed by the Dallas Symphony, 2005.

Me and Kesang Shrestha, Los Angeles, 2025.

Me and my niece Tara Arroyave at the *Transformers: The Last Knight* premiere, 2017.

Me and Woesel Sherpa, Malibu, 2009.

Me with friends and family at the 94th Academy Awards (Oscars). Left to right: Juan Arias, Mitch Smelkinson, Lisa Smelkinson, Stella Hopkins, me, Tara Arroyave, Aaron Tucker, and Natalia Tucker.
Dan Steinberg/Variety/Penske Media via Getty Images

My beloved extended family at Hotel Bel-Air Sunday brunch, 2025. Left to right: Bianca Arroyave, Tara Arroyave, Amelia Ysaguirre, Kesang Shrestha, Valentina Sabogal.

Me with my friends and family at the *Thor* premiere, 2011. Left to right: Tara Arroyave, Stella Hopkins, me, Tenzing Sherpa, Jr., Kesang Shrestha, and Tenzin Sherpa.
WENN Rights Ltd/Alamy Stock Photo

twenty-one

THE TICKTOCK OF VOICES IN MY HEAD

One afternoon, I had a call from my agent, Ed Limato of William Morris: "Hi, Tony. Oliver Stone wants to call you."

"Oliver Stone?" I was surprised. "Why?"

"He's making a film about Nixon."

"President Nixon?"

"Yes."

"Why is he calling me?" I couldn't think of any British role in a film about Nixon.

"He wants you to play Nixon."

I happened to know quite a lot about Watergate, having closely followed the news and Nixon's subsequent demise. I'd watched on BBC TV Nixon's resignation, his long, rambling farewell speech to the White House staff, and the famous V signs he gave before the helicopter whisked him away to obscurity. That was in August 1974; a week later I was in Manhattan to do *Equus*, and there were joke shops selling Nixon masks. Twenty-one years after that, my agent was telling me that Oliver Stone wanted me to play Nixon. But the idea was outrageous.

"Nixon? How? I'm British. Is Oliver Stone crazy?"

"No. He wants you to play him. Will you take his call?"

"Yes, of course."

Oliver called ten minutes later. He was somewhere in Europe. I had never spoken to him before, but I admired his films—*JFK, Born on the Fourth of July, Platoon.*

We had a brief conversation. He didn't mince words: "I want you to play Nixon."

"Nixon?"

"You got a problem with that?"

"Yes. I'm British. An American actor would be better, don't you think?"

"I want *you* to play him."

"OK. But why me?"

"Because you are nuts like Nixon. I've read some interviews you've done with magazines and newspapers, and you go on about paranoia and insecurities—that's Nixon. Listen, I'm coming into London on Saturday, staying at the Hyde Park Hotel. Meet me there for breakfast and we'll talk."

He hung up.

Jenni told me to use some common sense. "Don't say yes to that. You can't play Nixon. You'll make a fool of yourself."

She was right. Also, I think she was unhappy with the idea of my involvement in American films—and for good reason. She had no fondness for our previous life in California or anywhere in America. She felt like an alien there. I understood why she felt that way, but I was different. I'd dreamed of California as a boy. I loved the brutal vastness of the country, the brashness and toughness of the American people, the noise and energy.

WE DID OK, KID

It suited my nature. In New York and in Hollywood, I felt at home.

On Saturday, I met with Oliver Stone. It was a cold morning. As I put on my overcoat, Jenni said: "Don't be swayed. Just say no."

I walked up through Knightsbridge toward Hyde Park. Suddenly, I stopped at the Wellington Monument. I thought about the choice: Say yes to *Nixon* or no. Staying in Britain meant doing the usual plays in the theater and on television, Chekhov and Ibsen and whatever. Nothing to complain about—I was a lucky man in those days. But something didn't fit. *I* didn't fit. I had always been restless. And now I had an offer to work with the wild Oliver Stone. I didn't know if he was crazy, but I'd heard rumors that he was a tough director—courageous and outrageous . . .

Yes.

I arrived at the Hyde Park Hotel. Ed Limato had arranged the meeting for ten a.m. in the main restaurant. I sat and waited. Then Oliver came in and sat down. No warm, fuzzy friendliness. His first words: "So you're chicken, huh?"

"No," I said. "I'll play him."

"Great."

High five. All well.

"When do we start?" I asked.

"In three weeks, at Sony Studios in LA. But get out there two weeks before for fittings and tests. I'll send you some videos on Nixon. OK?"

"OK."

And that was it. There was no long conversation. Oliver Stone never bloviates, just tells you to take it or leave it.

Jenni was shocked and somewhat dismayed that I'd agreed to play the role. I understood her anxiety, but I wanted to return to America. That's the way it was.

Ten days later I left for California. I didn't know what I'd gotten myself into. The script was more or less completed. It was good. But I twisted and turned from positive to negative. Up and down moods. Too late now. I was in. The rest of the casting was underway. James Woods as Haldeman. J. T. Walsh as Ehrlichman. Joan Allen as Pat Nixon. Ed Harris as Howard Hunt. E. G. Marshall as John Mitchell. It was quite a cast.

There were fittings for wardrobe and tests for makeup. Oliver Stone gave me a number of videos of Nixon. I watched them in my obsessive way: Play. Rewind. Replay. I worked on Nixon's gestures and vocal patterns. At night I'd play the tracks of his voice, thinking that perhaps the sounds and images would pierce my brain.

At various points, I thought I might lose my mind. In rehearsal, there seemed to be no response to my efforts to get the accent right. A dialect coach was hired. She lasted two weeks. The woman appeared to me morbidly depressed and grim. Also she was a harsh, task-driven tormentor. Any mistake in pronunciation was greeted with a sigh, a long-suffering smile, and the words "No, no, no, that's wrong. You never get that right." She scribbled phonetic markings on my script; they looked like an ancient language. One day I asked her politely to leave me alone. I couldn't take any more. Just before taking her leave, she said: "Well, good luck. You'll need it, my friend."

Oliver heard about it and called. "What happened?"

I told him.

"Good. You don't need a coach. We have a table reading on

Friday. My PA will give you the address. It's in Santa Monica." He hung up.

A table read. Holy shit.

The PA called with the address and time for the table reading. A table reading is meant to be a guide for the director and producers. It's just a bunch of actors sitting at a long table. No acting required; you just read. Still, I dreaded the creepy ceremony.

The ticktock of voices in my head started their jabber: *You're not cut out for this . . .*

Friday morning. The reading. *Here we go.* In an upper room of an office building in Santa Monica, the entire cast assembled. An impressive bunch. I was a British actor among a powerhouse cast of American actors. I had never met any of them beyond brief handshakes.

I mumbled my way through the reading. No one seemed to take any notice. I wondered if they were deaf. The same voices were chirping away in the inner sanctum of my birdbrain head: *You'd better check out. Your wife was right. Why did you say yes to this?*

Two hours passed in this manner.

"That's it. Lunch break. Back at two."

No comment was made about my reading. As I was leaving the room, heading for the elevator, James Woods passed me.

"Great German accent," he said. He vanished into the elevator with J. T. Walsh.

I hung back. Didn't want to join anyone for a chatty lunch.

A minute later I went into the elevator. A big heavyset man hurried inside to join me.

"Hi. Paul Sorvino."

We shook hands. What else could I do? On our way to the ground floor, I said something inane: "Good reading."

Sorvino: "You think so? I thought it sucked."

Oh, OK. This didn't bode well.

"Shall I be honest?" Sorvino said. Before I could tell him that wouldn't be necessary, he said, "Your voice was all wrong."

We walked into the open mall and found ourselves standing in front of a Greek restaurant.

"Do you mind if I join you?" he asked.

We sat at a table near the window. Sorvino sat with his back to the window. I didn't feel like eating. He looked at the menu. The waiter came over. Sorvino ordered a kebab. I ordered a coffee.

"Do you mind if I'm honest with you?" he asked.

"No. Go ahead."

He gave me his assessment: "I'm saying this for your benefit. Your speech patterns are way off. I know Nixon. I'm an expert on the guy. Paranoia, Watergate, his Checkers speech—I know a lot about him. He was a fruitcake."

Suddenly I saw James Woods and J. T. Walsh standing outside. They were three inches behind Sorvino, the plate glass between them. Pulling antic faces—tongues out of their mouths, eyes crossed—they gestured at Sorvino. But the show was just for me; Sorvino was oblivious to them. He was chomping on his kebab, an eating event I'd prefer not to have witnessed. As he meticulously picked away at me, explaining the bleak mistake I'd made in agreeing to play Richard Milhous Nixon, pieces of lamb flew from his mouth. Finally, I got up, paid for my coffee, and returned to the office building. As I stepped into the elevator, Jimmy Woods and J. T. Walsh pushed in past me.

"Hey, was Fatso going at you?" Woods asked.

"Who?"

"Fatso. Your new friend, Sorvino the Sweats."

"I guess so. He thinks I am all wrong for Nixon."

"So? Fuck him. He's jealous. His big fat career never took off."

Back in the rehearsal room, I asked Oliver Stone if I could talk to him privately. We went into a small office, and I suggested to Oliver that it would be best if he fired me. Recast the role.

No reaction from Oliver.

"I don't want to spoil your film."

Pause. Then he said: "Has that fat slob been getting to you? You don't have to answer. I know he has. He's a baby. Don't take any notice of him, and no, I'm not firing you, and you're not going to walk. They are on your side, those guys out there—Jimmy and J.T. All of them. See, I told you that you were right for Nixon because you are nuts like him, paranoid, scared. So what? I was scared, still am. I saw enough crap in Vietnam, and I'll never forget it, so whatever screws you up from the past, childhood and all that shit, so what? Use it. Those are the broken pieces. Fuck that fat ass. Cut him dead."

I went back into the rehearsal reading room. Sorvino must have sensed that something had taken place, because he suddenly exploded and warned people not to mess with him.

The preparations continued, the makeup and wardrobe tests. Still flip-flopping with doubts, I reminded myself that nothing was ultimately of any importance. *It's a film! Who cares? Entertainment. Nothing of consequence. Popcorn.*

On Friday afternoon, the final checks were to be carried out in the Oval Office set. The makeup department worked hard to make the cast members look authentic. Just before being called on set, I glanced in the mirror. There was a vague look of Nixon, but that was all: The black suit. The hair.

What am I trying to prove? I asked myself. *That I am President Nixon? Forget it. I am not President Nixon. Schizophrenia. People who are mad sometimes believe they are Napoléon or Julius Caesar.* I didn't have to *be* him. I just had to act enough *like* him to make the story work.

As I walked toward the set for the final checkups, I felt a slight change. My shoulders hunched forward. I walked into the room, and the others looked at me. Oliver Stone said: "See? I told you that you are him. I told you when we met in London that you were as deranged and paranoid as old Richard Milhous. You did it."

"Huh," said Jimmy Woods. "This part is not too far removed from you, is it?"

Something clicked in my head then, and the film went smoothly. While we were making it I felt Nixon's presence almost as if he were looking over my shoulder, nudging me on. In the end, I'm glad I took it, as it helped expand my range, but I was certainly more comfortable with roles like those in the quiet Merchant Ivory films I'd done.

In *The Remains of the Day* and *Howards End*, in scenes with Helena Bonham-Carter and Emma Thompson, I played men who prioritized dignity and duty over love. That was not an uncommon choice for men of that era. And in both those movies, I felt that director James Ivory was able to get under the skin of a particular British way of life. Both films reveal the quiet tragedy that can result from a lifetime of self-sacrifice.

In *Howards End*, a family drama about class and convention

in Edwardian England, I played Henry Wilcox, a buttoned-up businessman who holds fast to old ideas of propriety even as it distances him from his family and keeps love out of his life.

A young kid, a runner on that film, told me, "You always play evil parts."

"What makes you say that Henry Wilcox is evil?" I said. "Do you know anything about Edwardian England? Where'd you go, Harvard? Didn't they teach you about the horrors of the world? And you're calling this character *evil*?"

For the part, I was dressed in a tweed suit. The hair and makeup team gave me a haircut and then one woman said, "They want you to wear a mustache."

"No!" I said. "I hate those things."

She put it on. I looked in the mirror. Staring back at me was a different person, a militaristic businessman. My voice changed immediately to that of an uptight Edwardian. The mustache made the character.

In *Remains of the Day*, set in 1930s England, I played head butler Mr. Stevens, a man who's so devoted to serving his employer that he overlooks his employer's complicity with the Nazis. Much later, he tries to reconnect with the head housekeeper, and yet all the years of pushing down his emotions make that difficult.

I'd read Kazuo Ishiguro's book *The Remains of the Day* before I even knew a film was being made. In Washington, DC, for an event, I was seated at a table with Isaac Stern, Gregory Peck, and legendary director Mike Nichols (who'd directed *The Graduate* and *Who's Afraid of Virginia Woolf?*). Nichols mentioned that he was going to be coproducing a film version of *Remains of the Day*.

"You should play the butler," he said.

"Me? I just read the book," I said. "I imagined a more Jeremy Irons type, not a chunky baker's son from Port Talbot."

"Well," he said, "I think you'd be ideal."

The director of the film turned out to be James Ivory, and he wanted to get me and Emma Thompson, whom I'd worked with on *Howards End*, and the rest of the gang back together.

The role was indeed perfect for me. Stevens the butler is a locked-up person. He can't understand how he could live without being of service. And he thinks, *Why risk the pain of living? Why risk the pain of love? Why risk the pain of being with another person?* He's got his life ordered. Stevens is quite safe in his home, his little kingdom. And that was me. (Of course, in a way, I am still that, just as I am Hannibal Lecter too. I am everything. Because we all are. All you need to do as an actor is access that part of what's inside you.)

At the end of the film, a pigeon flies into the house, and Stevens's new employer, Jack Lewis, catches and releases it. Stevens watches it fly away. People have wondered about the symbolism of that bird. To me, that's his soul. I imagine Stevens letting go in that moment and then probably going on in peace and living until he's ninety.

Early in the process, we shot a scene with Emma Thompson and myself in which she flirts with me and I keep telling her I just want to be left alone with my book. She asks what the book is.

"Would I be shocked?" she asks. She pries the book out of my hand and smiles at me, coming so close I could kiss her if I wanted to. And my hand reaches almost unconsciously for her hair, though I don't stroke it. My hand just hovers as I remain backed against the wall, frozen.

We shot that scene in about half an hour, with two cameras. It was raining outside, which helped the atmosphere. There's something about rain and death and mortality and love.

Sometimes on a set there will be an expert in the film's subject. For *Remains*, we had as our adviser an older man who had been a butler for both Princess Diana and Queen Elizabeth. He told me, "When you are in the room as the butler, the room must feel even emptier."

Our butler expert told us that if the queen said, "Good morning, John. How are you?" he would say only, "Very good, ma'am." They'd then discuss business of the day, and he would perhaps offer an opinion about a dish on a menu, but that's as far as he went in asserting himself. The job was all discipline. I knew how to be quiet, and I brought that skill to the role.

As I wandered about the huge English estate where we shot *Remains of the Day*, I noticed that in the beautiful library, there was a concealed door. "James, could I try something?" I asked. "Wouldn't it make sense for me to use that door?"

They'd already set up the scene so he said, "OK, well, all right, but how long will it take to set up again?" As it turned out, another hour. "OK, well, after lunch, you want to go through the door?"

I said, "Yeah, good."

And we did that.

"Well done. Cut," he said.

That's the height of praise coming from James Ivory. He isn't a great enthusiast. What he is, is an artist. When I arrived at the big house, I saw the whole staff lined up outside, all in black and white uniforms, waiting for the aristocrats to drive up, and it was a stunning visual image. *Just like a painting*, I thought.

In the early days of shooting, there was a scene in which I drive west to meet Emma Thompson's character.

"Can you drive?" James asked me.

"Yeah, I can drive."

"All right, well, just drive this way."

One take.

"And OK, we go over here."

I drove.

"Good. Once more."

Done.

In the restaurant scene we shot later, at an old Victorian seaside resort in North Devon, my character tries to convince Emma Thompson's character to return as housekeeper. After we cut, James Ivory said, "Wait, are you doing *me* in this? You sound like me."

"No, it's not you!" I said.

As I walked off the set, a crew member whispered, "But you are, right? Doing James?"

"Absolutely," I replied.

James arranged everything about those period rooms precisely and always adjusted for shots using delicate brushstrokes: "OK, move the flowers over here. Back again slightly. Angle the chair this way. Good. All right . . . "

Watching a great director work is still, to me, one of the most incredible magic shows. While I've seen many styles of directing be successful, I find myself most drawn to directors who have clear, precise visions. Some actors complain when they're given so little freedom of movement, but when you have a genius in the saddle, tight reins can be an actor's best friend.

Guy Ritchie has that meticulous eye, as do Steven Spielberg, Christopher Nolan, and Michael Bay. Spielberg came to my U.S. citizenship ceremony in April 2000, when I was sixty-two. He videotaped me taking the oath, and a woman sitting nearby commented on what a nice camera he had.

"I do bar mitzvahs as well," he told her.

When I get going naming actors I admire, it's hard for me to stop. Taron Egerton was phenomenal as Elton John in *Rocket Man*. Ed Norton. Billy Burke. Olivia Colman . . .

And Jonathan Pryce, whom I appeared with in *The Two Popes*. Jonathan and I are both Welsh; he's from the north and I'm from the south. One can have a lot of fun trying to prove that the South Welsh are the true Welsh and the North Welsh are . . .

Well, Jonathan has yet to put his case forward.

Mark Gatiss. Salma Hayek. Michael Gambon. Mark Wahlberg. Emma Thompson. Josh Brolin. Sean Penn. Winona Ryder. Robert Downey Jr. Judi Dench is probably the best actress there is. Sylvester Stallone I don't know too well, but I occasionally meet him in passing. I so admired his powerful determination to stay strong and tough, refusing to let anyone else be cast as the lead in his screenplay *Rocky*.

Michael Caine is another lifer who stayed the course. Like me, he found that movies let him enjoy his life more than theater did; for him, that means collecting art (he said once that he couldn't afford to do theater anymore because he'd developed a burning desire to own a van Gogh). I admire those who still do theater, too, of course, like the great Ian McKellen, whom

I was thrilled to appear with in *The Dresser*, a film directed by the wonderful Richard Eyre. We are roughly the same age, and he's unstoppable. I don't know if we will work together again. I certainly hope we do. That one film we made together was a highlight of my life.

From *Nixon*, I went on to do another unlikely part in *Surviving Picasso*. While I wasn't a particularly natural choice to play a macho Spanish womanizer, I was fascinated by the artist, and I loved hearing stories about him. In one, Richard Burton invited Picasso to lunch, and Picasso turned up with a retinue of people. Burton didn't speak Spanish or French, and he was concerned about paying for lunch for such a big group. He needn't have worried. When the check came, Picasso did a drawing on a napkin and handed it to the waiter, more than covering the bill with a stroke of his pencil. That was the panache he had.

Picasso took his young girlfriend Françoise Gilot, a great author and artist in her own right, to a hovel in Montmartre to visit an old woman who lay dying in her dank apartment. Her body was decaying. Her teeth had fallen out. Picasso gave her a kiss and some money.

As they left, Gilot said, "Why did you introduce me to that woman?"

He said, "In 1901, my friend the Spanish poet Carles Casagemas committed suicide over her beauty."

My mother at this time was in her early eighties and living on her own in Wales. When I got a call about being interviewed for the TV news program *60 Minutes*, the producer asked if I would be interviewed in Wales. They added that they would like to speak to my mother as part of the segment. She consented and they got her all made up and did her hair. The interviewer put her at ease. She was filmed outside our old house in Wern Road.

Well, none other than Sam Arrut, the soldier to whom my father had given a ride to the castle, was watching TV in his home in Miami and saw the segment. Seeing the house and my mother, he made the connection between us and his experience in Wales fifty years earlier. He contacted me through my agent, and when I returned to California, he and his wife flew to California to meet with me and my mother. We spent a wonderful day talking about my father and about those summer days in Wales.

After shooting the film about Picasso, I was in the running for a role in a film set in the wilderness. They were also considering Robert De Niro and Dustin Hoffman, and they made sure all of us knew about the others. I thought I'd know by a certain day. The day after that, I phoned my agent. "Any news? The deadline was yesterday."

"They're still waiting for Bobby or someone to make up his mind," he said.

"Well, look, I'll tell you what, then," I said. "Please call them and say thank you very much but I don't need the crumbs from the banquet table. I'm going to Arizona to see some friends of mine."

So I got in my car and I drove to Phoenix. I got there at about seven o'clock at night. And I felt this tremendous sense of peace. I didn't have to worry about those people anymore.

I no longer had to ask myself, *Do they like me? Am I going to get the part?*

As I was taking a bath before going out to dinner with my friends, there was a knock on the door of my room. My friend called, "Tony, can you pick up the phone in there? It's your agent."

My agent sounded giddy. "Hi, Tony, you got the part. And for more money. You should give up on parts more often."

The producers mentioned they wanted a different title for the film, as they felt the working title didn't sound exciting enough. And soon after, I had a dream. I saw a cliff with rock formations. When I woke up, I called my agent and said, "If they're looking for a title, call it *The Edge*." He said the producers told him, "Yes, we just thought of that this morning."

So before I knew it, Alec Baldwin and I were getting ready to shoot *The Edge* in Canada. I had just finished *Nixon* and *Surviving Picasso*. I'd been working nonstop.

I woke up one morning and collapsed. I thought I was having a heart attack, I was in such severe pain. I went down on one knee. I was taken to the hospital in Los Angeles and diagnosed with a herniated disc. The doctor said, "I'm not going to operate. Just rest and it'll go away." Well, I didn't take his advice. I drove straight up to Canada to begin working on *The Edge*.

As part of my preparation, I had to take swimming lessons, which inflamed the disc again. By the time we started shooting, I was in excruciating pain. When he saw me in agony, Alec Baldwin stopped the shoot.

"You can't go on doing this," he told me. "It's not worth it."

Then he went to the producers and said, "Listen, this is two hours of popcorn we're making. Meanwhile, this guy's dying. Get him into the hospital or I'm going to walk off the picture."

So I was taken to the hospital in Canada, and a doctor operated. When I woke up from the surgery, the pain had gone. "Can I go back to work now?" I asked. They made me wait two days, but then we were back up and running, and I wasn't in pain.

The Alberta wildlife was pretty unforgiving, and we had to spend a lot of time frozen to the bone. That was a tough film, but I enjoyed it. It was great working with Alec and Bart the Bear, who was also in, among other movies, *Legends of the Fall*, *The Bear*, and *White Fang*. He could really act, that bear.

The work kept coming. After filming *Zorro* with Steven Spielberg in Mexico, I flew up to New York to do *Meet Joe Black*. I was thrilled to be filming on the streets of New York City. I'm not given to the kind of sentimentality that William Parrish, my character in the film, has, and yet it was very easy for me to play him. He is strong, stubborn, a very rich, very powerful, business-oriented man who is bringing up two girls.

One of them is talking to him about marrying a man she doesn't love, and he tells her, "Love is passion, obsession, someone you can't live without. I say, fall head over heels. Find someone you can love like crazy and who will love you the same way back. How do you find him? Well, you forget your head, and you listen to your heart. And I'm not hearing any heart. 'Cause the truth is, honey, there's no sense living your life without this. To make the journey and not fall deeply in love, well, you haven't lived a life at all. But you have to try, 'cause if you haven't tried, you haven't lived."

In my own life, love had caused me tremendous amounts of pain.

Jenni and I had been together for twenty-five years when we decided to part ways. She saw me through the worst days of my drinking. She stayed with me when I stopped. And yet the marriage did not survive.

They warn you in AA that when you quit drinking, it's common for your partner to resent it even if they're grateful too. And I believe Jenni did resent it. We had a big fight one day when I brought some of my new friends home after a meeting.

"I can't stand these people!" I recall her saying when they left.

"Well, OK, I'll start drinking again. Would you like that?" I said, not kindly.

Of course it was annoying for her. She'd gotten the worst end of the deal when I was drinking. And now that I had a passion for sobriety, here I was suddenly hanging out with these "goody two-shoes," as she called them. For me, their company was lifesaving and endlessly fascinating, but for anyone on the outside, it was dead boring. I could see her switch off when I started talking about all I was learning about alcohol's effect on my life.

We'd bought a house in London, which she far preferred to Los Angeles. She had dolled it up quite beautifully. But I found myself staring at the curtains and thinking, *I'm going to die here.* I felt trapped in this kind of quasi-luxury. I thought, *I've got to get out.*

What it was that I felt closing in on me, I couldn't say. Perhaps a fear of death. The effect was terrible for her. She was married to somebody who was not to be trusted. She turned a blind eye to whatever I was up to. It was only years later that she knew about my infidelities. I don't know whether she took a lover too. I rather hope she did. I would never blame her for it. It would be some consolation to know that she found some happiness in those years in spite of me. It was sad because she deserved better than me, she really did. She brought a change in my life, and I blew it. I take full responsibility for that.

So I did another runaway, this time from my comfortable London home on Alexander Place in Kensington with Jenni. I did a film in Rome and then went alone to America. I look back on that with regret, sadness. I could have been better, but I wasn't.

When we got divorced, I was a mess. I was on the run from rocky dealings on films, broken relationships with women, my lack of trust, a neurotic insistence on being isolated. Sobriety had saved my life, and yet it felt as if something were dying inside me. How could that be? I had achieved everything I had set out to achieve. I had kicked alcohol. What was it that I still didn't understand?

twenty-two

THE CADILLAC SMILE

In 2000, I was made honorary mayor of Pacific Palisades. I was in a big parade, riding in the back of a car waving at everyone. Though I had a smile on my face, I kept thinking, *What the hell am I doing here?*

In the crowd that day, Stella Arroyave, the owner of Om Asian Fine Art and Antiques, waved to me. At the time, she was just a pretty face from a distance. Stella later told me that she said to one of her employees, "I just saw my future husband."

A year later, I came into her shop. I'd wandered in before, but hadn't met her. The gallery was filled with an eclectic collection of antiques, Buddhist deities, and furniture.

Stella greeted me from her desk; she was all smiles, a warm welcome. I expressed my interest in an eighteenth-century Indian dowry trunk and a few other magnificent pieces. I also admired a beautifully carved Chinese wedding chair, which Stella insisted on gifting me.

I offered to pay and asked if everything could be delivered the same afternoon.

"I'll do my best," she said.

She came up to the house that evening. We sorted out the decor and we chatted easily. I found myself attracted to her, and yet I knew I wasn't fit for anyone in my current state. I asked her if she was married.

"No," she said.

She recalls that, upon hearing that, I more or less pushed her out of the house. I didn't want to get involved. I didn't trust anybody.

And yet I couldn't get her off my mind. I found her beautiful, but more than that, I found her mysterious. She seemed at once to be intensely independent and warmly nurturing. She clearly was already living a big life on her own. I wanted to hear all about it. So I called her up the next day and invited her out for lunch. I called her the day after that, too, and the day after that. She apparently enjoyed my company but did not seem overly eager for our relationship to become serious.

I learned that she'd had a hardscrabble upbringing but had made a wonderful life for herself independent of any man. She'd traveled the whole planet, dancing on island beaches and exploring European capitals. She had a whole host of jobs and passions, the main two being an actor, and an art and antiques dealer. I also saw in her compassion and kindness such as I'd never seen before. She cared for her big family, was a loving sister, daughter, aunt, and cousin.

After a few dates, she shared her first impression of me that day at the Palisades parade. She said that even though I was smiling and waving, when she looked closely, she saw a very lonely man.

"You looked so lost," she said on one of our first dates. "I couldn't get over your sad eyes."

I said I was going through a divorce and all that, and yes, it was true I was not happy, and I was lonely, I guessed. But I insisted that I didn't want anyone and didn't need anyone.

Everything on the surface seemed fine. But Stella saw right through me. She refused to accept my explanations and started to deconstruct me piece by piece. And she worked on me.

"What is the matter with you?" she asked—not rhetorically but sincerely. "What really is wrong, deeply?"

"Nothing," I said. "I don't want to talk about it."

She said that by being so withdrawn, I was only hurting myself. She encouraged me to go to therapy. I'd never bothered to "seek help," as they called it out in LA.

My reaction: *Oh no! Not that touchy-feely stuff. Please. Get over yourself. Grow up. "Let's talk"? Hell no. Talk about what? Psycho-bubbles popping in the air? I am quite happy the way I am. Do I have regrets? Yes, a few. But not gut-churning regrets. I simply accept a deficiency in myself, a neurological tic in my brain. So what? I can't be bothered to stew on it. I'll figure my problems out myself. I'm strong. I've come this far. I can beat anything.*

That was my rhinoceros-armor-plated reaction to help or advice.

And yet, I found that the more I took Stella's advice, the happier I became. Over time, she got me to talk about my life, and she said, "I'm going to love you in spite of your not wanting to be loved."

She broke me wide open, helped me overcome the old feelings of regret and anxiety in a way that's set me free. "No matter what the past holds," she says, "you can recognize it and move on."

Illegitimi non carborundum.

I didn't really know Las Vegas when I got a call about recording a voiceover ad for the German magicians Siegfried and Roy. I'd made a trip there once in the late 1970s to see Frank Sinatra perform at Caesars Palace (terrific), and that was that. But when Rick Nicita, my agent at the time and a dear friend, called and asked me if I might be interested in doing the voiceover, I said I'd hear the duo out.

Siegfried and Roy were performing one of those vast spectacle shows at the Bellagio Hotel, an extravaganza with magic and big cats—white lions and white tigers, real predators. These two crazy guys had created the show and started out in modest venues with the usual troubles—a lack of cash and the struggle to survive—while trying to get into the big-time hotels. They'd had a run of luck with the smaller venues, but it was a mad publicity genius by the name of Bernie Yuman who'd put them on the map.

Rick Nicita warned me about him: "There is a business manager attached to this deal and he wants to meet with you to discuss money. I know you like to cooperate with these guys, but I am your agent. *Do not sign any documents.*"

This character, Mr. Yuman, came to see me in Ojai. Was he part of the Mob? I had no idea. I just remember that waiting for his visit that morning, I kept hearing Rick's words: *Don't sign anything. Don't sign anything. Don't sign anything.*

There was a knock on the door. Outside were three men who looked like something out of a gangster film. The man in the middle was dressed in black. As soon as I opened the door, he dropped to his knees.

"Please, Mr. Perkins! We don't have any money, but would you do the recording for my film?"

The other two men seemed embarrassed. "Bernie, get up," one said. "Get up off the floor."

So this groveling man was Bernie Yuman.

He got up and apologized. "I'm sorry, Mr. Perkins—"

The other man muttered: "*Hopkins*, Bernie. It's Anthony *Hopkins*. Not Perkins."

Before I could shut the door, the three men were in the kitchen. After two hours, the men left. I called Rick.

"I didn't sign anything," I said. "But I think Mr. Yuman took my wallet."

And that was my first encounter with Bernard Yuman.

Three days later I had my second encounter with him when he reappeared at my front door. With him were three other people. One was Muhammad Ali. This Yuman guy had been with the legendary boxer for years as his road manager. The other two people accompanying Yuman were Brian and Myra Greenspun. They were residents of Vegas. Brian's father was the late Hank Greenspun, who'd owned the *Las Vegas Sun*, and this Yuman character had made an offer to Hank to place an announcement for Siegfried and Roy's show on the front page of Hank's paper. It had never been done before. This was a newspaper, not an advertising journal. But so forceful was Yuman's selling power that Hank Greenspun surrendered.

With publicity like that (and, later, with my voice, I guess), Siegfried and Roy hit the jackpot. The Bellagio Hotel shows sold out.

Bernie went out of his way to help my mother when I brought her out to Los Angeles from Wales. Her loyal friends Eve and Gene Williams had done what they could, but they had their own families to take care of. She loved California and seemed to wake up and live when she was there. She also loved Bernie and his wife and the Greenspun family.

One weekend we took my mother to Las Vegas to see Siegfried and Roy, whom she couldn't get enough of. At the hotel, I said good night to my mother and opened the door to the room I shared with Stella. When I saw her sitting there, I felt myself break into a broad smile. I was just so happy to see her. She looked up and smiled back at me. I've always loved that smile. I call it the Cadillac smile, sometimes the Colombian Cadillac smile.

"What?" she said, confused by the look on my face.

"We may as well get married," I said.

"Married?" she said. "What brought this on?"

I knew Stella had never wanted to be married. She cherished her freedom. But with me, I argued, she had companionship *and* her freedom, because I, too, cherished my solitude. We loved each other's company. We liked the same things. We were playful together. We made each other better. We should get married.

"OK," she said.

"OK?" I said.

"Yes."

The wedding was lovely, a private affair out at the house in Malibu, with a pastor and a Buddhist monk officiating. My mother hadn't ever trusted me when it came to women. But she liked Stella from the start. They quickly went on to become great friends.

I loved looking around the party to see my mother chatting with Mickey Rooney, Stella's relatives chatting with my agents. What a gift to share that day with so many old and new friends.

Not long after the wedding, my mother died at the age of eighty-nine. Stella was with her to the last moment. My mother for some reason told me to leave the house that day. I think she didn't want me to watch her in her final moments. So, I left. About two hours later, I was in a restaurant eating lunch when my phone rang. Stella told me that my mother had just died.

"Oh," I said. "OK."

"Is that all you can say?" asked Stella, who was crying. I had the feeling that she was not only shocked by my bland response but even angered by it.

"Well, what can I say?" I replied.

She got off the phone to go and make arrangements, surely shaking her head at me.

But that was often the response I still had in moments that seemed to call for powerful emotions. It was the old trick I'd learned as a kid: Show nothing, especially grief.

At the funeral, the good reverend droned on and on. I wanted it to stop. Sitting there in the pew, I felt like I was suffocating.

And yet, in the days to come, I was able to reflect on what luck I'd had to enjoy so many years with her and her final years in the same city.

I was also glad she'd been able to see me make something of myself. The same year of her death, I was given a star on the

Hollywood Walk of Fame, the same street I'd walked down that very first day in Los Angeles decades earlier. The terrazzo sidewalk took me back to the terrazzo floors from my youth, the one in the kitchen of which my mother had been so proud and the one at the YMCA where I'd said my first lines onstage.

On the first, I'd vowed to prove my disappointed parents wrong.

On the second, a little Easter play had shown me how to do that.

Terrazzo. Terrazzo. Terrazzo.

In the mid-2000s, Stella and I decided to have some fun and do a project together. I wrote an experimental screenplay called *Slipstream*. The plot is stream of consciousness. Scenes have no obvious connections with one another; everything appears to be unrelated, haphazard, with no significant through line of action. And there is a film within the film. My character, screenwriter Felix Bonhoeffer, is witnessing the end of his own existence, unable to distinguish fantasy from reality. His own memories and clips from historical events flicker and explode into his awareness. Throughout the movie, he is pulled into the whirlpool of chaos.

After so many years of adhering to the conventions of plot, I wanted to play around and break the rules. I wasn't interested in making a statement. I simply wanted to poke fun at everything, to express my take on the world, a tragicomedy of the absurd, signifying nothing. I enjoyed playing around with the illusory experience of time, memory, and dreams.

While I was working on the film, I was given a lot of advice that I declined to take. The point wasn't to make a conventional movie that would enjoy conventional success. I wanted it to succeed on its own terms. And I believe it did. While the film didn't make much money and the reviews weren't great, I enjoyed the experience, and I stand by the movie because it was fun to do. Whenever I watch a movie, I think about what's happening just off camera. When John Wayne wanders back into the great open prairie at the end of *The Searchers*, I know that just off camera are piles of equipment, cables, lights, trucks, catering; the silent, invisible movie crew; and the great, cantankerous director John Ford waiting to shout, *"Cut!"*

To me, this is a great analogy for life. Sooner or later, the last word will be uttered. The epitaph will be "That's it! That's a wrap, everyone!" Everyone will wander off separately to his or her little box on the hill. In *Slipstream*, I used the movie as a stand-in for life itself. Is it all a dream? Perhaps.

Alas, I don't think I'm a good director. Plenty of actors are, but I'm not one of them. I don't have that objectivity. Trying my hand at it made me even more impressed with good directors. When I watch a Hitchcock movie, I'm in awe.

In *Psycho*, when Anthony Perkins as Norman Bates comes down from the house to the office, it's just one shot. He wants to invite Janet Leigh in for a sandwich. There's an awkwardness, and you see right away he's got a problem with women, the first clue. The way Hitchcock shoots the house, it's clear that this is the house of a monster. And in a scene where the detective goes into the office to look at the registry book, you see Tony Perkins hover over him like a great bird of prey, and you think, *That guy's going to be killed.* A brilliant shot.

In Hitchcock's 1943 film *Shadow of a Doubt*, Joseph Cotten comes to the home of his sister. His niece, Teresa Wright, is thrilled by her uncle Charlie's visit. She's fascinated by him. But when they're having dinner, as the dithering sister is rambling away, the light falls on his face in such a way that you can see that he's not a fun uncle but a killer.

Later he delivers a merciless monologue to his niece: "You go through your ordinary little day, and at night you sleep your untroubled ordinary little sleep, filled with peaceful stupid dreams. And I brought you nightmares. Or did I? Or was it a silly, inexpert little lie? You live in a dream. You're a sleepwalker, blind. How do you know what the world is like? Do you know the world is a foul sty? Do you know if you rip off the fronts of houses, you'd find swine? The world's a hell. What does it matter what happens in it?"

So many actors have stories about how precise Hitchcock was. Hume Cronyn said that in that film, he asked if he could move over a hair and Hitchcock said, "No, you'll be out of the light. Stay exactly where you are." James Stewart said that when they did *Rear Window*, he never left the set because he was obsessed with watching the way Hitchcock set up the lighting. And of course, Hitchcock could be ruthless when questioned. On the set of *Lifeboat*, Mary Anderson complained that he wasn't shooting her best side. He replied, "Miss, you're sitting on your best side." When an actor asked, "Mr. Hitchcock, what's my motivation?" he replied, "I'll tell you when you get a job."

Before we started shooting *World's Fastest Indian*, a biopic written and directed by Roger Donaldson about Burt Munro's at-

WE DID OK, KID

tempt to break the land-speed record on his motorbike, Stella said to Bruce Willis, "Can you keep an eye on my husband? Because he's nuts." She was afraid I'd try to do my own stunts, which I absolutely did.

I found Munro to be an interesting character. He was regarded as a strange eccentric, which he was, a real loner. He came from Invercargill in New Zealand. And his passion in life was that little motorbike he built that he called the Indian. People thought he was raving mad because he wanted to go to Bonneville Salt Flats and break the land-speed record. He was eccentric, but he wasn't stupid. My task was to become him even though we didn't look much alike.

When I met his niece, she said, "Uncle Burt told me, 'Always say yes to everything, and if you believe something, you're halfway there.'"

That philosophy can get you into a lot of trouble, of course, but Munro was a benevolent guy. He seemed to like everyone, and he loved kids. He was a good sport with a great sense of humor.

"My dad thinks you won't do it, you'll fail," a boy in the film tells Burt.

Burt vows to prove the father wrong.

"I believe you," the kid says.

"Well, thanks, mate," says Burt.

I admired Burt's spirit. Everyone in Bonneville was shocked when he brought out his homemade bike and said he was going to break the world record with it.

In our film, a man pulls out a piece of the bike and says, "What's this?"

"A cork from a brandy bottle," says Munro.

People thought he was crazy, but he did it, drove two hundred miles an hour and beat the world land-speed record.

One day on set, Roger Donaldson came up to me and said conspiratorially, "Is Stella here?"

"Not yet," I said.

"In that case," he said, "would you mind lying on the road and being dragged through the sand by this truck fender?"

"Sure," I said. And I let myself be dragged through the salt flats at forty miles per hour, laughing inside and thinking that I was more afraid Stella would see me doing my own stunts than I was of getting road burn.

A few years later, I was invited into the Marvel universe—I was given the part of Odin, Thor's father, the god of wisdom, poetry, war, death, divination, and magic. He and his son Thor, played by Chris Hemsworth, defend the godly realm against threats planetary, cosmic, and, sometimes, familial. Chris worked out four to five hours a day to build that body. He was a very nice guy, a very good actor, and there was no nonsense with him. No Hollywood crap. He's a good Aussie and he gets on with it.

Kenneth Branagh is extremely precise as a director. I'd seen him several times onstage and in films, and I'd met him years earlier when I'd worked with his then wife, Emma Thompson. He'd often been compared to Olivier and even played him in the film *My Week with Marilyn*. And I found his direction to be like Olivier's: professional, flexible, clever.

In some ways, those movies with big special effects feel a little bit NAR, to use Gregory Peck's term. I heard it from a man who in 1951 worked at a studio in London made up to look like a ship for the war film *Captain Horatio Hornblower*.

He came across Gregory Peck's script and noticed that *NAR* was written on certain pages. He gave it back to Peck, who thanked him.

"Mr. Peck, can I ask you what *NAR* means?"

Peck replied, "No acting required."

John Wayne said that in Westerns he didn't have to act much because the desert did a lot of the acting for you. I played Herod recently. We shot in Morocco in a huge empty arena built for chariot racing. They were going to add the horses in post-production. You watch the original *Ben Hur*, and the arena is full of extras and animals and life. Nothing against green-screen work, but I think you can tell the difference. There's something that you remove by substituting computer graphics. I wouldn't say it's deadening, but generally I prefer to be on location in a real place with real people.

These varied roles shot all over the world and in all different formats ultimately led me back to Shakespeare and to what I believe is the greatest part ever written for an actor: King Lear.

twenty-three

NOTHING WILL COME OF NOTHING

I'd first played Lear in 1986 at the National Theatre. It was an interesting production directed by David Hare. But I completely misjudged the way to play the king. I was forty-eight, far too young, and I felt I'd missed the mark. Thirty years later, I thought I would take another shot at the role.

In 2017, I was cast as King Lear in a film directed by Sir Richard Eyre. By that time I'd matured, and I had a better sense of how I wanted to play him. I felt confident that seventy-nine years of living had given me enough emotional information about the aches and pains of life, especially in old age, to do it correctly. I knew, perhaps too well by that point, how stubborn willpower could cause pain in others. Like the men in my family, Lear carries with him the locked-up rage and loneliness of his life. My grandfather's and my father's and my attitude so often amounted to *Oh, yeah? Well, then, screw you all!*

I also saw Lear as a man who'd been deeply hurt by women. The backstory for my interpretation was that Cordelia's mother had died giving birth to her, and Lear had locked his own grief at the loss deep within. He decided to raise Cordelia as a tomboy.

Being an old, scarred warrior, the irascible tyrant Lear had little or no tolerance for warmth or friendship. Not a stretch for me, as they say. The hardness of my father and his father were well embedded in me. The only trace of softness in Lear was his affection for Cordelia. His two older daughters, he knew, were conniving women. He saw through them. He knew they were greedy and ambitious for power. They held him in contempt, because they would never forgive him for what he was: a cold, iron-willed old soldier. He believed he'd taught his youngest daughter to be strong, warriorlike.

During the formal ceremony of dividing the kingdom into three parts for his daughters, he knows that the fulsome speeches of his two older daughters are exaggerated, meant to manipulate him into giving them large portions of the kingdom. He knows Regan and Goneril for what they are; he knows they rehearsed their false speeches of love and devotion.

He dismisses them after giving them their portions of the kingdom. The transaction is accomplished in a businesslike way. Then he turns to his youngest daughter, eager to hear her genuine profession of love and devotion. This will give him a sense of fulfillment and peace and, perhaps, a hint of love, something about which he knows little.

But Cordelia speaks the truth. She cannot offer her father full love. Her husband must now be the object of her love and devotion. At first, he thinks she must be joking. "Nothing will come of nothing," he tells her. "Speak again." When she refuses to bend to his will, he flies into a rage and banishes her as a way to bury his shock and humiliation.

Sometimes you see the first act of Lear played romantically, almost as if he's in love with his daughter. But sappy doesn't work for Lear. What works is blankness, rigidity. He refuses to accept love even as its absence is killing him. At the start of the play, Lear's heart is closed. He's the kind of man who labored in the Wales steelworks for decades, who built the West, who conquered nations.

The rest of the play is Lear's learning how much his cruelty has cost him. When he is banished and sets forth into the wilderness, a king of rags and tatters, the Fool gives him a horseshoe to wear as a crown. This symbol has always affected me in a powerful way. My father once told me about a beloved old horse he'd groomed every day. When the horse died, my father, then nineteen, broke down and cried. His father laughed at him, told him to be a man. My father kept one of the horse's shoes in our kitchen drawer, a talisman of fortitude.

Three weeks before starting rehearsals for *Lear*, I had taken part in an HBO series called *Westworld*. Oddly, on my last day, I came across an old horseshoe on a table in the props department. I asked the assistant props master if I could buy the horseshoe to use in *Lear*. He told me to take it, and that's what I used for the Fool's crown in the film.

In the end, when Lear drags Cordelia in dead—"She's gone forever"—I thought of my father's hardness in the face of death. "Yeah, well, we all go the way of all flesh," he liked to say. Like Lear, he hated to express softness or fragility. Lear, even when Cordelia dies, insists he's not going to weep. But then he breaks down, as my father, too, broke down. Even my grandfather Yeats wept when his favorite daughter, Jenny, died, before he brought the wall back up and refused to shed another tear for her or anyone else.

Lear, alone with his wise Fool, beaten and subdued, finally realizes that he mistreated the only person who truly loved him. In this production, the line that hit me harder than perhaps any other I've ever spoken was "I did her wrong."

Saying those words, I felt deeply, perhaps for the first time in my life, how I had hurt my own daughter, Abigail.

I did her wrong.

I remembered how as a baby she'd lit up when I walked into the room. I remembered how I said goodbye to her the night I walked out. I remembered how I had tried and failed to win her back later. I remembered how I had given up. And as Lear, but also as myself, I began to cry.

I wondered if something in me didn't break in my parents' house, something that limited my capacity to be a father. I thought back to that afternoon more than sixty years earlier when I was standing with my mother and my father, both silent and defeated, in that stifling, cramped kitchen behind the bakery, that crucial moment I realized that I would show them—

my mother, my father, anyone within earshot—that there was a power inside me that would transform everything.

That was the moment I decided there would be no more equivocating, no more waffling, no more hiding in corners. I would succeed. I stopped the *danse macabre* of collusion and agreement. No more. With that drive came a relentlessness that let me achieve so much and also that could be impossible for people I loved to bear.

After realizing I was unfit as a father for Abigail, I vowed not to have any more children, and I have kept that promise. I knew I was too selfish. I couldn't do to another child what I'd done to her. But in my old age, once I'd finally learned patience and kindness, I was finally able to be a kind of father figure. And I've found myself surrounded since then with people who are outsiders in some way. When you see someone who's suffering some terrible loneliness, you can say, "I know how you feel." You can't give them a shot and make them better. But you can be there.

One night Stella and I were watching the show *Doc Martin*, a medical comedy-drama set in a seaside town in Cornwall, and Stella turned to me, pointed at Martin Clunes's just-the-facts doctor on the screen, and said, "It's you!"

The character Doc Martin, as brilliantly played by Clunes, struggles to connect with people and never seems able to soften the blow of his honesty. In one scene, his girlfriend is going through a box of family photos and he says to her, "Why do people keep photographs?"

She says, "That's what people *do*, Martin."

How often people have said things like that to me!

Viewers have said that Doc Martin is likely on the autism spectrum. Stella's belief that I probably have Asperger's is likely right, given my proclivity for memorization and repetition (*BTX 698, terrazzo* . . .) and my lack of emotionality. But, like any stoic man from the British Isles, I'm allergic to therapeutic jargon. Even if the world might prefer I accept the Asperger's label, I've chosen to stick with what I see as a more meaningful designation: *cold fish*.

Life with Stella over the past twenty-five years has been full of revelations and adventure. We especially love rescuing stray cats. I even brought one back from the set of the exorcism movie *The Rite* in Budapest.

Doing this rescue work has healed the pain I felt losing a cat as a child. I once found a little gray cat, a stray. My mother let me keep her, and I named her Smoky. But one day a neighbor from the street, a Mrs. Worley, saw me playing with Smoky in the front garden. She opened the front gate and took that cat from me with only the words "She's mine." How I hated that woman! I can still remember the pain of that loss. A few months later, my mother brought a tabby kitten to the house, Celina. I loved Celina until she died in 1950. Stella and I have delighted in watching our older cats nurture our youngest, who came to us not long ago as an abandoned kitten. The will to live and help others survive is so strong.

In so many ways, Stella has helped me to unravel the knots and twists of my past. She keeps a sharp eye on me regarding my health and well-being. She also helped me rediscover a great passion. Stella found some old scripts with drawings, and she liked them. She asked me to paint pictures to give to the guests at our wedding. And I had so much fun doing those that, most days now, I paint or draw, as I enjoyed doing in my childhood. I don't know who I'm painting. One came out like Barack Obama. Others have looked like Kevin Costner, Sophia Loren. There's nothing meaningful in it.

I'm not trained, but I've developed little tricks, like putting white dots on the pupils to give eyes more life. I work on each painting for a few days, doing three or four at a time. I relish the freedom of it. I love color. It becomes a reflection of my own life. I listen to Greek music when I paint. I do it for fun and for free.

Ralph Waldo Emerson, in his famous Divinity School Address, said the way to God was through poetry, music, art, and nature. He and Henry David Thoreau, among others, created transcendentalism. He believed that if you touched one soul through poetry or art, all souls would be touched at the same time. Henry Miller said, "Paint as you like and die happy." And that is what I hope to do. I imagine that when the Oliviers told me, "Be so happy," this might have been what they meant.

twenty-four

KEEP YOUR TALENT IN THE SHADE

In 2019, Stella decided I should give back. She set up a series of meetings where I was to give advice to young actors and let them ask me anything they wanted. I protested for a few minutes. *I have nothing to offer! I have no philosophy of acting!* I quoted the American film actor Robert Mitchum for the thousandth time. Of acting for a living, he'd said, "It sure beats working." I reminded her that I'd do anything to avoid the mushy plague of sentimental guff and dewy-eyed hogwash smeared around in talks of Craft, the old darlings-and-loveys brigade.

Stella, as always, waited for me to conclude my tantrum and then watched me submit to her will. Not for nothing is her nickname "the Boss."

Friends love recalling the time when I was kept waiting all day in full costume and makeup on a film set, causing Stella, without my knowledge, to go into the control room and confront the producers.

"What is taking so long? *Anthony Hopkins,* who is in his *eighties,* has been waiting for hours while the six of you sit around this TV monitor with your kids in private school and your private jets and your backward baseball caps! You better move! You get him out of here!" I got called so fast, I didn't even have time to go to the bathroom before I was swept onto the set. They wrapped me in about five minutes.

Looking out at the hopeful faces in the Anthony Hopkins Artists Forum, all those young people summoned by the Boss, I began by saying that as a rule, I never offered insights into the mysteries of acting, because I didn't believe there were any. My main suggestion: Work hard, with a passion or even obsession. Then it became the wonderful game, the play of life upon life itself. And at its heart, acting was a job not so much different from any other job. Arrive on time. Don't keep others waiting. Learn the lines, don't bump into the furniture, and make sure you're squared up with your agent and your taxes.

I told them: The main thing is to believe in yourself. Believe in what you're doing. Live as if the future is the present. You need to tell yourself things like *I am successful.* The way Muhammad Ali said, "I'm the greatest fighter ever," you must say, "I am the greatest." I love the Dorothea Brande book *Wake Up and Live!* Thanks to her, I will often write on my script *Act as if it is impossible to fail.* Life is in session. This is not a rehearsal for the big event. This is the big event.

That doesn't mean we should be precious about our work.

I was asked by a Welsh director once: "You don't feel Welsh?"

"How is it supposed to feel?" I asked.

"Well, Welsh. Poetic. You know what I mean."

"Sorry, no, I don't know. I breathe oxygen just like everyone else."

When I hear young actors talking about doing only this or only that, I tell them that it's not yet time to be picky. They should take any job that comes their way. Don't wait forever for a better script. Believe that your life is all a matter of weaving; when you look back over the years, you'll see a tapestry. And in the meantime? They should read everything they can: The classics. History. Psychology. Sophocles. Schopenhauer. Nietzsche. Also: Watch old Hollywood movies. Steal from the greats.

Watch Bogart. He said, "Acting is six feet behind the eyes." He always had an air of loneliness about him. When he was shooting the 1950 film *In a Lonely Place*, he said to Gloria Grahame, a sexy young actress, "Keep your talent in the shade; keep it in the shadows." She cultivated a darkness, and it served her well in so many movies where she played doomed heroines.

To become an actor, you must be both tough and generous with yourself. There are no free lunches in this business. Learn your script backward and forward. You need to learn the pages in order to relax. That's the most important thing: Be professional. That means you say hello to the crew. You learn the lines. You show up on time. You look out for one another.

Once I heard a director loudly tell an extra, "You look like crap!" It made her cry.

"May I speak with you?" I said, taking him aside. "Who do you think you are, talking to someone like that? Apologize to her! And learn some manners. You ever do that again in front of me, I'll change the shape of your face."

A young actor recently said to me, "You're very friendly with the crew, aren't you?"

"What do you mean?" I asked. I had noticed that he didn't give anyone the time of day.

He said, "You talk to everyone." He seemed surprised.

"Yes, I do," I said, "because I don't even know how to take a photograph, but those guys put my stupid face on the screen and they put your stupid handsome face on the screen. The most important people around here are plugging in the lights, driving the trucks, and making sure the set doesn't crush us. That answer your question?"

That was the last time he tried to talk to me.

One famous young actor had a reputation for constantly showing up late. I never had that experience with him, and I told a crew member that.

"Oh, he's never late when *you're* here," the crew member said. "He respects you too much. We wish you were here every day so he'd never be late."

I'll never forget one hotshot actor who showed up late three days in a row. On the third day, the director said, "Don't bother changing clothes; you're done here. Your plane ticket is on the table." And that was an actor who'd been in the game for a while. Don't imagine anyone will put up with more than that from you.

And never whine. I have no patience for people saying life isn't fair. Of course it's not. If life were fair, I would have died forty years ago. If there were justice, I should have died many times before that too. But I'm alive. Not through my own will but through some kind of awakening of knowledge that came from deep within myself.

Remember what Olivier told me: When you're speaking onstage, even if it's just for a minute, during that time you're the star of the show. Be a king or queen! And for heaven's sake, speak up!

When I hear actors say things like "Acting is tough; it's almost like being in a battle!" I want to throw up. Some actors believe acting is dangerous. Some insist that they are so special, others must never look at them—"No eye contact, please." Bless their cotton socks.

If you don't like the job, sonny boy, give it up! I want to say to them. *And beware of that heavy door banging your slick little ass on the way out!*

Walk down the street, any street of any city block, and see how tough life really is. Witness the daily trudge of people trying to survive. At any supermarket checkout, there are older women bagging groceries for rude, cell phone–gabbing customers who are too busy texting to say "Thank you." On street corners, old men, veterans from forgotten battlefields, panhandle for cash. Meanwhile, actors make a living by saying, "Let's all dress up and pretend!"

I encouraged the forum members to check out the great Hollywood novel *What Makes Sammy Run?* by Budd Schulberg (who also wrote *On the Waterfront*). In the book, Sammy Glick, born in New York, goes to Hollywood to make it big. With ruthless ambition and drive, he claws his way to the top. But in the end, he's in his big mansion and all the stars have come and drunk all his booze and then gone home. And he's alone. Little Sammy Glick—he wanted success too much, and look what it cost him.

I told the forum actors, "Self-esteem is not the thing. You're here for *self-worth*. The more vulnerable and scared you are, the better. Don't try and be cool. The cool ones, you can see right through their masks. And you know who they are. You see them all over town. I know a couple of you work here at restaurants and hotels. Great—do the best you can with what you've got. Whatever grotty situation you live in, make the best of it. If it's too rough, find another job. Be open and it will happen. Just avoid the crust of bitterness and resentment. Don't let that become a shield. Because that's the end of your ability to be a good human being or a good actor."

The students made me set my ego aside to tend to them. The ego is the killer. It's the creator, but it's also the killer. In the past I was arrogant. I've come to a place where I am repelled by any shows of entitlement and I'm fascinated by how I could have lived like that for so long. I've exchanged some emails with Ryan Holiday, a brilliant young guy from Texas who wrote *Ego Is the Enemy*. I told him I feel like I haven't made all that many decisions in my life; I feel that I'm not actually the person driving the car.

Ryan shared what he'd learned from Seneca: "Soon we will spit out our life's breath. For a moment, while we still draw it, while we're in the human world, let's cherish our humanity. Let's not be a source of fear or danger to anyone. Let's cast scorn on injuries, harms, insults, and taunts; let's put up with brief annoyances. As they say, the moment we turn and look behind us, death stands right there."

While doing that artists forum, I felt that so acutely—that I must cherish my humanity, that death was standing right there. Speaking that way to the students became like peeling away layers of an onion. When there's a drought, you're left with piles of dried leaves. Speaking with those young people was like clearing away the dried-up foliage that could have set me on fire. It chipped away at residual barnacles of bitterness and anger. It quieted my mind.

Nothing against anger in the proper dosage. Anger gets you places. But I don't have much time for it anymore. I wake up in the morning and I look at my cat. He's quite happy being a cat. He doesn't want to be a puppy, doesn't want to be a bird.

"Dream big," I told the forum audience. "Nothing wrong with that. But remember that you are nothing. Your life is really none of your business. My life is none of my goddamn business." I told them that the important thing was to stay in the game. Whenever someone has tried to engage me in making fun of another actor, I say, "At least he's doing it! You're sitting on your ass watching."

I think often of the famous Theodore Roosevelt "Man in the Arena" speech from 1910. It's a speech my father liked to quote, as did Burt Munro from *World's Fastest Indian*.

> It is not the critic who counts; not the man who points out how the strong man stumbles, or where the doer of deeds could have done them better. The credit belongs to the man who is actually in the arena, whose face is marred by dust and sweat and blood; who strives valiantly; who errs, who comes short again and again, because there is no effort without error and shortcoming; but who does actually strive to do the deeds; who knows the great enthusiasms, the great devotions; who spends himself in a worthy cause; who at the best knows in the end the triumph of high achievement, and who at the worst, if he fails, at least fails while daring greatly, so that his place shall never be with those cold and timid souls who neither know victory nor defeat.

I told the young actors that their job was to be brave, to strip away the dross, the garbage, the dry rot. "Be awake, be aware, enjoy life!"

And on the day that I spoke those words, in front of them,

I broke down crying. Those students' humility and curiosity cracked me open like an egg. I found their drive and hope so inspiring. I felt moved by something beyond my puny knowledge, some great sadness and remarkable feeling of love and affection for each day of life.

I felt the great truth of Gerard Manley Hopkins's poem "The Leaden Echo and the Golden Echo":

> *How to keep—is there ány any, is there none such, nowhere*
> *known some, bow or brooch or braid or brace, láce, latch or catch*
>   *or key to keep*
> *Back beauty, keep it, beauty, beauty, beauty, . . . from vanishing*
>   *away?*
> *Ó is there no frowning of these wrinkles, rankéd wrinkles deep,*
> *Dówn? no waving off of these most mournful messengers, still*
>   *messengers, sad and stealing messengers of grey?*

That experience with the forum enriched my life and made me more conscious of my own mortality. To quote Ernest Dowson:

> *They are not long, the weeping and the laughter,*
> *Love and desire and hate:*
> *I think they have no portion in us after*
> *We pass the gate.*

Written and directed by Florian Zeller, a young French genius, *The Father* is a film about a man suffering from dementia—and about the passing of time and the pain of loss. In doing that movie, I felt myself in some way becoming my father as he was in his final days—the vacant stare, mouth agape, seeming to see things and hear voices.

Florian generously included songs in the film score that meant much to me, including "Je Crois Entendre Encore" ("I Still Believe I Hear"), an aria from Georges Bizet's 1863 opera *Les Pêcheurs de Perles* (*The Pearl Fishers*) that had made me cry when I first heard it as a little boy back in Port Talbot. What I feel every time I hear that song is at once that I am fully present and that I know absolutely nothing.

We shot *The Father* at a warehouse in Wembley. The way Zeller lit the apartment so moodily, with afternoon sun filtering into the room and street noise coming from below, was masterly. He captured the desperate horror of being trapped in your own brain. And Olivia Colman was so beautiful in the role of my daughter. I never add lines, but I did add a few words in that movie: "The wind and the rain." There was something powerful to me in the image of a storm outside and then the father in this still, quiet room.

My plan for playing this character was to speak very fast, like a man trying to catch up with his own thoughts. He is living in a totally confused world, so he's trying to show how clever and sharp he is at all times. That makes him cruel, often yelling at people. He keeps saying, "I don't need looking after! Leave me alone!"

In the course of the film, he gradually deteriorates to the point where he doesn't know where he is and he thinks everyone's stealing from him.

I tried to create a bit of a backstory for him, one in which he was disciplined, an engineer, tough, used to being in control. This is a man who tries to grab onto information even as his mind is falling apart. He doesn't even know his own name at the end. He's beginning to sense that death is close.

To reinforce this idea of who he was before, I asked the wardrobe department for a club tie or a military tie. In the first scenes, he's clean-shaven and wearing a jacket, trying to prove to himself that he's OK. The other part of his mind knows that he's going down into the hole.

I was reminded of a man I knew in the army, a major with a black mustache. He had highly polished boots and he'd been at the D-Day landings and the liberation of Bergen-Belsen. He was the most formal, disciplined man, but one day he put a bullet in his head. Something cracked in him. And yet, until the day he died, he projected an air of being completely in control.

So what I wanted to do with this man who was losing control was to play the opposite, to try to make him seem confident, combative. His monologues combined confusion and arrogance: "Who are you? What are you doing here? What are you doing in my flat? . . . You live in my flat? That's the best yet. What is this nonsense?" He also speaks of a daughter who's died as if she were alive: "The world is turning. You've always been that way. A worrier. Like your mother. Your mother was always scared. Always looking for reasons to be scared. Whereas your sister has always been much more . . . At least she doesn't keep badgering me . . . Where is she, by the way? Have you heard from her?"

His daughter had been killed years before. The audience knows that, and the other characters know it, but he does not.

Florian Zeller said, "Let's not give away too much at the beginning."

"Exactly," I said. "But from the very first scene, the audience knows this guy's in big trouble."

Watching that film for the first time, I became very emotional. I am close to that age. And the tragedy of dementia hangs over us all. Making that movie was almost too easy for me. I walked onto that set, saw the sunlight coming in, heard the traffic rumbling outside, and it was easy to feel myself dying inside this comfortable little apartment, not knowing what day it was. And my time with the forum had prepared me as nothing else could. I give credit to those young people for helping me reach that state of being.

Two years after the forum, I became, at eighty-three, the oldest person ever to win an Oscar, for *The Father*.

I wasn't at the awards ceremony that year from fear of COVID. I was also quite sure that the honor would go to the great Chadwick Boseman, who delivered such an exceptional performance in *Ma Rainey's Black Bottom* and who was taken from us that year, far too early. So sure was I that I wouldn't win, I was actually asleep in Wales when the announcement was made. My agent Jeremy Barber called and woke me up at four in the morning with the words "You won! You won your second Oscar!"

That day I posted a stunned thank you on social media. What I didn't say was that I feel I share that award with all the young actors of the forum. I believe that I was able to play that role in *The Father* with such vulnerability because they taught me how to be more open. I found their struggle to learn so achingly beautiful.

In sharing what I could with them, I finally overcame my aversion to the touchy-feely side of this work, and I found a whole new well of emotion in myself. More than ever, I feel the truth of the lines in the poem by W. B. Yeats, my favorite poet. That is my role now, to sit by the fire and remember.

When you are old and gray and full of sleep
And nodding by the fire, take down this book
And slowly read, and dream of the soft look
Your eyes had once, and of their shadows deep.

More and more these days, poetry sends me back to my childhood. When I read W. B. Yeats, I'm walking down a dreary road called Duke Street in Port Talbot, a morose little boy. I say two lines of Dylan Thomas and suddenly I can smell the warm bread in my father's bakery as if an oven had just been opened in the same room.

twenty-five

THE OLDER I GET, THE LESS I KNOW

Birth was the death of him. Again. Words are few. Dying too. Birth was the death of him. Ghastly grinning ever since. Up at the lid to come. In cradle and crib. At suck first fiasco. With the first totters. From mammy to nanny and back.

—SAMUEL BECKETT, *A Piece of Monologue*

The young live in the moment. They fall in love, have fun. Life for them is a party. But there is a dark figure waiting up on that distant hill for all of us. I'm at an age where I can see that vision more clearly. In a recurring dream, that distant figure is revealed to be my father, waiting to guide me down the long gray road across the moors of my childhood.

In 2024, I visited my father's grave in Christchurch, near Newport. Putting my hand on his gravestone, I said, "Rest in peace, Dickie Boy." He'd died at age seventy-two. I've already outlived him by more than a decade. And though he's been dead more than forty years, I find my memories of him crystal clear.

Although I am not given much to spooky stuff or sentimentality, as I stood by the grave I nevertheless had the odd feeling that he was behind me. And as sure as I'm sitting in a chair right now, I felt his hand on my back.

I turned. No one was around. Still, I felt him, the old man. He was there.

Loneliness is something I cherish. Not so much being alone, but loneliness itself. And yet, it had felt good to have my father there with me in that cemetery. Not judging this time. Not ranting. Just there. One old man with another old man. Eighty-six years after he fathered me, seventy-two years after he scolded me for failing out of school, forty-three years after his death, were he and I finally at peace?

A memory came back to me at that grave: I was standing on a cliff with my father. It was on the Worm's Head, in Gower, West Wales. I was twelve. I had an urge to jump off the cliff. Perhaps that's normal. *I'll jump and hit the rocks below.* It was just a thought. But as if sensing what was happening in my brain, my father put his hand on my right shoulder. There was rarely physical contact in those days, but he seemed to know I needed it then, and perhaps I need it now as I prepare to learn for myself what the old man called the Big Secret.

In a recurring dream, I'm standing on a shaky battlement. There's no way off it except by some rough, crumbling steps. I think, *How did I get up here? And how am I going to get down?* The quiet experience daily, even with the aches and pains of aging, is the aloneness of my inner life. What that means precisely, I have no idea, but I feel it is part of my father's life; yes, the old man and his life, long before I was even born, as if his past, even back to his own childhood, is in me and is mine. It is not just a spot of fanciful dream dust—it is real and located in the center of my body. I can describe it only as sadness. Not a sweet, "poor me" sadness; perhaps not even sadness, but something that pushes me onward to the end of the road. Perhaps it is a mixture of love and grief, the ground of all being.

Shakespeare, too, has laid some version of a hand on my shoulder from the moment I first heard his words spoken, in the darkened assembly hall in the grim Welsh boarding school where we heard the opening chords of William Walton's music and were shown the film of *Hamlet*.

Stella went to see a former Cowbridge teacher of mine a few years ago when she was making a documentary, and she asked him, "What was Tony like at school?"

"He never played cricket, never played football," he said. "We didn't know who he was. He never spoke to anyone. He was very, very quiet. And he was good at geography and good at music. He played the piano. But when he left school, within ten years he was onstage with Laurence Olivier."

That was the first time in my life that I realized how much had changed in just that decade. Drama school. Cardiff. Two years in the army. A quantum leap. And every year since, miracles upon miracles. I look at my life and remember that hapless little boy, and I think, *How did all this happen?* This is the thing that puzzles me about the mystery of life. I could never have organized any of this, or even imagined it. My life has been written by someone else, not by me. I don't know who's running the show, but whoever it is has an excellent sense of humor.

When I made *One Life*, the movie about Nicholas Winton, the British stockbroker who set up the Kindertransport that saved hundreds of Czechoslovakian children from the Nazis, I was inspired by his humility and grace.

He was once asked by a reporter, "Do you believe in God?"

He took his time replying. Then he said, "Well, the Germans are praying to God. The British are praying to God. The Americans are praying to God. Who knows?" He said we had no hope for the future unless we learned to compromise.

I found his story very moving, particularly as I remembered from when I was a kid the newsreels of the liberation of Bergen-Belsen, the walking skeletons. They're stuck in my memory forever.

A Buddhist friend of mine, soon after losing her mother, said of life, "It's all one long goodbye."

I love that. We can kid ourselves that we're important for a while. Red carpets, mindless drinking, the arrogance of success. But if you survive long enough, you come to the point: We come and say, "Hello," hang around, then say, "Goodbye, kids."

Accepting the Palme d'Or at Cannes, Meryl Streep said that watching clips from her films in the retrospective video felt like looking out the window of a bullet train, watching youth flash into middle age and then blur into old age. I often feel that way, and more and more I feel my earliest memories vividly.

One summer evening when I was still quite young, I crossed a small wooden cart bridge over Arnallt Brook at the end of Ty-Fry Road and meandered along the path past a farm and onward across the pasture fields to the Brombil Valley. I heard a voice drifting from a radio through an open window in the last house on the road. I can still hear it now, just as I can still smell the air of Margam Woods, where my aunt Lorna took me when I was four to see a field of bluebell flowers.

On that day, there were shafts of sunlight between the branches of the ancient beech trees, meadows of pale blues and vibrant greens. I ran into the thickness of the carpet and started gathering the flowers in large bunches while Aunt Lorna's kind, musical laugh echoed through the trees, delighted as she was by this little boy who couldn't sweep all the life and color he wanted up into his arms. For a moment, everything became still, as if we were inside a giant photograph. The dappled light, the rustle of the leaves, the sounds of all life froze into stillness.

Then I'm eighty-seven again, and, incredibly, still working. What's more, I've found that more often than not when it comes to work my age is an asset.

Olivier was once fired by Greta Garbo. He had no hard feelings. He said, "I didn't have it then. I hadn't found the middle of myself yet. But there comes a point when you know that you've found the middle, that you know how to do it. You have the reins of the chariot, like Ben-Hur."

I'll never forget seeing Yul Brynner on Broadway in *The King and I*. I believe he already had the cancer that would kill him. His voice was a bit croaky. When he came out for the curtain call, there was riotous applause. He looked out at the audience and saw that they weren't standing. In character as the king, he strode to the edge of the stage, put his fists on his hips, thrust out his chest, and jutted out his chin. His bald head gleamed in the klieg lights, and his eyes flashed with mischief.

"How dare you?" he thundered, glowering at the audience imperiously. "I am the king of Siam! Stand for me!" Laughing and clapping even louder, the audience leaped to their feet. Smiling, he grasped the hands of his costars and swept them all into another round of bowing.

I kept a little notebook for years in which I wrote things like *Act as if. Act as if. Act as if now.* I still like repeating mantras to myself, like "Today, I live in the eternal good and the eternal life. I lift my thinking above all sense of limitation. I turn to that power within which 'I can't' transforms into 'I can.' I have the wisdom, I have the knowledge, I have the energy and the power to reach my goals. Nothing can stand in my way."

Dreams spoken aloud have come true. When my father said I was hopeless, I denied what I was told by him and by my teachers. I said I would show them all, and I did. I dreamed a great future, and in doing so, I gathered a glorious future to me. I've found pure joy and freedom in art. I try to paint or draw every day, and I also play the piano every day for about two hours. In my old age, I've rediscovered the love of creating purely for its own sake.

While I have studied piano, when it comes to visual art, I find that if I think too much, it kills what I love about it. The great Stan Winston, a classically trained painter and sculptor and an Academy Award–winning makeup artist who collaborated with Steven Spielberg and James Cameron, once came over and looked at my paintings. He began asking why I put a face here, why I used a certain color there.

"I don't know," I said. "I have no training."

"Don't train!" he said. "Look, I've trained. I couldn't do what you do. Do it!"

For me, the less thinking, the better. Just show up and do it. Come on! We'll all be dead one day. Have a ball. Smile though your heart is breaking . . . have a laugh. We'll be dead a long time.

I tell people who are struggling that it can help to find photographs of themselves as children: Go back to that child whenever you're in doubt. Never forget the child in that photo, that little kid who knew so little and who perhaps no one believed in. It's important to remember who you are and where you come from. Never let go of it. If you're a farmer's daughter, hold on to that! Throughout my life I've felt like a con man, a trickster, and a highly successful failure. I agree with my detractors that I'm not smart enough to have created or planned any part of my life. Again: By all logic and common sense I should have died decades ago. How and why I am still here beats the hell out of me. Other people's resentments or hostility are understandable: "How did he do it?" Same question I ask myself.

Even as a young boy, I believed I was an impostor and never had a high opinion of myself. I was always on the run, never stopping to look back, a hobo and a drifter, a scraggy old alley cat on its ninth life. I lived by the old adage "Trust in God but keep your gunpowder dry." Live and let live, but keep your running shoes close for the big skedaddle. The Grim Reaper always gets the runner in the end, but we might as well make him chase us.

Now, though, I reflect on how hard I fought to be different from my father and grandfather and how much like them I couldn't help being. I hope against hope that I've found a way to be a man who's slightly kinder and gentler, more self-aware and forgiving.

A. E. Housman's poem "Is My Team Plowing" still reminds me of the mountains and woods of Margam.

"Is my team plowing
That I used to drive
And hear the harness jingle
When I was man alive?"

Ay, the horses trample,
The harness jingles now;
No change though you lie under
The land you used to plow.

Every year, my understanding of that poem deepens. After my mother's death, Stella arranged to have flowers placed on her grave at Forest Lawn every year on her birthday, November 16. I am so grateful to Stella for this tribute. To see the roses there taps something long-forgotten in me, some form of distant grief or regret. Regret is the word. *Why have I shut out so much?* No blame, no game. But the loneliness of those flowers, that image of life fading away, the mystery . . . What does any of it mean?

WE DID OK, KID

From that distant summer afternoon, that moment when I was a kid learning about death, I thought: *No, not me. I'll find a way out. Run now and don't look back . . . Run, rabbit, run, run, run . . . the farmer with his gun . . .* I now know that I was running away not from death but from life. What a paradox. And soon, I'll hear old winter's song . . .

The old, according to the young, tend to ruminate, going on and on about the good old days or the bad old days. When I was a young, know-it-all boy, I felt the same way about the old bores, the tedious old wrecks ranting about the good old days. I'd think, *I hope I'm not like that if I live that long.*

Now I have become that old man. Going back to the beginning—reliving it here—has given me an awakening, an appreciation of my good fortune and the summer days of my childhood. Now that I've set it all down on paper, I feel free to forget the past and focus on preparing to learn the Big Secret for myself. The laughable twist is that the past, as T. S. Eliot taught, doesn't forget us.

We have lingered in the chambers of the sea
By sea-girls wreathed with seaweed red and brown
Till human voices wake us, and we drown

TRIBUTES

It's a big daily surprise for me to wake up every morning and realize that I have lived such an unexpectedly long life. It's been interesting and fun. I've had a few laughs along the way. That's good. People have appeared, then disappeared. Memories of my father and mother are fading now. There is nothing poetical to say. Wake up and live. That's it—*live!*

One bright, sunny morning in a coffee shop in Los Angeles many years ago, I was trying to eat a breakfast of bacon and eggs. Feeling a bit under the weather, having not eaten for two days, I had to give up. A big two-day tequila hangover had dulled my appetite. My hands were shaking. That was a shock. I thought the shakes happened only in the movies, actors like Jack Lemmon overdoing it in *Days of Wine and Roses*.

The stranger sitting opposite me was Bob Palmer. I think he was my first real friend. I didn't need friends. That had been my way of life, but Bob had invited me to this unappetizing and greasy breakfast.

He was watching me.

"How do you feel?" he asked.

"Inadequate," I replied. That was the only word I knew. It had been stuck like a glass splinter in my head for as long as I could remember.

"Good. Because you *are* exactly that. You are inadequate."

That was a welcome slap in the face.

"What do you mean?" I asked.

"Can you predict what will happen in the next two seconds or minutes or half hour? Can you predict anything?"

"No."

"Right. That's why you have no power."

Bob took a sip of his coffee.

"We think we have power, especially drunks like us. We are a bunch of noisy know-it-alls, but we know nothing. We are just busted, disgusted, and not to be trusted. So what? Accept it. We are nothing. Give up the fight. There *is* nothing to fight, nothing to win and nothing to lose. No sweat, no big deal. Join the human race."

Suddenly, it all made sense. Peace.

My new life began slowly to emerge from the un-weeded garden of my past. A long process—almost fifty years of errors and small victories, sadness and unexpected happiness. From that point onward, I started meeting some new acquaintances who became friends.

Twenty-five years later I met my beautiful wife, Stella. We married in 2003, and she changed my life. We are opposites. She is a powerhouse of energy. Unstoppable. I drive her mad because I ask detailed questions about everything. Everything. My need to gather useless information drives her nuts. Slowly, slowly, she began, by example, to reshape a few of my thinking habits. She challenged me: Get out of the past. Live. Be healthy. Don't eat this. Don't eat that. Paint. Write music. Everything. *I can't.* Yes, you can. Just do it. Stop putting yourself down. Stop apologizing for everything. It has taken me some time to get a grip. Slowly, slowly, I'm getting there.

Our beloved house manager, Kesang, a Buddhist from Nepal, is the central energy in our home. She has been with us for twenty-two years. Kesang, her husband, Tenzin, and their two children, Tenzing Jr. and Woesel, are very important to our lives. Kesang comes in each day to assist Stella with the day-to-day household duties. Her presence brings peace. She is the calm, gentle breeze running through our home.

A year after Stella and I married, I met Aaron Tucker. He and his family had helped Stella when her antiques business struggled financially during the economic dip after 9/11. Our friendship has evolved over the years. Today, he's my closest friend and a partner in Margam Fine Art. We share common interests in film, music, literature, and art. Despite the age difference, we have a great deal in common. He and his elegant Russian wife, Natasha, are family.

Then came Tara, Stella's beautiful, highly intelligent niece. Tara came into our lives almost twenty years ago; I see her as a daughter. We have great banter. She calls me Sammy Slippers. I call her Mini-Boss. No respect. Bianca, Tara's younger sister, is my ally and defender when Tara and Stella get too bossy.

When they were young, Tara and her sisters survived breakups, fractures, separations, and some very difficult stuff. At one point, the family was wrecked—no money, no food, no clothes, no future. Fortunately, Oscar (Tara and Bianca's dad) has come a long way; he now lives in Colombia with Viviana, his new wife. I have deep affection for Stella's siblings

TRIBUTES

Amparo, Willie, and Oscar. Willie, the eldest, jumped into action during the aftermath of the 2018 Malibu fires. I'm forever grateful to him and Diana, his wife, for their unconditional support during that time. Everything has transformed beyond anything I could have imagined.

Our friend Jennifer Franklin has lived with us through twenty years of life's ups and downs and tribulations. I love her for her irreverent humor, for her courage and honesty, and for everything that she is. We have had many laughs along the way, laughs at the slings and arrows of outrageous fortune, and she will be with us forever.

My friend Jeremy Barber, also my agent, keeps me off the streets and out of trouble by finding me work in this acting business. We have great philosophical conversations and often laugh about everything. I am grateful for his support and hard work and for his enduring patience with my quirky ideas. He believes most people in this business—especially actors—are not wrapped too tight in the head.

Thank you to UTA's literary department for their role in bringing me to the venerable Simon & Schuster imprint of Summit Books. There I've had the pleasure of seeing my writing shepherded by the legendary editor Judy Clain, as well as her colleagues in the United States and abroad: Suzanne Baboneau, Ada Calhoun, Ian Chapman, Kimberly Goldstein, Kayley Hoffman, Jonathan Karp, Josefine Kals, Carly Loman, Kevwe Okumakube, and Tracy Roe.

Mitch Smelkinson, my entertainment attorney and friend, is married to Lisa Pepper, Stella's best friend of thirty years. Stella and Lisa are quite the duo. I often overhear their phone conversations where they laugh or cry about who knows what.

Mitch and Lisa have raised two magnificent daughters, Mia and Harper. Mitch keeps me in work and therefore, like Jeremy, keeps me out of trouble.

Thank you to David Garelick for handling our business affairs and keeping us safe. David, Debbie, and his children are always a part of our holiday celebrations.

Bernie Yuman and his wife and the Greenspun family visited my mother during the hospital stays at the end of her life, always bringing flowers and cookies. For that I am forever grateful. We don't meet often, but I always look forward to seeing them.

Stephen Barton, his wife, Margaret, and their young daughter, Abbey, an artist in her own right, are also close friends. Stephen is a brilliant, award-winning composer who supports and encourages me as a composer. His advice to me is always "Just go for it, don't hesitate, be bold, be outrageous." That's a great way to go. Stop analyzing and looking over your shoulder.

And Juan Arias, my assistant (nicknamed JOTS, for "Johnny on the Spot"). I must give this guy the credits in bold font. I did manage to get him a role in the film *The Two Popes*.

He was excellent. But then, predictably, he started to demand special amenities on film sets. (Not really. A joke we share.) JOTS is a remarkable young man, born in Colombia. His father gave him a tough education of homespun philosophies. "This is the youngest you will ever be, so enjoy each day." He smiles at everyone, knows everyone by name.

Dr. Maria Teresa Ochoa, Stella's compatriot, is an outstanding dermatologist at Keck Medicine USC. We've known Maria Teresa for almost twenty years; her company is always a source of great joy. We call her the "movable feast." She quietly looks out for us, facilitating any medical attention needed.

TRIBUTES

Brenda Nieto, a former Martha Graham dancer, now our private Gyrotonic coach, lives close by; she stops by often with her rescue dogs and thoughtful gifts. We love Brenda.

There have been a few serious injuries in my life as an actor—snapped and torn Achilles tendons, a broken ankle, a herniated disc, lower-back muscle rips and strains, results of my stupid self-belief that I could do my own stunts. At eighty-seven, I finally recognize the limitations of my body—the aches in my lower back and my legs. I still have strength and work out several times a week, but Stella insists I have physical therapy three times a week, and Annette Duggan is the one who came to my rescue. Annette is a wonderful physical therapist. I don't want to retire, nor do I want to be in a wheelchair. I must keep moving forward. Thank you, Annette.

A new addition to our home is Amelia, from Mexico, a jovial woman, always smiling. She takes care of our cats.

In Wales we have Ray Clark. We call him the Boyo. Ray spent some years in Afghanistan in action with the British forces, returned, and started his personal-security business. We have known Ray for almost ten years—a great man.

Then there is Eve—Eve Williams. All about Eve: She has been a friend of mine for well over fifty years. She managed the Ship Inn pub in Caerleon that my father leased in 1968. There were some raucous, jolly times in that place. Eve was married to her first husband then, but always standing nearby was Gene Williams. Eventually Eve and her husband broke up. Gene waited patiently, then one day popped the question. I went to their wedding. They both became close friends with my parents. They were grand days. I used to get on the train from London on Fridays and within two hours, I would be lapping it up in the bar. There was something about pubs that was always exhilarating. The booze. Ah, yes, the booze. That was the stuff that could change the world. I wouldn't have missed it. But never again. Eve and Gene were always there. My father died in 1981. He is missed by everyone. Eve still talks about him. Eve became my mother's closest friend. They were inseparable.

In 1978 BBC TV offered me a role in an excellent play. I traveled back to London from Los Angeles for rehearsals and a three-day filming session. The whole enterprise was a train wreck. A young actor in the cast was Julian Fellowes, the future author of *Gosford Park* and *Downton Abbey*. Julian was a remote figure in that group of actors. He barely spoke to anyone but silently witnessed the impending train wreck. Then, a few days into the rehearsal, he offered his opinion—I was being too passive, playing Mr. Nice Guy rather than advocating for myself and my fellow actors.

That was a kick in the head. But the man was right. I *was* playing Mr. Nice Guy. Having been one of the awkward squads over the years, I'd flipped my so-called record over to play the tune of Mr. Jolly Nice. That was a salutary lesson: No more Mr. Nice Guy. Julian and I became good friends. A few years later, he married. His son Peregrine was born, and I was asked to become godfather, an offer I could not refuse.

Having a family was the last event in my life. I always wanted to be alone, traveling freely and being independent.

I am deeply grateful to have my beautiful loving wife and this magnificent group of generous people who, by some osmosis or mystery, have changed my life. At eighty-seven I would find it mind-bogglingly weird to rest my feet on a veranda rail for too long, gazing at nirvana or my belly button. I'd go nuts.

These are the best of days to wake up each day, look up at the sky, and say, "Good morning, world. Here I am again, the youngest I will ever be. Let's have a laugh today."

In January 2025, as this book was going to press, Stella and I lost our home in the Palisades Fire. It wasn't a "grand" house, but there were a few things we valued. Now they have vanished. So? Everything vanishes in the end. Onward. We'll probably drift around as we always have done. I told my grandfather I wanted to be a drifter. It worked that way, I guess, and it's been a pretty good life. *No complaints*, I tell myself. *Keep kicking the old tin can. Be bold and mighty forces will come to your aid. Life is in session.*

Appendix

ANTHONY HOPKINS'S COMMONPLACE POETRY BOOK

When I am asked for any kind of advice, I am usually stumped for an answer. I never want to come on as heavy or serious. How can *I* advise anyone?

I don't know the Rules of the Game. I have *never* known the rules of the game—because my own life has always been a bit of a muddle and a bit of a puzzle and I don't mean it in a bad way, because my life has been pretty good really, so far. Looking back almost fifty years ago, I remembered it was a bright December morning in Los Angeles when it suddenly occurred to me *that my LIFE was none of my business*; and, even more unsettling, I realized that it *never* had been any of my business. It's hard to explain but I sensed that some other thing, some other element had overseen my existence. Most peculiar. I still can't explain that wake-up call, because that is what it was—a wake-up call, and it was my first breath of freedom from the feeling of hopelessness.

My solution had always been, "So what?! Who cares?! Stay silent. Never get involved. Keep your head down. Feel nothing"—and that numbness seemed to work for a long, long time.

But then, again, way back to my almost forgotten school days, there had been another surprise: I'd been summoned by our English Literature teacher to stand before a classroom of schoolboys. Why? To read a poem to them. A poem? Me? "*Yes, you.*" I was fifteen. I didn't know anything about poetry. Poems were boring, but I had been invited by the teacher to *recite* one to that room of morose, listless schoolboys. Why did he call on me? I had become an expert at staying below the radar. I was the invisible man. Don't look at me. Don't speak to me. But now, for some reason, I'd been rumbled. I got up from my hiding place, the school desk at the back of the classroom, and reluctantly shuffled toward the schoolteacher's desk. I stood there like a fool. Now what?

The teacher handed me a hefty volume of *Palgrave's Golden Treasury*. That was enough to make you run for the hills. But anyway, the book was open and there was the poem I was to recite. It was John Masefield's "The West Wind." I stared at the page. I didn't know what to do.

"*Well, go on,*" said the teacher. "*Read it.*"

Well, I took a breath and I started reciting the poem to that silent classroom of indifferent kids. I avoided eye contact with them because I didn't want to acknowledge their indifference. But, suddenly, I was drawn into those opening words of the poem, as if they had come from some other life buried inside me.

The rhythm of the poem, the words, the cadences deeply affected me. That surly bunch of bored classmates were strangely quiet. Spellbound? I don't know about that, but they did seem impressed. I cannot, for the life of me, explain why I was able to read and be deeply moved almost to tears. That would have been a minor disaster: Crying in front of a bunch of sullen boys. Boys don't cry. When I'd finished reading, I gave the book back to the teacher.

There was a silence, a stillness, and the teacher—Mister Arthur Codling, that was his name—said: "*Well done. Excellent. Well read.*" He told me to go back to my desk and sit down.

It was the only praise of good report I had ever received. After the class was over, Mister Codling gave me the book. That was a gift, and that was my introduction.

So here I am today and the only advice I can offer anyone would be: Listen to music. Any music. Or read. Read anything. Books. Poems. Whatever it is. I started to read Charles Dickens's *Great Expectations* when I was ten. Why? I don't know. It was a struggle, but I did it, then I read his novel *Oliver Twist*.

Poems have a bad reputation, or so I've been told, but I happen to like them.

I wouldn't push my choices on anyone, but I happen to like poets such as T. S. Eliot, Maya Angelou, Ezra Pound, W. H. Auden, Langston Hughes, Philip Larkin, Dylan Thomas, William Shakespeare.

I read Fitzgerald's *The Great Gatsby* in school. That was another "personal" identity thing. Why? It was an American novel. It had nothing to do with my life. Why would I latch on to an American novel set in the nineteen twenties? The last words about the broken dreams, the loneliness of Gatsby—*and so we beat on, boats against the current, borne back ceaselessly into the past.* I don't presume to compare myself to the hope in Gatsby's

APPENDIX

heart. But I think it was *hope* and *hopelessness* that took over my life and delivered me to this point in my surprisingly long life.

Music also played a large role in my life. Poulenc's *Stabat Mater*, Beethoven's *Ninth Symphony* (especially Leonard Bernstein conducting it in Berlin), Franco Corelli singing *Tosca*, Maria Callas (who was in great pain during that part of her life) singing Bellini's *Norma*. Toscanini, Jacqueline du Pré—Brahms Cello Concerto. Horowitz playing the Rachmaninoff Third.

I am no snob about any of this culture stuff. I just happen to enjoy odds and ends of music. All the above. Lotte Lenya, Sinatra, Dolly Parton, Leonard Cohen, Gary Brooker / Procol Harum. Etc.

The pages that follow contain some of the poems I learned as a boy, but also, the effect they had on my father. He used to ask me to recite some of them. He had no education himself, but he did have a wonderful gift for learning poetry. He told me once, not long before he died, that poetry helped him find relief from his depressions and anxieties. It gave his restless energy something to hold on to, I suppose. His favorite was Omar Khayyam's *Rubaiyat*:

The Worldly Hope men set their Hearts upon—
Turns Ashes—or it prospers; and anon,
Like Snow upon the Desert's dusty Face,
Lighting a little Hour or two—is gone.

As I Walked Out One Evening

W. H. Auden

As I walked out one evening,
    Walking down Bristol Street,
The crowds upon the pavement
    Were fields of harvest wheat.

And down by the brimming river
    I heard a lover sing
Under an arch of the railway:
    "Love has no ending.

"I'll love you, dear, I'll love you
    Till China and Africa meet,
And the river jumps over the mountain
    And the salmon sing in the street,

"I'll love you till the ocean
    Is folded and hung up to dry
And the seven stars go squawking
    Like geese about the sky.

"The years shall run like rabbits,
    For in my arms I hold

The Flower of the Ages,
    And the first love of the world."

But all the clocks in the city
    Began to whir and chime:
"O let not Time deceive you,
    You cannot conquer Time.

"In the burrows of the Nightmare
    Where Justice naked is,
Time watches from the shadow
    And coughs when you would kiss.

"In headaches and in worry
    Vaguely life leaks away,
And Time will have his fancy
    To-morrow or to-day.

"Into many a green valley
    Drifts the appalling snow;
Time breaks the threaded dances
    And the diver's brilliant bow.

"O plunge your hands in water,
    Plunge them in up to the wrist;
Stare, stare in the basin
    And wonder what you've missed.

"The glacier knocks in the cupboard,
    The desert sighs in the bed,

And the crack in the tea-cup opens
   A lane to the land of the dead.

"Where the beggars raffle the banknotes
   And the Giant is enchanting to Jack,
And the Lily-white Boy is a Roarer,
   And Jill goes down on her back.

"O look, look in the mirror,
   O look in your distress:
Life remains a blessing
   Although you cannot bless.

"O stand, stand at the window
   As the tears scald and start;
You shall love your crooked neighbour
   With your crooked heart."

It was late, late in the evening,
   The lovers they were gone;
The clocks had ceased their chiming,
   And the deep river ran on.

Ithaka

C. P. Cavafy

As you set out for Ithaka
hope your road is a long one,
full of adventure, full of discovery.
Laistrygonians, Cyclops,
angry Poseidon—don't be afraid of them:
you'll never find things like that on your way
as long as you keep your thoughts raised high,
as long as a rare excitement
stirs your spirit and your body.
Laistrygonians, Cyclops,
wild Poseidon—you won't encounter them
unless you bring them along inside your soul,
unless your soul sets them up in front of you.

Hope your road is a long one.
May there be many summer mornings when,
with what pleasure, what joy,
you enter harbors you're seeing for the first time;
may you stop at Phoenician trading stations
to buy fine things,
mother of pearl and coral, amber and ebony,
sensual perfume of every kind—
as many sensual perfumes as you can;

and may you visit many Egyptian cities
to learn and go on learning from their scholars.

Keep Ithaka always in your mind.
Arriving there is what you're destined for.
But don't hurry the journey at all.
Better if it lasts for years,
so you're old by the time you reach the island,
wealthy with all you've gained on the way,
not expecting Ithaka to make you rich.

Ithaka gave you the marvelous journey.
Without her you wouldn't have set out.
She has nothing left to give you now.

And if you find her poor, Ithaka won't have fooled you.
Wise as you will have become, so full of experience,
you'll have understood by then what these Ithakas mean.

The West Wind

John Masefield

It's a warm wind, the west wind, full of birds' cries;
I never hear the west wind but tears are in my eyes.
For it comes from the west lands, the old brown hills.
And April's in the west wind, and daffodils.

It's a fine land, the west land, for hearts as tired as mine,
Apple orchards blossom there, and the air's like wine.
There is cool green grass there, where men may lie at rest,
And the thrushes are in song there, fluting from the nest.

"Will ye not come home, brother? Ye have been long away,
It's April, and blossom time, and white is the May;
And bright is the sun, brother, and warm is the rain,—
Will ye not come home, brother, home to us again?

"The young corn is green, brother, where the rabbits run.
It's blue sky, and white clouds, and warm rain and sun.
It's song to a man's soul, brother, fire to a man's brain,
To hear the wild bees and see the merry spring again.

"Larks are singing in the west, brother, above the green wheat,
So will ye not come home, brother, and rest your tired feet?

APPENDIX

I've a balm for bruised hearts, brother, sleep for aching eyes,"
Says the warm wind, the west wind, full of birds' cries.

It's the white road westwards is the road I must tread
To the green grass, the cool grass, and rest for heart and head,
To the violets, and the warm hearts, and the thrushes' song,
In the fine land, the west land, the land where I belong.

The Leaden Echo and the Golden Echo

Gerard Manley Hopkins[*]

The Leaden Echo

How to keep—is there ány any, is there none such, nowhere
known some, bow or brooch or braid or brace, láce, latch
or catch or key to keep
Back beauty, keep it, beauty, beauty, beauty, . . . from
   vanishing
away?

Ó is there no frowning of these wrinkles, rankèd wrinkles
   deep,
Dówn? no waving off of these most mournful messengers,
   still
messengers, sad and stealing messengers of grey?
No there's none, there's none, O no there's none,
Nor can you long be, what you now are, called fair,
Do what you may do, what, do what you may,
And wisdom is early to despair:
Be beginning; since, no, nothing can be done

---

[*] A distant cousin of mine!

To keep at bay
Age and age's evils, hoar hair,
Ruck and wrinkle, drooping, dying, death's worst, winding
sheets, tombs and worms and tumbling to decay;
So be beginning, be beginning to despair.
O there's none; no no no there's none:
Be beginning to despair, to despair,
Despair, despair, despair, despair.

The Golden Echo

Spare!
There is one, yes I have one (Hush there!);
Only not within seeing of the sun,
Not within the singeing of the strong sun,
Tall sun's tingeing, or treacherous the tainting of the earth's
    air.
Somewhere elsewhere there is ah well where! one,
Óne. Yes I can tell such a key, I do know such a place,
Where whatever's prized and passes of us, everything that's
fresh and fast flying of us, seems to us sweet of us and
swiftly away with, done away with, undone,
Undone, done with, soon done with, and yet dearly and
dangerously sweet
Of us, the wimpled-water-dimpled, not-by-morning-matchèd
    face,
The flower of beauty, fleece of beauty, too too apt to, ah! to
    fleet,

APPENDIX

Never fleets more, fastened with the tenderest truth
To its own best being and its loveliness of youth: it is an everlastingness of, O it is an all youth!
Come then, your ways and airs and looks, locks, maiden
    gear,
gallantry and gaiety and grace,
Winning ways, airs innocent, maiden manners, sweet looks,
loose locks, long locks, lovelocks, gaygear, going gallant,
girlgrace–
Resign them, sign them, seal them, send them, motion them
    with breath,
And with sighs soaring, soaring síghs deliver
Them; beauty-in-the-ghost, deliver it, early now, long before
    death
Give beauty back, beauty, beauty, beauty, back to God, beauty's
self and beauty's giver.
See; not a hair is, not an eyelash, not the least lash lost; every
    hair
Is, hair of the head, numbered.
Nay, what we had lighthanded left in surly the mere
    mould
Will have waked and have waxed and have walked with the
    wind
what while we slept,
This side, that side hurling a heavyheaded hundredfold
What while we, while we slumbered.
O then, weary then whý should we tread? O why are we so
haggard at the heart, so care-coiled, care-killed, so fagged,
so fashed, so cogged, so cumbered,
When the thing we freely fórfeit is kept with fonder a care,

APPENDIX

Fonder a care kept than we could have kept it, kept
Far with fonder a care (and we, we should have lost it) finer, fonder
A care kept. Where kept? Do but tell us where kept, where.–
Yonder.–What high as that! We follow, now we follow.–
Yonder, yes yonder, yonder,
Yonder.

A Psalm of Life

Henry Wadsworth Longfellow

What the Heart of the Young Man Said to the Psalmist.

Tell me not, in mournful numbers,
    Life is but an empty dream!
For the soul is dead that slumbers,
    And things are not what they seem.

Life is real! Life is earnest!
    And the grave is not its goal;
Dust thou art, to dust returnest,
    Was not spoken of the soul.

Not enjoyment, and not sorrow,
    Is our destined end or way;
But to act, that each to-morrow
    Find us farther than to-day.

Art is long, and Time is fleeting,
    And our hearts, though stout and brave,
Still, like muffled drums, are beating
    Funeral marches to the grave.

APPENDIX

In the world's broad field of battle,
    In the bivouac of Life,
Be not like dumb, driven cattle!
    Be a hero in the strife!

Trust no Future, howe'er pleasant!
    Let the dead Past bury its dead!
Act,— act in the living Present!
    Heart within, and God o'erhead!

Lives of great men all remind us
    We can make our lives sublime,
And, departing, leave behind us
    Footprints on the sands of time;

Footprints, that perhaps another,
    Sailing o'er life's solemn main,
A forlorn and shipwrecked brother,
    Seeing, shall take heart again.

Let us, then, be up and doing,
    With a heart for any fate;
Still achieving, still pursuing,
    Learn to labor and to wait.

O, That This Too, Too Solid Flesh Would Melt (from *Hamlet*)

William Shakespeare

O, that this too, too solid flesh would melt
Thaw and resolve itself into a dew!
Or that the Everlasting had not fix'd
His canon 'gainst self-slaughter! O God! God!
How weary, stale, flat and unprofitable,
Seem to me all the uses of this world!
Fie on't! ah fie! 'tis an unweeded garden,
That grows to seed; things rank and gross in nature
Possess it merely. That it should come to this!
But two months dead: nay, not so much, not two:
So excellent a king; that was, to this,
Hyperion to a satyr; so loving to my mother
That he might not beteem the winds of heaven
Visit her face too roughly. Heaven and earth!
Must I remember? why, she would hang on him,
As if increase of appetite had grown
By what it fed on: and yet, within a month—
Let me not think on't—Frailty, thy name is woman!—
A little month, or ere those shoes were old
With which she follow'd my poor father's body,
Like Niobe, all tears:—why she, even she—
O, God! a beast, that wants discourse of reason,
Would have mourn'd longer—married with my uncle,

APPENDIX

My father's brother, but no more like my father
Than I to Hercules: within a month:
Ere yet the salt of most unrighteous tears
Had left the flushing in her galled eyes,
She married. O, most wicked speed, to post
With such dexterity to incestuous sheets!
It is not, nor it cannot come to good:
But break, my heart; for I must hold my tongue.

Aedh Wishes for the Cloths of Heaven

W. B. Yeats

Had I the heavens' embroidered cloths,
Enwrought with golden and silver light,
The blue and the dim and the dark cloths
Of night and light and the half light,
I would spread the cloths under your feet:
But I, being poor, have only my dreams;
I have spread my dreams under your feet;
Tread softly because you tread on my dreams.

Fear No More the Heat o' the Sun
(from *Cymbeline*)

William Shakespeare

Fear no more the heat o' the sun,
Nor the furious winter's rages;
Thou thy worldly task hast done,
Home art gone, and ta'en thy wages:
Golden lads and girls all must,
As chimney-sweepers, come to dust.

The Love Song of J. Alfred Prufrock (excerpt)

T. S. Eliot

I grow old . . . I grow old . . .
I shall wear the bottoms of my trousers rolled.

Shall I part my hair behind? Do I dare to eat a peach?
I shall wear white flannel trousers and walk upon the beach.
I have heard the mermaids singing, each to each.

I do not think that they will sing to me.

I have seen them riding seaward on the waves
Combing the white hair of the waves blown back
When the wind blows the water white and black.
We have lingered in the chambers of the sea
By sea-girls wreathed with seaweed red and brown
Till human voices wake us, and we drown.

Vitae Summa Brevis Spem Nos Vetat Incohare Longam

Ernest Dowson

The brief sum of life forbids us the hope of enduring long.
—Horace

They are not long, the weeping and the laughter,
Love and desire and hate:
I think they have no portion in us after
We pass the gate.

They are not long, the days of wine and roses:
Out of a misty dream
Our path emerges for a while, then closes
Within a dream.

Ecclesiastes 1:5, 9, 11

The sun also rises, and the sun goes down,
And hastens to the place where it arose.
. . .
That which is done is what will be done,
And there is nothing new under the sun.
. . .
Nor will there be any remembrance of things that are to come
By those who will come after.

Seneca

Soon we will spit out our life's breath.
For a moment, while we still draw it, while we're in the
  human world,
Let's cherish our humanity.
Let's not be a source of fear or danger to anyone.
Let's cast scorn on injuries, harms, insults, and taunts; let's put
  up with brief annoyances.
As they say, the moment we turn and look behind us,
Death stands right there.

Adlestrop

Edward Thomas

Yes. I remember Adlestrop—
The name, because one afternoon
Of heat the express-train drew up there
Unwontedly. It was late June.

The steam hissed. Someone cleared his throat.
No one left and no one came
On the bare platform. What I saw
Was Adlestrop—only the name

And willows, willow-herb, and grass,
And meadowsweet, and haycocks dry,
No whit less still and lonely fair
Than the high cloudlets in the sky.

And for that minute a blackbird sang
Close by, and round him, mistier,
Farther and farther, all the birds
Of Oxfordshire and Gloucestershire.

Elegy Written in a Country Churchyard

Thomas Gray

The curfew tolls the knell of parting day,
    The lowing herd wind slowly o'er the lea,
The plowman homeward plods his weary way,
    And leaves the world to darkness and to me.

Now fades the glimm'ring landscape on the sight,
    And all the air a solemn stillness holds,
Save where the beetle wheels his droning flight,
    And drowsy tinklings lull the distant folds;

Save that from yonder ivy-mantled tow'r
    The moping owl does to the moon complain
Of such, as wand'ring near her secret bow'r,
    Molest her ancient solitary reign.

Beneath those rugged elms, that yew-tree's shade,
    Where heaves the turf in many a mould'ring heap,
Each in his narrow cell for ever laid,
    The rude forefathers of the hamlet sleep.

The breezy call of incense-breathing Morn,
    The swallow twitt'ring from the straw-built shed,

APPENDIX

The cock's shrill clarion, or the echoing horn,
    No more shall rouse them from their lowly bed.

For them no more the blazing hearth shall burn,
    Or busy housewife ply her evening care:
No children run to lisp their sire's return,
    Or climb his knees the envied kiss to share.

Oft did the harvest to their sickle yield,
    Their furrow oft the stubborn glebe has broke;
How jocund did they drive their team afield!
    How bow'd the woods beneath their sturdy stroke!

Let not Ambition mock their useful toil,
    Their homely joys, and destiny obscure;
Nor Grandeur hear with a disdainful smile
    The short and simple annals of the poor.

The boast of heraldry, the pomp of pow'r,
    And all that beauty, all that wealth e'er gave,
Awaits alike th' inevitable hour.
    The paths of glory lead but to the grave.

Nor you, ye proud, impute to these the fault,
    If Mem'ry o'er their tomb no trophies raise,
Where thro' the long-drawn aisle and fretted vault
    The pealing anthem swells the note of praise.

APPENDIX

Can storied urn or animated bust
    Back to its mansion call the fleeting breath?
Can Honour's voice provoke the silent dust,
    Or Flatt'ry soothe the dull cold ear of Death?

Perhaps in this neglected spot is laid
    Some heart once pregnant with celestial fire;
Hands, that the rod of empire might have sway'd,
    Or wak'd to ecstasy the living lyre.

But Knowledge to their eyes her ample page
    Rich with the spoils of time did ne'er unroll;
Chill Penury repress'd their noble rage,
    And froze the genial current of the soul.

Full many a gem of purest ray serene,
    The dark unfathom'd caves of ocean bear:
Full many a flow'r is born to blush unseen,
    And waste its sweetness on the desert air.

To Be, or Not to Be, That Is the Question (from *Hamlet*)

William Shakespeare

To be, or not to be, that is the question:
Whether 'tis nobler in the mind to suffer
The slings and arrows of outrageous fortune,
Or to take arms against a sea of troubles
And by opposing end them. To die—to sleep,
No more; and by a sleep to say we end
The heart-ache and the thousand natural shocks
That flesh is heir to: 'tis a consummation
Devoutly to be wish'd. To die, to sleep;
To sleep, perchance to dream—ay, there's the rub:
For in that sleep of death what dreams may come,
When we have shuffled off this mortal coil,
Must give us pause—there's the respect
That makes calamity of so long life.
For who would bear the whips and scorns of time,
Th'oppressor's wrong, the proud man's contumely,
The pangs of dispriz'd love, the law's delay,
The insolence of office, and the spurns
That patient merit of th'unworthy takes,
When he himself might his quietus make
With a bare bodkin? Who would fardels bear,
To grunt and sweat under a weary life,

APPENDIX

But that the dread of something after death,
The undiscovere'd country, from whose bourn
No traveller returns, puzzles the will,
And makes us rather bear those ills we have
Than fly to others that we know not of?
Thus conscience doth make cowards of us all,
And thus the native hue of resolution
Is sicklied o'er with the pale cast of thought,
And enterprises of great pith and moment
With this regard their currents turn awry
And lose the name of action.

The Lake Isle of Innisfree

W. B. Yeats

I will arise and go now, and go to Innisfree,
And a small cabin build there, of clay and wattles made;
Nine bean-rows will I have there, a hive for the honey-bee,
And live alone in the bee-loud glade.

And I shall have some peace there, for peace comes dropping slow,
Dropping from the veils of the morning to where the cricket sings;
There midnight's all a glimmer, and noon a purple glow,
And evening full of the linnet's wings.

I will arise and go now, for always night and day
I hear lake water lapping with low sounds by the shore;
While I stand on the roadway, or on the pavements grey,
I hear it in the deep heart's core.

When You Are Old

W. B. Yeats

When you are old and grey and full of sleep,
And nodding by the fire, take down this book,
And slowly read, and dream of the soft look
Your eyes had once, and of their shadows deep;

How many loved your moments of glad grace,
And loved your beauty with love false or true,
But one man loved the pilgrim soul in you,
And loved the sorrows of your changing face;

And bending down beside the glowing bars,
Murmur, a little sadly, how Love fled
And paced upon the mountains overhead
And hid his face amid a crowd of stars.

Remember

Christina Rossetti

Remember me when I am gone away,
    Gone far away into the silent land;
    When you can no more hold me by the hand,
Nor I half turn to go yet turning stay.
Remember me when no more day by day
    You tell me of our future that you plann'd:
    Only remember me; you understand
It will be late to counsel then or pray.
Yet if you should forget me for a while
    And afterwards remember, do not grieve:
    For if the darkness and corruption leave
    A vestige of the thoughts that once I had,
Better by far you should forget and smile
    Than that you should remember and be sad.

CREDITS

"As I Walked Out One Evening" by W. H. Auden (Page 323) Copyright © 1940 by W. H. Auden. Reprinted by permission of Curtis Brown, Ltd. All rights reserved.

"Ithaka" from C. P. Cavafy (Page 326): *Collected Poems, Revised Edition* translated by Edmund Keeley and Philip Sherrard, edited by George Savidis. Translation copyright © 1975, 1992 by Edmund Keeley and Philip Sherrard. Reprinted by permission of Princeton University Press.

ABOUT THE AUTHOR

Sir Philip Anthony Hopkins, CBE, is one of Britain's most recognizable and prolific actors. He began his career onstage, working under Laurence Olivier, before moving on to star in various critically acclaimed films. Throughout his six-decade-long career, Sir Anthony has become known for acclaimed appearances in notable films such as *The Silence of the Lambs*, *The Remains of the Day*, Marvel's *Thor*, *The Father*, and many more. He most recently starred in the series *Those About to Die* and he will star in an upcoming biopic about the Maserati family directed by Academy Award winner Bobby Moresco. Sir Anthony has received numerous accolades for his outstanding performances, including two Academy Awards, four BAFTA Awards, two Primetime Emmy Awards, and a Laurence Olivier Award. He currently resides with his wife, Stella, in Los Angeles, California.